OFFICC

A V. B

James Walvin

the only game

FOOTBALL
IN OUR TIMES

James Walvin

Longman

PEARSON EDUCATION LIMITED

Head Office:
Edinburgh Gate
Harlow CM20 2JE
Tel: +44(0)1279 623623
Fax: +44(0)1279 431059

London Office:
128 Long Acre
London WC2E 9AN
Tel: +44(0)20 7447 2000
Fax: +44(0)20 7240 5771
Website: www.history-minds.com

First published in Great Britain in 2001
© James Walvin 2001

The right of James Walvin to be identified as Author
of this Work has been asserted by him in accordance
with the Copyright, Designs and Patents Act 1988.

ISBN 0 582 50577 1

British Library Cataloguing in Publication Data
A CIP catalog record for this book can be obtained from the British Library

Library of Congress Cataloging in Publication Data
A CIP catalog record for this book can be obtained from the Library of Congress

10 9 8 7 6 5 4 3 2 1

Typeset by Fakenham Photosetting Limited Fakenham Norfolk NR21 8NN
Printed and bound in Great Britain by Biddles Ltd

The Publishers' policy is to use paper manufactured from sustainable forests.

In some cases we have been unable to trace the owners of copyright material and we would
appreciate any information that would enable us to do so.

CONTENTS

PUBLISHERS ACKNOWLEDGEMENTS

The publishers gratefully acknowledge the material on page 203, paragraph two, which comes from David Conn's book, *The Football Business* (1999).

ACKNOWLEGEMENTS

I could not have written this book without
the critical help of a number of people,
notably a formidable team of women at
Pearson. They have been led by Heather
McCallum, whose initial idea prompted me to
write the book, and whose attention to
progress has seen the book emerge in its
present form. Magda Robson was a wonderful
editor and helper at all times. Two others
at Pearson who proved staunch backers at
different stages were Anna Vinegrad and Sally
Greene. Helen Hodge brought copy-editing
clarity to the process. I am, as ever,
immensely grateful to my agent, Charles
Walker, at Peters Fraser and Dunlop, for his
help and advice.

This book is about England and English
football. I have wrestled throughout with the
complexities of the division between England
and Britain, in this context especially
between *England* and *Scotland*. I hope I have
used the words precisely throughout.

Finally, I dedicate this book to the memory
of the two men who first gave me the
football bug (but many more precious things
as well); my father, James Walvin,
(1910-1952) and my grandfather, Robert Wood
(1890-1960).

James Walvin
York, September 2001

01

This island now

Turn right out of our house and the road quickly drops down to the river. Take an early morning stroll along the river bank and you'll encounter a camouflaged army, lurking in hideaways every few hundred yards; knots of silent fishermen clad in waterproofs. Continue north along the river from the city centre and you quickly reach the well-manicured and lavish playing fields of a local public school. Turn left from the house and walk towards my place of work; the road leads between a large golf club and a huge spread of playing fields, mainly for cricket and football. As I write this, I can look out from my study at the top of the house, and see the local race-course stadium. Relaxing, a mile away, on my son's back lawn, we're sitting on the remains of the playing pitch of the town's professional football team.

Here I am, living on the southern edge of a famous northern city, surrounded on all hands by reminders of sport. Yet most of the time, I don't even notice it or think about it. I suspect most people don't. It is part of the way we live – part of this island now.

England has changed incalculably in my own lifetime; so much, so fundamentally that it's impossible to know where to begin. Yet beneath the changes – below the surface of a society which at times seems even to have been uprooted from its own history – there are some remarkable survivals. Fewer are more pervasive, so ubiquitous, than the passion for sport, but even that has changed. What follows is an attempt to write about one particular English sport – football. It is the same game my grandfather watched a century ago (same rules, same clubs, same curious obsessions) yet it is also very different. But this game, the national game, has changed more in the space of a mere ten years than any time in its history.

The greatest show on earth

Of course, football is not simply an English game; it is a British (and global) sport. But this book is about the *English* and their passion for (sometimes their revulsion against) the national game of football. By profession I am an academic historian and much of what I say is clearly shaped by my training and my occupation. *The Only Game* is not, I hope, simply a piece of history, but rather a personal commentary on the recent past. I don't pretend to hide my lifelong attachment to one particular team. My father and grandfather supported the team I follow; my two sons and now my grandson do the same. There is nothing special or unusual about that. In fact it is this peculiar *family* tradition, part of the social DNA of millions of people, which makes football fans so numerous, so obsessive and also so hard to explain to non-believers. Yet it would be wrong to claim that the footballing fraternity rolls on, year after year, unchanging and unwavering. The fans, like the game they follow, have changed fundamentally in the recent past.

Today, one of my brothers – raised like me to think only of one team – emails his reactions to the latest game or football story. But he lives in Jakarta, rising in the wee-small hours to watch the game I watch live in England. Another friend, raised in Leeds, emails from New York

The fans, like the game they follow, have changed fundamentally in the recent past.

with his own views on the current state of play. Again – nothing unusual here; it is all part of the way many people live. But it is very different from the way we used to live.

I set out to write a book which would make sense of *recent* changes in the game, in terms of football's longer history; to portray its recent past forged by the longer traditions of football stretching back to the late 19th century. The more I researched, however, the clearer it became that I faced an altogether different problem. Football since the late 1980s has been completely transformed. In many respects the game has been wrenched loose from the historical and social fabric which brought it into being. Yet these massive changes were also responsible for making football the greatest show on earth. Blame it on the Premier League. A small group of elite English clubs, playing among themselves with an eye to European competitions, filling their ranks with players from all corners of the world, and all backed by the staggering commercial power of television and global corporations have, within little more than a decade, changed the national game beyond recall. Yet it remains, obviously, the same game.

Outside the showbiz dazzle of the major clubs, the basics of English football look much as they always did; armies of young men and boys playing simply for the love of the game; hundreds of thousands trekking to watch games at weekends. A closer look however reveals that even here, down at the grass roots of the people's game, football has changed and not always for the better. The full extent of the football revolution is perhaps best measured by considering the game's global appeal. Football is more popular today than ever before. Few places on earth have been able to resist the temptations of televised games beamed in from the other side of the globe. The curious exception is the USA, despite enormous support among young women, college teams and Latino immigrants. Even at the height of the US World Cup in 1994, enthusiasm for football in the US was, in the words of Archie Macpherson, 'about the same as it is for the Communist Party'. Those who try

Sunday morning football © Lawrence Griffiths/Allsport/Hulton Deutsch

to foster American enthusiasm for the game despair: 'Americans think that any guy who runs around in shorts kicking a ball instead of catching it has to be a Commie or a fairy'.

Why another book on football? At times it seems there are more books than players. Why *is* so much time spent writing about sport – and why *this* game in particular? After the boom in football literature over the past twenty years, what more is there to be said about the game? In addition to countless books, football news, reports, profiles and gossip fill the dailies and weeklies, magazines, fashionable journals, celebrity glossies. Football has even crept into financial journalism. It is impossible to escape from the game. It has crept into the nation's front room, flickering on television sets throughout much of the year, with scarcely a month's break in mid-summer. Sometimes, even the cricket season is overshadowed by major international football competitions. For the devoted football fan, it is a dream; endless television-borne matches flitting in and out of the house, most days of the week, most weeks of the year. For those indifferent or hostile to the game (silent but brooding millions whose tranquillity is often disturbed when least expected by football on their TV screen) football is an unfathomable irritation. They remain perplexed by the attention the game attracts, and by the boisterous enthusiasm of its followers. Not long ago, it was once possible to escape to remote corners of the land (or even remote corners of the globe) to get away from football. No longer. Football now bounces from satellites into radios and TV sets in the most inaccessible corners of the globe. Fans seem to pop up in the most remote spots; in the Sudanese desert, high in the Himalayas and deep in various rainforests. Can this really be the same game I have followed since 1948, and the team I have watched for more than 50 years? At one level it obviously is: same game, same club, same ground, same name, same rules, same city. Thereafter, however, things begin to look very different.

For those indifferent or hostile to the game ... football is an unfathomable irritation.

A different game

For a start, football *feels* very different in the new century. The first odd sensation is watching my money disappear into the maws of a massive commercial enterprise, a handsome sum (the equivalent of five hours of the minimum wage) for two tickets (if you can get them), simply to watch a cosmopolitan team of young millionaires play football. The fans around me also look different to the fans of my childhood memories. Today they are festooned with the costly favours of the team I follow – but now they wear football shirts ('£45 please', said the young woman on the club's superstore cash desk). The simple red and white scarves which my brother and I tucked into our gabardine school raincoats have gone. So too have the wooden rattles we swung over our heads. They vanished soon after the ration books. The old school bell we used for special occasions made its farewell appearance at an FA Cup semi-final in 1957; the clapper came off, flying like a bullet into the packed crowd.

As a schoolboy, the men around me at football matches swore but, as far as I can recall, it was all pretty simple: bloody, bugger, sod – that was about the range of it, and nothing worse than I heard from less 'respectable' members of the family circle. But going to a major football match today is sometimes like joining a squad of young soldiers. Every conceivable swear-word trips readily from the lips, hurled at opponents, officials and sometimes at home players, often in an orchestrated chant clear enough to people outside the ground – and audible to armchair viewers watching the game on TV.

Football *sounds* different – at least to me. I cannot remember when chanting among thousands of fans began – at some time in the 1960s I suspect – but the cacophony of a big modern game is, again, different from before. The massive shouts of pleasure, excitement – anger even – are still there of course; many times I came home from a game in the 1950s with my head ringing from the noise of the past two hours. But I have no memory of the orchestrated chanting and singing so common at the modern game, some of it vulgar and sometimes racist.

The players even *looked* different. Today's top professional footballers are – with a few exceptions – sleek modern athletes, with kit to match. Look at old photos, say of professional teams in the 1950s, and they, including the greatest of players, look more like working men in ill-fitting, baggy football kit.

Today's top professional footballers are sleek modern athletes, with kit to match.

That is precisely what they were: men plucked from working-class communities and briefly given the status of a professional footballer. Not only do the players look different, they even sound different. Until very recently, players in English football teams were overwhelmingly British. The first team I followed in the late 1940s was predominantly English, the captain was Irish, and a couple of Scots added the exotic flavour to the team. Their successors, ten years on, consisted of nine Englishmen and two Irishmen. Today, it is hard to keep track of that team's national composition – French, Dutch, African, West Indian, Norwegian, Welsh. Listing the nationalities is pointless because the fact is so obvious – English elite football has become a cosmopolitan workplace.

The stadium we file into is, at once, both the same (it has the same name, located on exactly the same spot) and yet utterly different. What I pay for a seat today would, as a schoolboy, have been enough to get me through the turnstiles for 500 matches. (One shilling versus £25.) The cost of a modern match programme (£2) would have paid for 40 schoolboys through the turnstiles. But it is hardly the same place. The stadium itself is unrecognisable, its modern form the culmination of periodic transformations which have, bit by bit, swept away every physical feature of the 1950s and 1960s. Again, this is true right across the modern game. Clubs with traditional names, their history stretching back for the best part of a century, now boast ultra-modern stadiums, perched on small pieces of urban land occupied since the late 19th century. Some new stadiums are wonderful functional flights of architectural fancy. Others are just big; cavernous bowls ringed by cramped, moulded-plastic seating, scarcely enough room for fans in winter clothes to wedge themselves between their neighbours. For all the physical discomforts, there is something indescribably exciting about a packed modern football stadium – the colours, the noise, the dazzling lights. I get an initial buzz of excitement seeing it from a distance. It is very different from those dark grey monuments of the earlier game; banks of concrete and brick terracing, spliced and broken up by metal barriers to lean on, with a small area under corrugated-iron cover and an even smaller area reserved for seating, an old-fashioned 'scoreboard' at the back of the terrace looking more like a railway signal box. As you shuffled in and out of the stadium, there was always that inescapable disinfected smell of the urinals.

Even getting to the grounds is different. I used to travel on special buses, and to away games on football specials on the railways. Huge convoys of Manchester Corporation buses lined the city centre, primed for fans heading to the stadium. Later they lurked close by the ground, waiting to absorb the tidal wave of fans pouring out of the stadium at the end of the match. Now I go by car (and modern tram). Judging by the motorways crowded with cars and coaches (bedecked in football favours) converging on the city, most other fans also travel by road.

The haves and the have-nots

It is, then, a very different game. Echoes of all these changes can be seen not just in the Premier League but clean through all the ranks of the professional game. In the lower leagues, the crowds are thinner, the stadiums less lavish, the players less gifted (and much less well paid), the noise less deafening; the whole affair much less in the public eye. National media attention is devoted almost uniquely to major clubs and their players. However good the players and teams in the lower leagues, however vital they might be to the health of the professional game at large, they occupy only walk-on parts in the great media circus which has become the modern game of football. Local radio, local TV and local newspapers cover local or regional games. But such coverage hardly begins to compare with a full spread in, say, *Hello*. At times, players in the lower leagues must feel they are mere noises off-stage in a footballing drama played out before an audience of tens of millions. But it is in the nature of the footballing beast that he wants to be in the full glare of modern publicity. To receive such attention, to be fêted in so lavish a fashion, is to be to be successful, acclaimed – and to be rewarded on a scale which was unimaginable little more than a decade ago. Today's successful footballer (always the tiniest of minorities) enjoys rewards beyond the dreams of avarice.

The rich elite clubs, bloated with money from major corporate deals, form merely the peak of a massive footballing pyramid. Although they catch the eye – and secure the lion's

Today's successful footballer enjoys rewards beyond the dreams of avarice.

share of media attention (and, of course, the lion's share of all the money in the game) – they are, in all sorts of ways, utterly untypical. The Premiership is both different from its professional forebears and quite unlike the rest of football played in England. The major teams are utterly divorced from their immediate footballing ancestors. They bear the same name, colours (sometimes) and address – but much else is unrecognisable. Elite clubs are also quite unlike smaller, less successful professional clubs – millionaires, again, mixing with worthy, workmanlike fellow citizens – but no one imagines they are one and the same. More striking still is the gap between the elite clubs and amateur footballers.

The rich English clubs play precisely the same game as millions of fans who turn out, week after week, to play for their local clubs (a pub, a workplace, a school), but it forms a curious contrast. Both rich and poor footballers play by the same rules, same pitch size, same duration, same passions – but they are also utterly different. This may seem to be simply a matter of money. But the financial difference is on such a *scale* that it lifts elite players into a cultural and social world beyond the ken of their footballing peers elsewhere. The best (and therefore the richest) of footballers move in a world of popstars and lottery winners. Sunday park footballers are ordinary men (and, increasingly, women) from all walks of life, but unbridgeably beyond the lavish lifestyle of the players whose skills they admire and would love to emulate. Football has become, very recently and very quickly not so much the 'game of two halves' as the game of two worlds: the haves and the have-nots. At the top of the footballing firmament there struts a small band of Premiership clubs and their well-heeled players. At the bottom of football's social system there are millions of players (no one really knows how many) getting by

> ## Not so much the 'game of two halves' as the game of two worlds.

as best they can; through personal effort (and money), having to endure playing facilities which are inadequate and which have got worse year by year since the 1980s. And all is made possible by the dogged commitment by small bands of volunteers (schoolteachers, club and league secretaries, parents and others), scattered across the country and who form in effect football's hidden army. Unseen, unrecognised and unrewarded, they are the worker bees of the footballing system, the drones who make everything possible.

The Premiership

Football has clearly changed beyond recognition. But by concentrating on the elite game, critics and commentators so often overlook the game at the grass-roots of society. It is there that we find the people's game thriving much as it has throughout the 20th century. Yet the story of football in the 1990s is the story of the Premiership, and of the massive changes it has brought in its wake, through all levels of the game. The Premiership has major repercussions clean down to the smallest of local leagues and to school football. When a small band of tycoons planned before 1992 to create a super-league of major clubs, breaking away from the century-old League structure, they and their corporate supporters had no idea of two major revolutions they were about to unleash. Firstly, though they clearly anticipated a more profitable future under their new arrangements, they had no idea of the *scale* of the financial harvest they were about to reap. It proved, like the coming of commercial TV itself, a licence to print money. Secondly, they could never have predicted the massive changes they would bring about throughout the national game (not least because they gave no thought to the game outside their own corporate concerns). Many of those changes were to harm the popular game of football. The profits accrued to the major clubs; the cost was borne by the game at large.

Complaining about the Premier League has become a cottage industry itself. Authors, journalists, politicians – and above all, fans – hurl regular barbs at each and every aspect of the Premiership. It is a system which invites criticism. Bloated with massive profits (leeched from fans and corporate deals), the major clubs present a deeply unattractive image to the world at large. The major clubs' grasping corporate greed is quite at variance with football's traditional profile. But the rich clubs still have their friends, for they find sympathetic company, and mutual pleasure, with some of the world's most rapacious businessmen. The richer clubs make fat cats look anorexic. To recite the Premiership's failings is easy enough, and hardly provides an excuse for a new book. All this has been said before, more bitingly, by earlier critics.

The richer clubs make fat cats look anorexic.

The Premiership arose from English football's worst epoch. In the mid-1980s English football had been brought to its knees by a string of major footballing

Paolo di Canio © Gary M Prior/Allsport/Hulton Deutsch

disasters. Played in old, ugly and dangerous stadiums, football was marooned by a rising tide of hooliganism, the whole sorry scene capped by a chorus of foul racial abuse. English football was a *problem* more than a sporting or spectator pleasure. England's major teams were banned in Europe, and their fans dreaded wherever the game was played. Here was the national game which created alarm at home and shame abroad. Yet no one seemed capable of solving the game's endemic troubles. I was one of many who despaired of what had happened to the game I had grown up with and which, by the mid-1980s, had been transmuted into an ugly and dangerous problem.

Football entered the 1990s in a state of flux. Within ten years, however, it had made the most dramatic of comebacks and had become *the* most lucrative sporting forum England had ever known. Or rather the Premiership had become the most lucrative of English sporting activities. It was a staggering upheaval, and one which is easily overlooked, today, when the prime complaint is about the dizzying financial harvest reaped by the Premier clubs and their players.

Two factors were responsible for this transformation. Firstly, the Hillsborough disaster in April 1989 led to a far-reaching investigation headed by Lord Taylor. His report initiated the most extensive physical and social reconstruction of the game for a century. For the first time since the game's inception, the interests and well-being of football fans were placed at the top of the agenda. Secondly, senior clubs wanted to break loose from the old League system which had barely changed over a century, in order to secure a more profitable future. They found an ally in the form of fledgling satellite TV, and together the two created what was to prove to be an unimaginably lucrative liaison. From relatively modest financial beginnings, the Premier League and their TV backers began to rally corporate support, developing marketing strategies and devising club-based products which proved amazingly successful.

Those last-minute, eve-of-flight purchases vital to every successful holiday – a pair of Manchester United socks.

Odd as it may seem, there were large numbers of people willing to pay inflated prices for Arsenal towels, Leeds United duvet covers, and Manchester United wallpaper. Odder still, such people were not limited to local fans, but popped up across the nation. Later, as the marketing and TV coverage expanded, huge numbers of fans all over the world were anxious to gobble up club products. Major clubs opened their own supermarkets at their grounds (and even at airports) to sell their produce. Everything the football fan might need – those last-minute, eve-of-flight purchases vital to every successful holiday – a pair of Manchester United socks, for example. At times, even the most hardened football fan had to pinch him/herself: was this really the same game of a mere ten years ago?

The changing face of England

It would be foolish to deny the successes of the Premiership. Fans have returned to the game in growing numbers. Some clubs have effectively sold *all* their tickets for the entire season long before the first game kicks off. And people want to see televised Premiership football in unprecedented numbers. When Manchester United won the European Champions League in May 1999, the TV audience peaked at 19 million people. Inevitably perhaps, Premiership spokesmen often illustrate their success by pointing to the game's profits, and to the clubs' stock-market standing. This is hard and undeniable evidence. But it is also deceptive. For all the money, despite the millions of TV fans, and notwithstanding the legions of football fans worldwide, all is *not* well with the English game. Football in England is fissured and weakened by a number of serious structural faults. And many of those faults have been brought about by the seismic impact of the Premier League. Yet we need to probe more deeply than this. Football has not changed in isolation. England itself has changed and in recent years football seems to have held up a mirror to the changing face of England.

> **Football in England is fissured and weakened by a number of serious structural faults.**

There was plenty of hard empirical data to confirm the pessimism about British life. In most comparative tables, the British were shown to be well down the league – and slipping. The British, who once ruled the world, whose industries had once dominated, whose finances had been pre-eminent, and whose leaders once expected to sit at the head of the world's tables, now found themselves marginalised and often ignored. Here was a nation adrift on a sea of its own self-doubt. In the 1980s, football seemed a perfect metaphor for national decline.

The people who prided themselves on giving most modern games to the world now could rarely compete with the best on an equal footing. The game of football posed some curious problems. All this seemed to change dramatically in the 1990s – a decade of unparalleled footballing success at home – of returning fans (to modern stadiums), of attractive English club teams, with devoted fans in all corners of the world. But what made those teams so appealing (and successful) was not their *Englishness*, but their *cosmopolitan* mix. At the very time the British continued to be cautious about involvement in Europe, the national game had become increasingly European. Firstly, its major teams had been thoroughly infiltrated by foreign (mainly European) players. Secondly, the driving ambition behind all the major clubs was to play in European competitions. Thirdly, the commercial and financial power of the game was hugely enhanced by the televised integration of the national game into European schedules (indeed of global viewing). The national game had clearly become European and international.

The national game had clearly become European and international.

The story of football in the 1990s, according to the gloss painted by the proponents of the Premier League, was an unparalleled success story. But there was also a different tale to be told – a tale which surfaced wherever fans or critics met, or when they put pen to paper. From fanzines to the heavy weeklies, from Sunday morning footballers through to secretaries of schoolboy leagues, a very different story emerged. And when in 1997 the new Labour government launched its *Football Task Force*, those complaints were given a thorough and well-publicised airing. All was clearly not well with the national game of football. Most striking was the terrible state of football's grass-roots – its pitches and facilities, its crucial foundations. In common with the social fabric of urban life at large, the infrastructure of football had experienced a dramatic and alarming decline. How could this be, at a time when the game was attracting more money than ever before, more money indeed than anyone had dreamed possible? The 2001–2002 season has a domestic television contract worth more than one *billion* pounds (Manchester United are expected to earn £40 million from television alone; they could play throughout the season in an empty stadium and still make millions). Defenders of the Premiership are right to point to the dazzling volumes of money flowing through their coffers. But they need also to look to other corners of the game to present a more rounded picture.

This book is intended to do just that – to put the footballing events of the past decade into some sort of context. The 1990s marked a dramatically new phase in the history of English football. That decade also set in train a number of massive changes for the game far beyond the costly stadiums of the Premier clubs. The most staggering change has of course been the amount of money involved – for the lucky few. No less important (and closely related) has been the transformation of the game into a global passion. A game which, little more than a century ago, was the preserve of English public schoolboys and British working men has become the passion of untold millions worldwide. Teams which were once the footballing representatives of particular cities – or even parts of a city – now find their games and results watched by millions on the far side of the earth. It is, to say the least, a curious story. Today a small band of English football teams play for millions – for millions of pounds and for millions of fans. For most of those fans, football is the *only* game.

Football ... causeth fighting,
brawling, contention, quarrel-
picking, murder, homicide and
great effusion of bloode, as
daily experience teacheth.

Philip Stubbs, *Anatomy of Abuses* **(1583)**

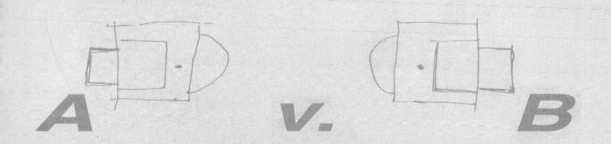

Famous English Football Players, 1881 © Vin Mag Archive

Gentlemen and players
Pre-1914

The folk game

In 1888, a history of football claimed that

The game of football is undoubtedly the oldest of all the English national sports. For at least six centuries the people have loved the rush and struggle of the rude and manly game, and kings with their edicts, divines with their sermons, scholars with their cultured scorn, and wits with their ridicule have failed to keep the people away from the pastime they enjoyed.

Games of football had been played throughout Britain for centuries before the rise of the modern game. Folk games of football, some of which survive to this day, punctuated the local and religious calendar. It was generally a rowdy game, with complex local rules and conventions: a highly ritualised game popular among young men. A crude ball, often an inflated animal bladder, was chased by teams of indeterminate size through villages and towns, scores counted when the ball reached its destination (a church porch, for example). It was a turbulent ritual, dangerous to life, limb and property, and to social tranquillity. Time and again, from the 14th century onwards, football was banned. Yet it managed to survive a succession of prohibitions and banishments. Feast days, holidays, wakes, fairs, all spawned games of football. Injury, damage (occasionally death) were all associated with these folk games.

Historians have found hundreds of such football matches, and efforts to curb or stop them, between the late Middle Ages and the origins of the modern game in the 19th century. The colourful evidence for pre-modern football is rich in anecdotal detail and has been repeated time and again by lovers and historians of the game. Most quoted of all perhaps is William Fitzstephen's description of Shrove Tuesday football in the city of London in 1174.

> After the midday meal the entire youth of the city goes to the fields for the famous game of ball. The students of several branches of study have their ball; the followers of the several trades of the city have a ball in their hands. The elders, the fathers, and men of wealth come on horseback to view the contests of their juniors, and in their fashion sport with the young men; and there seems to be aroused in these elders a stirring of natural heat by viewing so much activity and by participation in the joys of unrestrained youth.

All the game's basic ingredients are here: young men playing, older men watching, and the noisy passion of play and spectating.

The classic example of folk football was perhaps the Shrove Tuesday football match between the parishes of All Saints and St Peter's in Derby (hence the expression, a local 'Derby'). 'Teams', consisting of hundreds on each side, engaged in a game which lasted for hours as each side sought to drive an inflated pig's bladder through the porch of their opponents' church. Bystanders and property were at risk from the roving turbulence of the waves of young men locked against each other. This was just one of many similar folk games (Welsh 'knappan', Cornish 'hurling'), all generally tough and physical play, played among young men on particular high days and holidays.

Each side sought to drive an inflated pig's bladder through the porch of their opponents' church.

Descriptions of such games pepper contemporary social and legal accounts, especially when damage and injury took place. Many traditional folk games of football were however much less turbulent than this, being instead highly ritualised, with rules, conventions, referees and even clubs – long before the evolution of the modern game of football.

Football matches could be found across the face of pre-industrial England, but they did not constitute a *national* game. Football formed part of a colourful mosaic of folk games and pleasures, wakes and fairs, festivals and revels, which formed the popular recreational culture of the common people for centuries. Folk football was also an expression of local identity and rivalry (one village or parish versus another). But football as a game was also disliked; one scholar has counted 23 edicts issued *against* football in England and Scotland between the 14th and the 17th centuries. Such edicts seem not to have worked however, for the game of folk football continued right through to the 18th and 19th centuries.

The massive social and economic changes we know as the industrial revolution transformed the old games of football into the game we know today. The rapid rise of an urban and industrial society, and the increasingly widespread enclosures in rural England, helped to deny the common people access to land where they had once played traditional games. In the towns and cities of industrial England, large gatherings of young men, keen to enjoy traditional turbulent pleasures, were clearly a potential threat to peace and order. This was part of a much broader concern about how to police large crowds of people. As a result, the old folk games declined in the early 19th century. Where the games survived, they needed to be disciplined and able to fit in with the regulations of the new cities.

The old games did not go willingly, though. Players and supporters of folk football vigorously opposed the game's suppression, and in places police had to use force to stop local football games. Despite all this, folk football managed to survive in places. Shrove Tuesday football continues to this day in Ashbourne, Derbyshire and elsewhere.

A new, more disciplined game began to appear in the 1830s and 1840s.

Such examples are unusual, however, and throughout the first fifty years of the 19th century traditional folk football was in retreat. In its place, a new, more disciplined game began to appear in the 1830s and 1840s. Matches were arranged – often with a purse for the winner – between teams of youths, with clearly marked-out pitches and an agreed set of rules for the game. In 1841 in Bolton an announcement was made that

> Twenty Boltonians are prepared to play at foot-ball with twenty of the best men in the Rifle Regiment now stationed at Bolton, for £10 a side; to come off on New Year's Day, in the neighbourhood of Bolton . . .

Such matches were arranged by formally constituted football or sporting clubs, by groups of men in the army, by men gathered in taverns or from the workplace, joining together to play like-minded local groups. Sometimes one sport spawned another; cricket clubs begat football clubs, for example. In addition, such groups had to agree about the rules of play (the nature and size of the pitch, the timing and duration of the match). Often it was simplicity itself. The game at Hampton in Arden, played 'for a bottle of wine and dinner each' was to take place on a pitch in which

> The length between goals to be ten score yards, width of goals ten feet, height six feet, and to be the best of three goals.

Less organised forms of football, notably 'street football', continued, despite efforts to curb or ban them: impromptu games, usually among boys, playing according to no real set of rules, but involving indeterminate teams of boys.

Here was an informal, spontaneous and ubiquitous game which seemed to defy all efforts to suppress it. New laws governing the new cities and towns tried to drive street football away. A Highway Act of 1835 levied a fine of 40 shillings for

> playing at football or any other game on any part of the said Highways, to the Annoyance of any Passenger ...

Backed up by various local bylaws, such legislation allowed the new police forces to prosecute street footballers, but there is, again, abundant evidence to show that boys continued to play football in city streets. Though the traditional games of football had withered, they had not vanished.

The public schools

Football in the early years of the 19th century was also popular among boys from a more privileged world. The English public schools had played their own varieties of football for centuries. By the mid-18th century the game was established at Eton, Harrow, Westminster, Shrewsbury, Winchester, Marlborough and Charterhouse. On the whole, it was a game run by the boys, not by the masters. In fact school authorities tended to dislike it as much as authorities disliked street football; it was often subversive, generally rowdy and sometimes threatening. In his frequently quoted denunciation, Samuel Butler, Head of Shrewsbury from 1798 to 1836, said football was 'more fit for farm boys and labourers than for young gentlemen'. Between 1827 and 1836 the famous Eton Wall Game was banned because of its violence. Traditional games of football at Winchester were little less brutal. Like floggings and faggings, the violence of the public school games was simply a fact of life.

Like floggings and faggings, the violence of the public school games was simply a fact of life.

Harrow School team, 1867 © Hulton Getty.

By the mid-19th century, however, these undisciplined and rough games of football had been pulled into order within the Public Schools. Indeed football, along with other games, emerged as a key element in disciplining gangs of growing boys. This revolution is commonly associated with the work of Dr Thomas Arnold, Head of Rugby from 1828 to 1842, though much of the process was actually the work of his disciples. From the 1830s onward, there emerged a new generation of Heads and Housemasters, anxious to revitalise their schools, and who realised the importance of games. Sport became the agency that established a chain of command, from Head, to Housemaster, to team captain, to boys. Within the game, boys – the players – were given a strict code of discipline. What had once been rough and tumble, *ad hoc* and sprawling became, by the 1850s, a highly regulated and codified game of football (though it still differed from one school to another). By mid-century games had become a central feature of public school education, responsible for building 'character' and manliness, fostering team play and spirit and prizing sporting and athletic prowess above all else.

> **What had once been rough and tumble became a highly regulated and codified game.**

When the Clarendon Commission investigated the public schools in 1864, it heartily approved of 'their love of healthy sports and exercise' which, the Commission felt, was responsible for teaching Englishmen 'to govern others and to control themselves'. The critical decade for public school sports was the 1850s. A string of reforming Heads ensured that the school days of public schoolboys were filled with energetic sporting activity. Sport became an end in itself, each sport and team dressed in its custom-made kit, their 'colours', jerseys, 'caps' (the origins of football international caps), blazers, waistcoats and custom-made boots. The schools spent huge amounts of money on acquiring playing fields, a habit later picked up by the grammar schools and, at the end of the 19th century, by the new compulsory Board schools.

The enthusiasm for sport was contagious, as young public school masters moved on to other schools, taking with them the sporting values acquired under the major reforming Headmasters. In the same way, the cult of sporting prowess was transplanted from the public schools into Oxbridge colleges, into the armed forces, the Church, and into the Civil Service, both at home and in the empire.

Public schoolboys graduated from their schools with an enthusiasm for sports, determined to play as long as they were able, and keen to encourage others to adopt their sporting passions. Thus did rowing and cricket become a passion at Oxbridge, and at new schools staffed by young men from the older schools. There was a remarkable expansion in the number of public schools across the country, and all were influenced by the cult of sports. Looking back from the late 1880s, Montague Shearman noted that football, like athletics, had taken root in schools between 1850 and 1860, 'as part of the regular athletic curriculum, and as the chief school game of the winter months'.

Football had one major problem, however. The older schools played football according to different codes and conventions. Teams and games tended to be organised among men from the same school, or who agreed to a particular school's footballing code. In the 1840s students at Cambridge tried to codify the rules of the different games of football they had learned at school, but the early teams and clubs (Sheffield 1857, Blackheath 1858) tended to follow different rules. Although old-school sporting loyalties died hard, codification of football began to emerge in the 1850s, culminating in 1863 in the formation of the Football Association in London. Even then, the game looked odd to modern eyes. Handling the ball was allowed in certain circumstances, and many wanted to maintain the old practice of 'hacking' – in which 'any player on the opposite side should be at liberty to charge, hold, trip or hack him, or wrest the ball from him'. Without hacking, thundered the representative from Blackheath,

> you will do away with all the courage and pluck of the game, and I will be
> bound to bring over a lot of Frenchmen who would beat you with a week's
> practice.

Blackheath men's insistence on 'hacking' led them to break away from the FA and, in 1871, they were instrumental in forming the Rugby Football Union. Thus was the Association game – soccer – left to develop on its own.

In the 1870s the newly rationalised game of football began to spread throughout the country, through the formation of local clubs, regional associations and simple one-off football matches. By the end of that decade, football had begun to generate enormous popularity, 'as much the national game of winter as cricket is of summer'.

Football remained a tough, physical game. It was also a *gentleman's* game (hence the offence of 'ungentlemanly conduct'). It was a game in which men of the educated, propertied and privileged classes learned not only to develop physical, sporting perfection, but also how to work as a team and, of course, how to command those placed in their care:

> to command a division, lead a cavalry charge, bear the brunt of battle, the hardships of the field, or accept the responsibilites devolving upon the men to whose hands is entrusted the government of the nation.

Working men

But what about the *other* game of football – the popular folk game of the common people? New restrictions on football, imposed by local bylaws and the enclosure of common lands, were compounded by a new industrial discipline. Regulated by the clock, and dominated by the mechanical pace of the new industries, the personal and communal lives of working people began to change. The discipline of the new machine age was not universal, however, and old cultural habits often stood firm in the face of industrial and social change. But the trend was unquestionably *away* from the old patterns of traditional sports and pastimes, as more and more working people found their time consumed by work. Now their free time tended to be doled out by employers – allocated to weekends and specified holiday periods (though there were fewer holidays than ever before). And it was in these periods of leisure time that more and more working men drifted to the game of football.

This 'democratisation' of football began in the 1870s. The game which had been streamlined and reformed by the gentlemen of the public schools began to attract players and spectators from very different social backgrounds. Football clubs mushroomed, especially in the Midlands and the North. In Sheffield 34 clubs sprang up in the 1870s; the Lancashire FA represented 40 clubs formed in the ten years 1870–1880. Many football clubs simply did not survive the initial years of enthusiasm (among them the 'Flash Ramblers' and the 'Accrington Heroes'). Some regions remained oddly unaffected by the dramatic rise of football's popularity in the 1870s, but the game had clearly put down its roots as a popular, increasingly plebeian game, and with great commercial potential.

MANCHESTER UNITED F.C.

Manchester United, 1905 © Popperfoto

Crowds got bigger and bigger. Only 2000 spectators watched the first FA Cup Final in 1872, but in 1880 the first Lancashire Cup Final attracted 9000 spectators. By then, football had clearly begun to attract major investments, notably in stands and enclosures. By 1880, the game had begun to take on a recognisably modern shape. It had also begun to develop the distinct geographic and social bases which were to survive throughout the 20th century.

The centre of footballing gravity shifted from the public schools to England's industrial heartlands. Take, for example, the FA Cup. Until 1882, the Cup had been won by public school men and their teams. But in 1883, Blackburn

> **By 1880, the game had begun to take on a recognisably modern shape.**

Olympic defeated the Old Etonians, the winning goal scored by Jimmy Costly, a cotton spinner. It is true that many professional men continued to play the game in the last quarter of the nineteenth century but there was a seismic shift in football's support and composition. Increasing numbers of working men turned to the game which their forebears had enjoyed as a popular folk or street game, but where that had been turbulent and undisciplined, now it was rational and regulated. For a brief period in the 1870s and 1880s, both working class and public school footballers converged on the same game.

What enabled these working men to turn to football was the mix of free time and spare money. The economy had begun to yield spare cash to growing numbers of working people. Real wages rose by about one third in the generation between 1875 and 1900, most markedly in the last decade of the century. This was especially striking in Lancashire, where the buoyant textile industry yielded a much improved working-class wage. It was no accident that Lancashire was home to the newer forms of popular culture: the trips to Blackpool, the creation and rapid proliferation of the corner fish-and-chip shop, and, of course, the emergence of numerous football teams.

Saturday, day of sport

More and more working people also benefited from the freeing of Saturday afternoon from work. As early as 1867, Thomas Wright ('a working class engineer') noted that

> it is now a stock saying with many working men that Saturday is the best day of the week, as it is a short working day, and Sunday had to come ...

After one o'clock lunchtime, as the factories emptied, 'the younger apprentices and other boys immediately devote themselves to the business of pleasure'. Over the last 25 years of the century, the increase in the number of working men with leisure time on Saturday afternoons was striking in the Lancashire textile trades, for example, although much less noticeable in London and in Liverpool with their pools of casual labour. In both cities, the formation and proliferation of local football clubs and leagues came later than in textile Lancashire.

Sunday, of course, had been traditionally safeguarded by defenders of the Sabbath. Thus Saturday established itself as *the* day for sporting activity, and especially for football. In places, some of the old popular recreations existed alongside the new patterns of the industrial world; 'St Monday' (working men taking time off on Monday, when they felt like it, for their pleasures) continued into the 1850s and 1860s. But the drift towards Saturday being the *natural* day free from work was unmistakable. It was, for example, clearly reflected in the magazine *Bell's Life* reports of sporting activity. From the 1850s to the 1860s the games and recreations reported in that magazine showed a marked shift from being a predominantly Monday activity to a Saturday one. When football became ever more commercial in the 1870s, the drift to Saturday was clinched. By the mid-1870s the very great majority of all football matches reported in *Bell's Life* took place on Saturday.

> ## When football became ever more commercial in the 1870s, the drift to Saturday was clinched.

Sunday games were forbidden to the footballing fraternity, not least because large numbers of the new football clubs sprang from churches and Sunday schools, but also because the FA (moralistic from the first) took an early stand against it. Rule 25 decreed that

> Matches shall not be played on Sundays within the jurisdiction of this Association.

This ban was not rescinded until 1981. Of course this did not prevent boys from playing on Sundays whenever the opportunity arose, as a letter to the *Preston Herald* complained in 1884.

> On Sunday the parks are visited by numerous gangs of young lads, who vie with each other in the use of obscene language whilst indulging in their wonderful game ... Surely the police would not be exceeding their duty in trying to put down all football playing in the public streets and parks.

The clubs

Football was further transformed in the course of the 1880s. Clubs, associations, knock-out competitions and leagues proliferated in that decade. Team play, individual skills, coverage in the burgeoning popular press – all these and more lured ever-larger crowds to the roped-off football pitches. The bigger games began to attract vast crowds and local entrepreneurs were quick to construct viewing stands (and to charge entrance money) for the swelling armies of spectators. Spectators, in their turn, were willing to pay to watch the game, and were spending more and more money on other forms of popular leisure (music halls, seaside trips). As football's popularity grew, as the revenue it generated increased, skilled players began to realise that here was a way of earning a wage.

Skilled players began to realise that here was a way of earning a wage.

> No word of ours can adequately describe the present popularity of football with the public – a popularity which, though great in the metropolis, is infinitely greater in the large provincial towns ... it is no rare thing in the North and Midlands for 10,000 people to pay money to witness an ordinary club match, or for half as many again to assemble for a 'Cup Tie'.

But how had all this come about, in so short a period? Where precisely did the football clubs spring from? A number emerged from existing sports clubs, notably cricket clubs, whose members wanted to keep together, and to play, in winter. Sheffield Wednesday (cricket was a well-established sport in Sheffield) and Preston North End both began life in this way. Something like a quarter of the early football clubs sprang from churches. Barnsley, Bolton, Everton and

Southampton all began like this. The workplace also spawned a number of clubs which survive today in a professional form: Stoke City, West Bromwich Albion, Manchester United and Arsenal. Other football clubs emerged from public houses (which many other clubs used as changing rooms).

But what inspired men to form sports clubs in the first place? There was an undoubted element of middle-class, educated influence at work. Men inspired by the public school sporting culture were often anxious to encourage sport among working men. Keen to encourage healthy play, to cultivate the ideal of team above self, they were also influenced by an attachment to the belief that sport was good for physical well-being. Men steeped in this ethos worked throughout the country as clergyman, teachers, businessmen and professional soldiers (at home and abroad). Ex-public school men were everywhere, and were especially important in founding sports organisations, notably the FA (1863). Yet the story is uneven, and not all the games enjoyed by public school men successfully translated into working-class communities. Sometimes, public school men even *resisted* the spread of their favourite sports among local working men.

Large numbers of football clubs sprang from within working-class communities with little or no prompting from public school footballing enthusiasts. Often, the urge to form a football club came *up* the social ladder. Working men sometimes sometimes asked their 'betters' to help them financially or to provide contacts and organisational experience, in order to form a club. Often too, working men broke *away* from a club when they found it unsympathetic. Men in Christ Church Football Club in Bolton split from the church in 1872 when the vicar sought to make his continued support for football dependent on church attendance. More common perhaps, clubs were created with help from a variety of quarters. Aston Villa was formed by young men linked to the Aston Villa Wesleyan Chapel in Birmingham; they played on a field owned by a local butcher and they changed in a local pub.

To recap, then, there was a powerful working-class attachment to sport which long predated the rapid growth of modern football clubs. And there were men and organisations already in place, throughout working-class Britain, able to make use of the new-found leisure time and spare cash, and to tap into the growing popularity of organised sports in order to establish football teams and clubs. There was in effect a profusion of cultural changes which came together to drive forward the rise of popular football in the last quarter of the nineteenth century. The tide of sporting enthusiasm which lapped across England from the 1870s onwards was spread by a marked movement of people. This was most apparent in the textile districts of Lancashire, which were the heartlands for the modern

The textile districts of Lancashire were the heartlands for the modern game of football.

game of football, and which saw the game spread from Darwen, to Blackburn, to Bolton and Preston, thereafter throughout the Lancashire textile region, thence to the country at large.

The modern game

The formation of hundreds of football clubs by 1900 was part of a remarkable episode in the history of British sports. In the second half of the nineteenth century, *thousands* of sports clubs mushroomed across the face of Britain. Angling clubs (in Sheffield alone rising from 180 in 1869 to 500 in 1914), curling clubs (in Scotland), golf clubs (from one, Blackheath, in mid-century to 1200 by 1912), rugby clubs (from 32 to 481 between 1871 and 1893), while lawn tennis clubs increased from one in 1872 to about 1000 in 1914. The story could be repeated from one sport to another, from athletics to hockey, from bowling to badminton. The first football club, Sheffield Football Club, was founded in 1857; by 1914 there were 158 professional clubs, in addition to 12,000 boys' clubs. In football, as in all other sports, a framework of local, regional and national administration quickly emerged to monitor, regulate and control the game. Local games were governed by County Football Associations, national issues by the London-based Football Association, which eventually joined the international association (FIFA) in 1906. The proliferation of such large numbers of clubs and their parent associations in turn led to a multiplication of competitions and leagues – in all sports, not just in football. There was, for example, a veritable explosion of competitions among cricket clubs in the north of England in the late century. But even that was dwarfed by what was happening to football.

The most influential form of competition was the FA Cup, inspired by C.W. Alcock, an old Harrovian, and based on the 'knock-out' principle of Harrow's

'Cock-House' competition. Such competitions were common in most of the major public schools, attended by the men who, in 1871, agreed to establish the FA Cup as a competition for their own football teams. Not surprisingly, for the first ten years the winners of the Cup were men from the public schools. Along with the inauguration of football matches between England and Scotland (beginning in 1872), the FA Cup saw a rapid codification of existing football rules and a dramatic upsurge in the game's popularity. Teams, players and fans seemed to thrive on the sudden-death thrills of the Cup. That, and similar international knock-out competitions, have remained the most exciting formula of the game from that day to this.

> ## Teams, players and fans seemed to thrive on the sudden-death thrills of the Cup.

In the course of the 1870s, the game we know today came into being. Football's rules were laid down: the size of the pitch and playing conditions were specified, the crossbar was introduced (as was the goalkeeper), and a formal break authorised at 'half time'. The rules even specified the size of the ball. Old confusions, about handling the ball and about hacking, were swept away. Henceforth it was clear to everyone exactly how the game should be played, what was permissible and what was unacceptable. Footballers knew that they had to abide by an agreed set of rules, and the FA gave itself power to penalise, punish and ban players who transgressed, to 'rule out of the game any player who persistently infringed the laws'. Referees had controlled games in the FA Cup from 1871, and by 1880 that official was given a permanent role on the football field. The year after, shin-guards were first introduced, and not before time; the offence of 'violent conduct' had also entered the rulebook. A number of players – including Old Etonian Lord Kinnaird – had developed reputations as tough, aggressive players. Teams began to acquire their own distinctive playing strip, though sometimes this was varied and to modern eyes looks odd. In the Darwen team in the FA Cup in 1878–1879, one or two players

> ... wore long cloth trousers, with braces over a dark shirt. Those who boasted knickerbockers, had these useful garments made from old trousers cut down. Their shirts were of all kinds, and two of their prominent players wore sweaters.

Lord Kinnaird, who played in an extraordinary *nine* Cup Finals and won five winner's medals, played for the Wanderers and the Old Etonians in long white trousers, a quartered cap – and sporting a long red beard. At the 1882 Final, he stood on his head in front of the stands. Later, he was to become High Commissioner of the Church of Scotland.

The element of competition clearly prompted excitement, and generated still more enthusiasm for football both in England and Scotland. For a start, football often reflected older, traditional rivalries. Football teams from pub and church, from the Sunday school, the workplace and trade union drew upon men's local loyalties, and pitched them in competition with rivals round the corner, across the city or, later, in other towns entirely, in a pattern that echoed centuries-old rivalries. But now football had moved away from the prototype of its gentlemen founders to find a new centre of gravity (in the north) and a new social tone: plebeian where previously it had been propertied. Though the rules had become standardised, a new *kind* of game was emerging; one which was rooted ever more securely in working-class communities in the major industrial areas, and which was able to draw large crowds of spectators. Where

> **Team play, careful defensive play and a determination to win became football's characteristics.**

once the game had revolved around the individual, allowing the 'dribbler' to have his own way, to play as he wished, to be his own man, the new game – especially from the 1880s – saw a marked change of tactics. Team play, careful defensive play and a determination to win became football's characteristics.

Professionals and amateurs

The key proponents of these new tactics were the Scots, with an emphasis on the passing game, where the ball was kept on the ground. The game in Scotland paralleled the changes in England. By 1881 it was remarked that one cannot go into a single village or town in Scotland without seeing the practice grounds and goalposts of the now omnipresent football club.

More than that, Scotland also dispatched south growing numbers of young men to play in the expanding English game. From the 1880s onwards, and right to the present day, the role of the Scot (as player and coach) was critical to English football. Scots also took the game round the world. There were huge numbers of Scots on the move in search of work; if they played football, they had an added skill they could trade in the labour market.

By the 1880s, football had begun to attract very large crowds, and skilled footballers expected to be paid for entertaining such numbers. The issue of professionalism had surfaced, posing a fundamental challenge to the values and ethos of football's founding fathers. The ideals which had inspired football among public school men were the very essence of amateurism – of enjoying games for their own sake. Gentlemen did not play for money (not least because they had no need to). By the mid-1880s, after fierce argument it was realised that, much as it was disliked, professional football had arrived and needed to be regulated, not banned. In 1885 professional football was accepted, grudgingly, and hemmed in with a battery of regulations. Thereafter professional footballers had to defend their interests against bureaucracies and individuals unsympathetic to professionalism and rarely willing to accept the players' legitimate interests. Today, in a world of millionaire footballers, it is easy to forget the exploitative relationship which has characterised the lives of most professional footballers throughout the history of the game.

> Gentlemen did not play for money (not least because they had no need to).

English football teams of the 1880s clearly needed a regular structure for their games. After 1888 they had the Football League, which was itself increasingly professional in interests and tone – a fact which drove men of the 'old school' ever more surely towards an overtly amateur game and which was best expressed by the gentlemen amateurs, the Corinthians, founded in 1882. Both north and south of the border, the structures of the modern game were now in place. It would be wrong, however, to think solely of the professional game. Professional football clubs were (then as now) an elite. Beneath them, there were thousands of clubs, and teams (all of them of course subject to the control and authority of the FA). The popular amateur base of football was massive, and was expanded late in the century by the introduction of compulsory education and the encouragement of football among young boys at school. Even when a school had only a bare, rough playground for recreation, schoolboys played football. The end result of all these changes was that, by the 1890s, football was an inescapable feature of urban life. It was played in parks, on spare land and local fields, in rough streets and school playgrounds. Most memorably, of course, the game was played in the new football stadiums which began to dot the urban skyline.

The fans

By the late 1880s the crowds turning up to watch professional matches strained the physical fabric of the game. Crowds got bigger and more numerous as the number of clubs grew. The graph of football attendance went ever upwards, especially in the early years of the new century. There had never been such crowds, so ubiquitous, so clamouring, so demanding and so frequent. Not perhaps since the crowds at the Roman spectacles had such numbers flocked to public entertainment.

In 1875 only two games attracted crowds of more than 10,000 people. Within ten years that had risen to 18. In 1885, 27,000 had watched a cup tie between Aston Villa and Preston; in 1888, the Cup Final at the Oval attracted a crowd of 17,000 people. After 1892, the Surrey Cricket Club would not allow their turf to be damaged by football and the Cup Final moved north, to an athletic stadium in Manchester which housed 45,000 people. In 1895 it moved south again, to Crystal Palace, where crowds grew year by year. By 1913, 120,000 watched the Final. The most dramatic rise in attendance (helped by the opening of custom-built stadiums) was in the 1890s. In 1888–89, 31 cup ties attracted 200,000 fans. Six years later, 63 matches drew 1,200,000 people. Knock-out competitions were the most popular, but the new football league, playing on a regular weekly basis, accumulated huge numbers of spectators across the season. In the first season of the football league, 602,000 people watched the games between the 12 leading clubs. Five years later the figure had reached almost two million, dominated, not surprisingly, by the major teams in the big cities and conurbations.

The early days of roping-off a field and charging an entrance fee, gave way to creating embankments of earth with steps cut into them, and building a simple stand for protected cover. (Not until the last 25 years has British football seen fit to protect *all* its spectators against the guaranteed misery of British winter weather.) Between 1889–1910, 58 clubs moved into new facilities, often on land already in use for sport. British cities were now home to the latest of sporting venues: custom-built stadiums, the amphitheatres of modern international sporting passion and rivalries, local and international (especially between England and Scotland). But the fans' comfort was not an item on the designer's drawing-board. Nor, despite the large numbers of spectators, was professional football a profitable business for the men who invested in the new stadiums. Football clubs became limited companies, mainly to raise money to build new facilities, but in 1908–1909 only six of the 62 prominent clubs paid a dividend to their shareholders. Even then, football authorities limited the return to 5 per cent. Most investors agreed: 'No one who is out for business return would look at football shares.' Some clubs gave their profits away. Celtic, for example, gave their money to Catholic charities. There were, inevitably, branches of the football business which might yield a profit to local businessmen, from rent, catering and the like. Yet most investments in the game saw a return only in the form of enhanced local status and prestige. Not surprisingly, the great majority of the backers of football clubs were businessmen – small groups of local shareholders, sometimes family groups. Football did not, however, conform to normal business patterns and expectations. There was, quite simply, no other business like it. Wages for the players were low, profits for the shareholders were infrequent and small-scale. Yet millions of fans poured through the turnstiles by the end of the nineteenth century, their money apparently evaporating before it reached the pockets of players or directors.

No one who is out for business return would look at football shares.

By the early 20th century, football was a mass game; a game which had entered the bloodstream of millions of (mainly working-class) men and boys and on which they spent whatever spare cash came their way. It was, at once, a local routine; 'just being there to support your team and to identify yourself with thousands of others who felt the same'. But it was also a passion; a

noisy, raucous, sweaty affair which made staid men bellow in anger or excitement; sensible men said the most stupid of things, and even 'gentlemen' took
on an utterly different – loud and sometimes crude – persona when packed
into their favourite football ground. The 'fan' thus came into being (the term
itself adopted from US usage for baseball supporters). Baden-Powell for one
did not like what he knew of football crowds:

> Miserable specimens ... learning to be hysterical as they groan or cheer in
> panic unison with their neighbours, the worst sound of all being the hys-
> terical scream of laughter that greets any trip or fall by a player.

Fans learned about games by advertisements in shop windows, on billboards
but, most important of all, through news and adverts in local newspapers.
This was, after all, the age of a new mass literacy and compulsory education.
It was also a period of British life characterised by the rise of the popular
press; cheap daily and weekly, national and local newspapers, available on
street corners, which devoted ever more space to sport, and especially to
football. The game was also accessible, thanks to new transport systems. If
fans could not get to the games on foot, they travelled by omnibus and by
trams which snaked their way around British cities. But most important of
all, of course, they travelled by train. The national, cheap train system
enabled fans and teams to criss-cross the entire country. Fans in their thousands packed the special trains heading for distant football matches. Working
men from northern industrial cities descended by the trainload every year for
the Cup Final in London. For millions of people, the football trip to London
remained an annual event, like a trip to the seaside, for which they saved
throughout the year. Likely as not, it was the *only* trip they made to the
capital.

Entrance prices for most weekly matches were low. Though cup ties saw
admissions rise to 1/–, most games could be seen for 3–6 pence. Between
1890–1915 the minimum entrance fee stood at 6 pence (lower for women and
boys) and was within the range of most working men. Even the poor felt able
to set aside money for football. A Dundee newspaper noted in 1908 that 'no
matter how slender the finances of many households, the male must have his
sixpence to witness the football ...'. Very bad times (notably unemployment)
naturally affected local attendances, but the rise in attendance at football
matches clearly shows that more and more men before the First World War
were willing and able to spend their spare cash on football.

Cup Tie — Albion v Luton, Hove, December 20, 1919 © Popperfoto

WILES
19
25 PRESTONVILLE R?
BRIGHTON.

The crowds streaming towards football grounds were remarkably varied. The well-to-do, tradesmen and the middle class, with a sprinkling of women, mingled with labouring men at the games. But from the mid-1880s onwards the crowds became more obviously working class. Even the Cup Final was affected. In 1886 the *Athletic News* thought the 'working class elements are in the majority'. The evidence is confusing, but on the whole the fans at the grounds seem to have been primarily young working men, a scattering of more prosperous and older men, and some women. That is exactly what we see when we look closely at the photographs of early football crowds.

They descended on the grounds wearing their teams' 'colours', with placards and banners, noisily making their way to and from the railway stations. Newspapers often told of ribald and vulgar chanting and responses, and out-bursts of bad behaviour. There were also more serious disorders, sometimes because of overcrowding, but also because of the crowd's dislike of the referee or his decisions, or animosity to the club and management. Dubious or unpopular decisions sometimes forced the police to protect the referee on his way home. One referee told how he was threatened

> by a body of dirty low blackguards . . . [who] threatened to smash my (adjective) jaw when the game was over.

After the game he was abused by umbrella-waving women, something was thrown at him, and he had to be rescued by local gents. Such incidents seem to have been rare, though insults hurled at the referee for his decisions became a footballing ritual.

The policing of football crowds became an art in itself.

Fans often hurled verbal insults at each other. When tempers flared, they threw objects at their opponents. Sometimes visiting players were attacked. Crowd trouble, however, was more likely to be caused by overcrowding, when hoards of people were forced to spill onto the playing pitch. Even before the turn of the century, the problem of crowd control had become a feature of English football, taxing the police and footballing authorities, and erupting with some-times tragic results. From the first, the police were involved with football. Indeed the policing of football crowds – the logistics of marshalling such huge bodies of humanity to and from the railway stations, in and out of the grounds – became an art in itself. The wrong chemistry (poor police management, excessive numbers of fans, or unpredictable events – a collapsed barrier, for example) inevitably led to football's periodic disasters.

What was remarkable was that such large crowds gathered, peacefully, for a simple 90 minutes of football. In the thirty years before 1914 the game had gone full circle, passing through the reforming hands of the public school pioneers, to return whence it had originated – as the game of the common man. Now, as well as being massively popular throughout urban Britain, it had also become a professional game (though many, many more footballers simply played for love of the game), it was highly commercial and it was a subject of remarkable interest in the press.

03

Coming of age
1914-1939

© PA Photos

O n the eve of the First World War there was no doubting football's remarkable popularity. It was watched by millions, played by tens of thousands, was the site of an expansive professionalism (despite the hostility of the founding fathers). Football was simple; it had simple rules, and was an ideal game which new fans (and players) could turn to and play or watch without too much trouble about the game's complexity. It thrived as a popular street and park culture among armies of boys and youths. It was also a game which had already spawned an extraordinary range of commercial interests, from the newspaper 'football special', to cigarette cards and custom-made kits. Football was also the source of a major gambling industry. The game was a ubiquitous, noisy and, in many parts of urban Britain, simply inescapable social activity which had, for millions, taken on a life of its own. Football stadiums fringed the cities, its major players were 'stars' (though generally humbly paid), and its professional teams and their international counterparts inspired passionate loyalty (and enmity). Football teams were the object and occasion of local pride and attachment. The game also represented that peculiar, ill-defined but tangible animosity between north and south, and between England and Scotland. Rowdiness, horseplay, vulgarity, vocal obscenities – all and more swirled around the game of football. Sometimes those footballing passions spilled over into crowd turbulence and street disorders. Like the fans in general, these troubles overwhelmingly involved young men. Football was also a game which seemed to characterise that most distinctive of British phenomena – social class in action. For all the presence of the well-to-do in boardrooms, notwithstanding the old tradition of public school football, the game had become primarily a sporting passion of the urban working-class male. These features were to characterise football throughout the 20th century.

The First World War

Football of course had its critics. Some fretted that there were too many spectators, not enough players, that the lack of physical activity might sap the strength and resolve of the hardy British imperial 'race'. The young football fan, hunched on the terraces, a cigarette between his lips, did not impress those critics wedded to the public school ideal of athleticism. They disliked crowds of men flocking to football matches

in their workaday dirt, and with their workaday adjectives on their tongue.

Yet the game also attracted 'respectable' support. In 1914 football was even given the seal of royal approval when the King watched the Cup Final. On the outbreak of war, football, unlike many sports, did *not* suspend its activities, waiting instead until the end of the season in 1915. The wrath of the game's opponents became vituperative:

we view with indignation and alarm the persistence of Association Football Clubs in doing their best for the enemy ... there is no excuse for diverting from the front thousands of athletes in order to feast the eyes of inactive spectators who are either unfit to fight or unfit to be fought for. . . .

Such criticisms were unfair, for football 'did its bit', lending its organisation and stadiums for recruitment of men to the services. In fact wartime served to illustrate the universal popularity of football. Not surprisingly, millions of recruits were football fans, and the game thrived in all corners of the war. The famous football match at Christmas, in no-man's land in 1914, was only the most spectacular example of impromptu and organised games among soldiers in all the major theatres of war. The Germans, French and British all sent footballs to the front lines for the troops' recreation and pleasure. It was the same on all sides. Life for British prisoners of war in Germany was brightened by football matches. Austrian prisoners won over their Russian guards to the game, while the French soldiers became attracted to football by watching games played between British and Belgian soldiers. Looking back, proponents of sporting manliness thought that the war had proved the value of games.

> `Wartime served to illustrate the universal popularity of football.`

> If the first 100,000 British soldiers in the war had not been sportsmen, they would not have known how to take defeat and eventually turn back the Germans.

The flaw with that argument was that the Germans were no less enthusiastic than the British about team sports.

Even in the midst of that terrible slaughter, the old chivalric images of sport flitted in and out of wartime writing. A master from Marlborough, mourning the death of yet another former pupil, wrote

> *Aye, Marlborough knows you played the game*
> *Dying you set the gem on her.*

For another victim, he wrote

And now you've played a grimmer game;
Old England called – you heard and came
To shot and shell, to fire and flame.

In public school mythology, sporting prowess and leadership went together. And so it proved – but with disastrous consequences few had foreseen. The men who administered most formal sporting organisations were utterly committed to the war, and saw no reason to continue with their regular sporting activities. Any effort, especially among healthy young men, that was *not* directed against the enemy ought to stop.

The professional game simply faded away as the war dragged on and as attendances simply drooped under the force of mass enlistments. But football matches continued throughout the war – charity matches, friendlies, regional games and an endless series of ad-hoc matches. Despite the critics, despite the social snobberies directed at it, football's reputation as the British national game had been amply confirmed.

The inter-war game

In the twenty years between the wars, football consolidated this claim. Moreover it did so in a society experiencing some remarkable changes in contemporary popular culture. Millions poured each week into the new cinema palaces, tens of millions of people bought their own radio set (generally on hire purchase) to listen to the BBC. In summer, armies of Britons took to the trains or motor coaches for their annual trek to the seaside resorts. Yet all this was at a time of marked unemployment, especially after 1921. For those in work, however, real wages rose and working hours were reduced; for them there was more money and more time for leisure. Football boomed. Professional football clubs increased in numbers, and so too did the spectators. In the process, the social geography of the game began to change. Football clubs in London and the Midlands now challenged the northern teams, both in their following and success, led most spectacularly by Arsenal. Even so, football's centre of gravity, its cultural heartland and the source of its greatest inspiration and support, remained in the north. Some northern clubs undoubtedly suffered but the steadfast loyalty of football fans in those communities blighted by local unemployment was remarkable. Football was a game able to rally its fans in the most depressed and deprived of circumstances.

There was in effect a post-war football craze. It even spread to women. In England, women's football had developed a distinct following as early as the 1890s, though it remained more a curiosity for the men, however serious the players' intentions. It was, in part, an attempt to enter the world of contemporary masculinity. But it made little headway until immediately after the First World War; there were an estimated 150 women's teams in 1921. But women's football had always offended the masculine ethos of the FA and in 1021 they banned it, deeming it to be 'unsuitable' for women and 'not to be encouraged'. Women's football also flourished in France. Contemporaries often described the 1920s as 'crazy years', and George Bernard Shaw was not alone in regarding the passion for sports as the craziest venture of all.

The game of football itself changed. The inter-war years saw the introduction of important tactical and rule changes (the offside rule, long 'throw-ins', the emergence of new defensive plans built around the centre-half). The game also seemed physically tougher. Football fans with long memories thought that the game was more physical than at any time since its codification in the 1880s.

> It is a long time [wrote one journalist in 1926] since I watched a game in which the elbow and the foot were used to stop a man so often.

When Walsall played Arsenal in the Cup in 1933, it was claimed that no one could

> have complained had five of their men, at least, been sent off the field in the first quarter of an hour ...

The toughness of inter-war football alarmed some observers. Teams regularly squared up to each other, and referees were blamed for not being firm enough. What made it worse in the eyes of such critics was that this took place at a time when industrial militancy was thought to be a growing national problem – football seemed to be holding up a mirror to the troubled face of British life.

The toughness of inter-war football alarmed some observers.

The 1920s and 30s witnessed the emergence of the modern football manager.

Club managers had prevously been administrators rather than trainers and were often described as Secretary Managers. The most successful was Herbert Chapman of Huddersfield Town and Arsenal.

In the 1920s Chapman raised Huddersfield Town from a modest club (almost out of business) to the most successful club of that decade. A modest player, (the pattern for so many great managers), Chapman had been banned for illegal payments (to the defunct Leeds City), but bounced back at Huddersfield with two Championships and an FA Cup win. He was promptly wooed by Arsenal, which he quickly established as the most successful team of the 1930s (though Chapman died in 1934). Arsenal won three Championships in a row, and became a new *kind* of football club: glamorous, eye-catching, always in the media eye, and able to buy the best players available. Their star players were able to capitalise on their metropolitan fame by making sponsorship deals and promoting a host of products. The club modernised the Highbury stadium, and provided the best of contemporary facilities for players and fans alike. Arsenal were a stylish club on and off the field – where most others remained dour and practical. They were also very successful. As a result, they were much envied ('Lucky Arsenal') – and disliked.

Arsenal dominated English football at a time when tactics revolved around *preventing* goals. Many of the 1930s stars were defenders (Manchester City's goalkeeper Frank Swift for example) and one obvious consequence of this defensive mentality was that goals became rarer. Older critics thought the game had become less tough than in its pioneering days, though contemporary 'hard men' were infamous. The hardest of all, Frank Barson, was even sent off in his own testimonial. Indeed many games are remembered because of their physical aggression as much as their skills or scores. Having said that, the most eye-catching players were always the star attackers, none more memorable than Dixie Dean of Everton and England who managed to score 82 goals in the 1927–28 season, and an amazing career total of 473 goals in 502 matches. No player since has come remotely close to such a strike rate, and all that at a time of disciplined defences and intimidating defenders. Whatever tacticians decided in the dressing room, fans clearly wanted to see goals; goals excited the crowds – however much the purist might purr about skilful defenders, then as now, defenders were rarely as memorable or as exciting as a goal-scoring forward. Dixie Dean, like Alex James at Arsenal, made good money for sponsoring products, and both men were considered glamorous stars with a great deal of commercial potential. Along with a small band of star footballers they represented a new kind of player who was both professional and commercial, thought their extra earnings look paltry set alongside the riches of modern stars.

Herbert Chapman personified the rise of professionalism among football managers, though they were always (and still are) severely restrained by their Directors, often local businessmen who felt that business success automatically qualified them for football management. It was to be a feature of the professional game throughout the century. After a fashion it was understandable. Men who invested their hard-earned cash in football clubs felt it reasonable that they should have a say in the running of the club. Thick-skinned directors managed to unite both the fans and the players in a healthy distrust of the local football board. But it was the 'hands-on' manager, intimately involved in the physical and tactical preparation of his players and teams, who spearheaded some of the major improvements in the nature of English football before the Second World War.

Despite finding new strength and support in the urban habitat, football continued to be governed by men of the old school. Football's administrators were steeped in the ethos and ideals of their youth (they were after all Victorians), generally resistant to change, disliking many aspects of an increasingly professional and commercial game. Nor were they much interested in football outside the British Isles. They were 'little Englanders' (even when not English), secure in the knowledge that they had shaped the modern game of football, and confident in what had become the tried and tested regimes of the domestic game, notably the annual rituals of leagues and the Cup. Their initial reaction to almost every innovation was resistance and refusal (to betting and the pools, to Sunday and women's football, to approaches from footballers abroad).

Football's administrators were 'little Englanders'.

Football's ruling elite within the FA also showed remarkable distaste for professionalism, and gave undue attention and consideration to the amateur game. So too did many others of the 'old school' (that commonplace phrase is itself an indication of the power which 'old schools' came to exercise in British life). The quality press, for example, continued to cover the amateur game as if the days of Edwardian public school athleticism survived intact.

The spirit of the footballing amateur, best expressed by the Corinthians, remained a powerful feature of the game after 1919. Even as late as 1960, a major publication on the history of football devoted 12 out of 22 chapters to 'The Amateur Game'. In the inter-war years, this was not so much because there were, (as there are today), many more amateur footballers than professionals (football in state schools, on streetcorners and in parks), but rather that the young men of the late Victorian and Edwardian public schools had become the elderly patriarchs of football. It was, in part, a common generational issue – a game which was, inevitably, of and for the young but governed by the elderly. Those older administrators were, by upbringing and inclination, generally out of sympathy with many of the developments in the modern game. This was especially striking at two important levels: football as the game of the common man, and football as a professional game. Socially, the FA remained utterly removed from the poor industrial communities in which the popular game thrived; similarly they remained fundamentally at odds with the professional game. Such tensions between what might be called rank-and-file sentiment and the spirit of administration was not unique to football. It was a divide, rooted in social class, secured by schooling, and given a polish by Oxbridge education, which haunted many English institutions.

The football business

Professional football was transformed after the First World War by the rapid emergence of radio broadcasting, and by the proliferation of a new print media which paid increasing attention to football. The best footballers became 'stars', their articles 'ghosted' in newspapers, magazines and the sporting pages, their faces made famous by film, advertisements, photography and cigarette cards. They were now able to supplement their earnings by a range of commercial activities. In a game which tightly restricted players' wages, a club's ability to provide outside earnings for their better players proved a major incentive in the movement and transfer of footballers. Wages were generally poor however. Most players did not receive the maximum wage of £9 a week (reduced to £8 in 1922), plus small bonuses. As low as these may seem, they were much better than the pay of ordinary working men, including skilled men, from whose ranks most professional footballers had risen. As late as 1939 skilled engineers were paid only £3/10/0 for a 47-hour week.

Footballers were tied to their clubs by restrictive contracts which allowed them no freedom of movement to take their skills and earning capacity elsewhere. They might even find their non-footballing activities *curbed* by their contracts. In 1924, for example, Harold Gough of Sheffield United took a pub, with an eye to retirement. The club promptly stopped his wages (and insisted on repayment of all his wages since he took the pub), put him up for transfer for an excessive fee, and Gough never again played professional football. The Players Union (founded as early as 1907) was powerless in the face of such tight contracts and such obdurate club management. Today, when we discuss the freedoms and rewards of the modern player, we need to recall the harsh lot of most professional footballers throughout much of the history of the English game. They were shabbily treated, generally poorly paid, discarded when surplus to requirements, and ill-regarded by their employers.

The Players' Union, based in Manchester, was, not surprisingly, disliked by football's authorities, especially when it talked about strikes and forging links with other trade unions. There were serious divisions within the Union (and among the players), notably a north–south divide, and between the stars and the 'rank-and-file' players. The union's main efforts went into securing compensation (for injuries, ill-health, wrongful dismissal and the like), but it remained weak and financially insecure. Many players were reluctant to join, even resenting the 2/– subscription fee. In the words of Stanley Matthews,

> You could buy a few pints of beer for a couple of bob, and some of the boys thought more of their pint than of Mr Fay's [the union Secretary] arguments.

Thanks to Fay's efforts however, the union grew in strength, helped by a more appreciative press. By 1939 there were almost 2000 members.

Professional footballers were in a peculiar position. They worked under a draconian employment system, which was itself out-of-kilter with even those severe times. Yet they played their football before growing numbers of spectators. Times were hard in the world at large, especially in many of the working-class communities most wedded to the game. But what was happening to the money coming into the game? No one, now, doubts that attendances at football matches increased between 1919–1939.

Even in regions blighted by unemployment, attendances remained unexpectedly high.

Even in regions blighted by unemployment, attendances remained unexpectedly high. There were armies of fans attached to football Supporters' Clubs, but many could not afford to go. The cruellest of scenes is the one captured by the Pilgrim Trust's account of the Liverpool unemployed, keen to watch the game but with no money to get in, enjoying only the vicarious thrill of watching others going into the grounds.

Clubs' financial turnover increased, though only the bigger clubs managed to pay all their bills (the largest of which was players' wages) from gate money. Smaller clubs covered their costs from the sale of players. Then, as now, the game was divided between big and small, between rich and poor. However packed the terraces, the resulting income rarely seemed to pay more than the clubs' basic costs. Nor did the money go into the pockets of the directors or shareholders.

In this financial setting, the bigger clubs, notably Arsenal, rose to prominence in the 1930s, clubs financially capable of sustaining a national scouting service, and able to buy the best players from smaller clubs who were obliged to sell to keep themselves solvent. Then as now, there was a crucial link between the game's major clubs and the smaller fry. Both needed each other: the one for talent, the other for money. Yet to phrase it like that is to simplify. At times, the football business seemed economically irrational. Those who were likely to make the *best* living from the game were the ancillary groups – manufacturers and traders in football equipment, journalists, broadcasters, advertising people. It seemed ironic that those most directly involved in the game – the players, management, training staff and even the directors – took home only modest returns for their efforts or investments. Nor was the money invested in improving the physical fabric of the game. The professional stadiums, with a few exceptions, remained uninviting and bleak, offering little shelter or protection, no warmth and scarcely enough room or elevation to see a game properly. For this fans paid one shilling. When packed, those grounds were positively unpleasant, uncomfortable and often very dangerous. On the eve of the Second World War, they remained Victorian and Edwardian institutions struggling to cope with the new cultural and popular demands.

The inter-war audience

In full flight and full voice, football fans were much as before: noisy, partial, often vulgar and sometimes troublesome.

Football fans headed towards football grounds by all possible means of transport. At a Cup tie in Swindon in 1925, huge crowds converged on the ground in 'charabancs, cars, motorcycles, push-bikes, horses and traps and even donkey carts'. By the 1930s, fans were organising buses and motor coaches to take them to matches. Some even walked, used the trams and buses for criss-crossing the cities. Most important of all, it was the train which made modern football possible. Suburban and inner-city train systems plus the mainline trunk routes enabled football fans to travel in unprecedented numbers. When the railway companies did not provide trains at a reasonable (excursion) fare, attendances at matches inevitably fell. Teams themselves used the same systems to get to matches.

Football trains took on something of a carnival atmosphere and spawned an extraordinary, colourful and often boozy culture among the travelling fans. Compartments were festooned with colours and posters announcing the groups travelling inside. Bradford City fans heading for Burnley in 1921 announced themselves variously as 'The Swankers', 'The Toffs', 'Jock's Pals' and various other names. In 1928, the trains heading south from Huddersfield to Wembley were decked with balloons, banners and slogans. When West Ham returned from the first Wembley final, they travelled home in a tram lavishly decorated with coloured electric lights which spelled out the club's nick-name, 'The Hammers'.

Fans were famous for loading their railway carriages with ample beer for the journey – not surprising, since pubs had often been closely involved in the growth of football teams. However, there were many men who promoted football because they thought it *distracted* working men from the temptation to drink – they might now spend Saturday afternoon at the match instead of inside the pub. But many managed to do both, drinking on the train to away games, and in pubs after the game was over. Landlords often asked for extended licences to serve fans after major local games. Games were often advertised on posters *inside* town pubs, and there is plenty of photographic evidence to show that fans took bottles of beer into the grounds. Fuelled by beer before the match, or having enjoyed a few pints afterwards, football fans soon developed a reputation for coarseness and vulgarity. Hats and caps were thrown in the air in excitement, crowds spilled over the fences on the field in celebration, fans threw objects (snowballs, orange peel and rotten fruit) on to the pitch – and chanted insults at unpopular players, officials, and especially referees of a 'superior' social class. As the *Preston Herald* complained, fans

Northern fans catching the train down South © Popperfoto

were heard to bellow 'Punch his *** ribs in, punch his *** legs off', and other filthy rhymes. Big games, then as now, were infamous for their noise and players confessed that they could be inspired or dispirited by a crowd's vocal support. Sheffield's Hillsborough was infamous for its 'Hillsborough Roar'. Crown enthusiasm sometimes got out of hand, and grounds were sometimes closed. Milwall was especially prone to crowd disorders in the 1930s.

Fans turned out in their team's colours and favours, waving bells and rattles (often borrowed from the workplace) to add to the crowd's cacophony. Street vendors were generally on hand to sell the appropriate items and colours to fans heading matchwards. Time and again, it was remarked that fans wore the most amazing items for football matches. In the words of one commentator in 1928:

> People dress themselves up in strange garb, carry painted umbrellas, blow
> bugles, swing rattles and handbells, and perform in a manner they would
> never think of doing at any other time.

Works' bands often added both to the noise and to the local sense of occasion. Sometimes fans offered their own rendition of favourite contemporary songs from the music hall. Football magazines printed the words of songs for fans to sing at matches, including, in 1927, 'The Wearing of the Green' and 'My Old Kentucky Home'.

Time and again the FA had to intervene – to warn clubs about their fans, to threaten fans with punishment, to prosecute wrongdoers (especially those who attacked referees). In fact the numbers of major incidents was small, and the authorities' response was generally reasonable. The behaviour of the fans in the inter-war years was, in general, more peaceable, more disciplined, more accepting of regulation and marshalling than it was to be later. Fans guarded their 'own' corner of the ground, and might barrack players and officials, but the territorial feuds, accompanied by foul-mouthed (and racist) abuse and violence which erupted from the 1970s was absent. Hence the shock among older football fans when faced by the hooliganism of the late 20th century. Football before 1939 was clearly part of the social fabric of English life, but it was rarely discussed or treated as a *problem* in the way that was to become so commonplace later on.

What helped to transform the game of football in the years to 1939 was the press and the radio. Newspapers were especially important. Daily

Now the London press gave the game a new national platform and status.

newspapers, but especially the Sunday papers, devoted ever more space to football and other sports. The local press had been important for its football coverage in the late 19th century, but now the London press gave the game a new national platform and status. Millions of people learned about football, followed the games and the clubs, and learned about the stars without ever seeing a single game. They were informed, tantalised, even titillated, by reporters who relayed the inside story of football to a vast reading public.

Local newspapers were especially important in fostering interest in local football clubs and seemed to have been responsible for maintaining and furthering local and regional passions and prejudices, favouring the home town or region versus all-comers, especially traditional rivals. Substantial proportions of local newspapers were devoted to football, and town after town had its own 'Pink' or 'Green' editions on Saturday evenings, with complete reports and results of the nation's games within minutes of the matches ending. When new newspapers aimed at working-class readers were launched, they inevitably promised substantial sports coverage, especially of football. The new popular national papers flaunted their sports coverage: 'Four pages of sport', boasted the *News of the World* – and half of those four pages were devoted to football.

Saturday night specials ran a results service (in the years before the process was taken over by radio and later television), while Sunday and Monday editions offered a complete guide to results and to league tables – spiced, in the popular press, with columns of gossip about the game. Headlines followed the popular trend, developing that snappy, wise-cracking style which later became something of an art form. The 'FA in blunderland'-type headline of 1930 evolved into alternately bizarre/funny/ridiculous/attention-grabbing headlines of the 1980s and 1990s, i.e. '*United Supporter to be next Pope*' (a comment on Newcastle United-supporting Cardinal Hume), or '*Yanks 2 – Planks 0*' (when the USA beat England in 1993).

Some inter-war editors disliked professional football and tried to promote the amateur game instead, but such men were exceptions to the general rule that

Only 5 Weeks to Win Film Prizes

SUNDAY·PICTORIAL

THE GREAT SUNDAY PICTURE NEWSPAPER

—for boys and girls on page 27.

BOLTON WIN THE CUP AGAINST A KEEN DEFENCE UNDER DIFFICULT CONDITIONS

Bolton players (white shirts) getting in some effective headwork.

The referee, players, Red Cross men and others intermingled when play was interrupted.

The King acknowledging the cheers of the crowd which had invaded the pitch.

A fine clearance by a West Ham back. Play was keen to the end.

A West Ham player intercepting a pass. The team showed precision, giving displays of neat combined work, but clearly were hampered by the crowd on the touch-line, whose presence prevented effective passing or speed work.

Bolton men waiting while police, mounted and on foot, clear the ground.

Printed and Published by SUNDAY PICTORIAL NEWSPAPERS (1923), Ltd., 23–29, Bouverie-street, London, E.C. 4.–Sunday, April 29, 1923. Telephone, Central 3440.

editors were keen to let professional football dominate the national and local press. Even local papers gave increasing coverage to the national, professional leagues, well beyond the confines of the home town.

The newspaper circulation wars of the 1930s led to dramatic changes in the nature and content of football reporting. The rather staid, factual accounts of the more serious newspapers gave way to the sensational, blood-and-thunder style of the mass dailies and Sunday papers. Sunday newspapers in particular found that football – at least when presented in a sensational fashion – rivalled crime and scandal as popular items among their millions of readers. Particular papers, and certain journalists, developed their own style of crusading, punchy football journalism, generally to the great irritation of club and football officials. Club chairman and administrators were regularly lampooned – even in death (e.g. 'Football dictator Cuff dies'). The *Athletic News* had previously been *the* journal for football ('The *Times* of football'), but by 1931 it had been effectively destroyed by the new popular press who were prepared to give their readers not detailed, factual descriptions of games (so basic to the *Athletic News*) but a spicy commentary, laced with heavy-handed judgement and crusading style.

On the eve of the Second World War, the popular newspaper coverage of football would have been recognisable and familiar to anyone glancing at today's popular press. Though today's coverage has gone much, much further than any inter-war footballing populist would have dared to, it was a tradition first established in the 1930s. Journalists on local newspapers often enjoyed a cosy relationship with the home football club. They travelled to games with the teams (many still do of course). Too critical a report or story could lead to banishment or a club's refusal to cooperate on stories, briefings and gossip, so vital to the work of the football reporter. Often the press overcame the problem by couching critical questions in the form of letters from the public; in general, though, football writers had to tread a fine line between the club and their journalistic instincts. Today some of the coverage looks curiously dated – if not downright implausible:

> Great excitement was evident at Ascot-under-Wychwood on Saturday evening when it became known that Ascott-under-Wychwood FC had beaten Charrington in the semi-final of the Chipping Norton Hospital Cup.

The inter-war interest in football was also increased by the remarkable rise of the football pools. For a long time, the pools troubled football's authorities, with their innate dislike of gambling. After a series of false starts and despite efforts to resist them, the football pools took root in the 1920s and blossomed in the 1930s. They proved enormously successful. Some five to seven million people a year spent £30 million on the pools, the figures traced in sales of Post Office postal orders to gamblers. In Liverpool, home to Littlewoods and Vernon's, the football pools formed a major industry, employing 30,000 people, most of them women. Newspapers developed special columns for investors in the pools, predicting games and offering advice about how to win the fortunes promised by the pools' companies.

This newspaper coverage and the pools system were both made possible by an increasingly sophisticated modern telegraph and telephone system. Though it may seem mundane today, in the mid-1920s it was astonishing that a football report could be for sale on the streets of a provincial city a mere hour after the match had ended on the other side of the country. This same process of modernisation (in news gathering, print and distribution) fuelled the rise of the popular press in the inter-war years. The major nationals (*Express, Mail, Herald, Mirror*) sold millions of copies each day. The popular Sunday papers had an even higher circulation, and it is there that we find football given saturation coverage. Up to 10 per cent of a newspaper might be given over to the game. When a popular newspaper's fortunes flagged, it invariably sought to restore its sales figures by devising a new approach to the game, or by increasing the pages devoted to football. As newspapers, notably the Sundays, wrestled with each other for circulation, each found new footballing angles. By turns they were flattering or abusive, investigative or sensational, and sometimes simply inventive in ways familiar to modern readers of British tabloids. In the process, the style changed. The older tradition of football coverage, serious, thoughtful essays and reports by authors keen to write well and sensibly about the game, gave way to a more direct, snappy and sometimes vulgar style of writing. Some of its major exponents were influenced by the new sporting (notably boxing) journalism in the USA. Popular British newspapers, in ferocious competition with each other and always anxious to steal a publishing march on their rivals, went from strength to strength. Sometimes they gave bad taste a bad name, and always seemed able and ready to hurt the feelings of the old guard who dominated the game. If sales figures are anything to go by, the British reading public loved it.

Journalists were part of a team effort to sell newspapers, and the fact that football was widely used for that purpose is itself the greatest possible testimony to the importance and popularity of the game itself. Football could carry newspaper success (or failure) along with it; it was a host which nourished and sustained a totally different industry and enterprise. Yet they both needed each other, and it is hard to disentangle the fate of the one from the other in the years after 1919, much as the story of the modern game has become enmeshed with the history of TV.

Radio also stimulated the popular curiosity about football. By 1939, nine million people paid for a radio licence, and many more listened to that rich, plummy diet crackling from the wireless sets in the front room. After an initial reluctance (rooted again in the social bias of the founding elite within the BBC) more radio time was devoted to football by the late 1920s. Broadcasters however faced opposition, notably from the League (and some quarters of the press) who feared that football broadcasts would erode attendances – ignoring the evidence that for armies of house-bound fans, sports broadcasting was a wonderful godsend. From the first, there was established that tetchy relationship between English football and broadcasters which remained a recurring problem throughout the century. Yet for the listeners at home, football broadcasts remained popular, as did the discussions and other programmes devoted to the game.

> **For armies of house-bound fans, sports broadcasting was a wonderful godsend.**

Football was also promoted by that other major cultural revolution in the inter-war years – the boom in cinema attendance. Filmed coverage of major games became a staple item in cinema newsreels. There were also occasional films which involved football clubs, much as football began to make appearances in contemporary fiction, though it never attained the elevated cultural

status of cricket. Similarly there were specialised sports and footballing periodicals, offering serialised footballing stories alongside conventional reports
of the games and its stars. More important perhaps was the proliferation of
schoolboy literature. Fictional and fantasy football was a central ingredient
in that vast range of comics, magazines and journals aimed at the eager
schoolboy and adolescent reader. Like the game itself, schoolboy literature
about football came, in part, from the public school tradition which reached
back to the mid-19th century, more especially to *Tom Brown's School Days*.
Not surprisingly, it was a form of literature which praised the amateur above
the professional, which found its footballing heroes within the world of priv-
ilege and social standing, and discovered that valour and selflessness, team-
spirit and fair play invariably resided among the men from the old schools.
It was, however, as far removed as could be from the world of the millions
who played the game and who crowded the professional stadiums.
Nonetheless it clearly fostered images of the game which embedded themselves in the public memory. It is impossible of course to know the *precise*
influence of this fictional, fantasy football aimed at the young, but it formed
one of many overlapping cultural forces which served to keep football, in all
its forms, firmly in the public eye (at least among males).

North and south

By 1939 the people's game had entered domestic life and had become the vernacular of millions. It was a national institution in which vast numbers of
people claimed an interest and a passionate allegiance. Its crowning and ter-
minating game – the Cup Final – was even attended by the monarch or his
representative, leading to endless jokes about how the royals managed to
secure scarce tickets. What gave the game its edge, the force which honed its
passion and its wit, was its local, regional and social commitments and
divides. Above all else perhaps, football came to express that visceral divide
between north and south which dated back to the pioneering days of the
modern game. The new national press played up these divisions for sales
purposes, and football seemed riven by this north–south fault line (though no
one could actually locate its position). More easily pinpointed of course was
the persistence of the old England–Scotland rivalries, though this was something different. Football's rivalries were expressed most clearly at the
Wembley Cup finals after 1923 (no one has satisfactorily explained how the
opening game, with 200,000-plus swirling around in a 100,000-capacity stadium failed to turn into a disaster). With the tickets split between competing

finalists, tens of thousands of working men packed the excursion trains heading for London from the north and Midlands. Of the 34 teams who played at Wembley before 1939 only three came from the south. The Cup Final became an occasion for provincial working men to strut around the capital and its major sites en route to the game. In the early years, many also converged on the Cenotaph to leave their team's colours in memory of the war dead from their home town. In what became an annual ritual, the press portrayed images of hoards of northerners sweeping south. Like an alien army, these train loads of football fans were a reminder of another England – harsher, less comfortable, less refined – hundreds of miles north of the capital. This was especially true in the 1930s when the north seemed to bear the brunt of recession, and the pleasures and fun of a day trip to London stood in sharp contrast to the hardships and uncertainties of life back home. It is true that football rivalries were most aggressively on display for the visits of Scotland and its armies of fans. But year after year the press reported on (and embellished, or even staged) the 'northern' antics of football fans on the loose in London, and the vocal animosity shown to visiting southern teams (especially Arsenal) when they played in the north.

Like an alien army, these train loads of football fans were a reminder of another England.

Arsenal's success in the 1930s – its relentless gathering of trophies, its relatively well-heeled players (courtesy of outside sponsorship) and its general metropolitan style, contrasted with what football fans elsewhere regarded as their own down-to-earth qualities, rooted in the industrial landscape of the north and Midlands. The south (and especially London) was soft; the north was tough and gritty. It was of course an unreal caricature which paid no attention to the privations of London's working-class communities, and the teams they backed. Real or not, such feelings were part of the warp and weft of football before 1939. The rivalries between towns, within towns, between north and south, were more important than the sense of national identity which football (and other sports) expressed at international venues. There had been a residue of post-war national sentiment still lapping through the country in the early 1920s, but the picture had changed quite markedly by the 1930s when the game was characterised by a mosaic of regional and local footballing passions.

Here then was a game – the national game – which consumed huge amounts of time, energy, money and interest among millions of British people (men in the main, but some women too). It was also a game which had come of age. In the period 1890–1914 football had remained an uncertain force, distrusted by those who worried about the raucous collective voice of masses of working men, by people who were fearful about the simple presence of such huge crowds, and who saw in the game's boisterous rowdiness and vulgarity an incipient plebeian rebelliousness. By the Second World War much of that worry had gone, not least because the game itself was more stable, more comfortably settled in the routines of urban and industrial life. Of course football continued to send out the occasional worrying social ripples, but they were entirely contained by a society which was itself generally stable, despite the disruptive forces unleashed by the depression and its consequent social distress. The opening of Wembley in 1923 saw a vast crowd test the stadium and the police to the limits – yet all ended peacefully. The 1923 Cup Final was testimony to what the British had become: a highly disciplined urban, industrial people whose work, politics and pleasures were characterised by an orderly and good-humoured acceptance.

Some critics argued that the passion for football, on the terraces, in the pub and workplace, served to support social harmony – a 'social balm' which diverted tensions and passions which might otherwise have taken a different route. Such arguments – variants on the theme of religion as the opium of the masses – ignored the fact that radical discontent was often expressed most severely in areas where football was most popular.

Football had never found unanimous support, of course. From the pioneering days of the modern game to the present, football faced ranks of vocal opposition. Voices expressing contempt and distrust served as a harsh descant to the better-known vocal enthusiasm for the game throughout these years. Despite attracting a range of snobbish and political objections football had secured an unrivalled social role: a game which expressed many of the best features of sporting endeavour, and provided harmless and cheap entertainment for millions who often had little else to enjoy in return for their toils.

Harmless and cheap entertainment for millions who often had little else to enjoy.

On the eve of the Second World War football was 'respectable' to a degree that its older fans could hardly have predicted. The game had secured its first knighthood, was securely rooted in the compulsory school system, and had spawned some of the century's most enduring sporting heroes. For all its boisterousness, despite its vulgar humour and vocal aggression, football represented the English (and the British) at their most disciplined. Tens of thousands of people were herded from train and tram, thence into stadiums, which were often so crowded they offered only a partial view of the game itself. For such meagre pleasures – a mere 90 minutes – endured in harsh conditions, the fans queued and travelled for hours. They were a remarkably stoic bunch. They were to need all the stoicism they could muster between 1939 and 1945.

Some people think that football
is a matter of life and death
... I can assure them it is
much more serious than that.

Bill Shankly in *Sunday Times* 4 October 1981

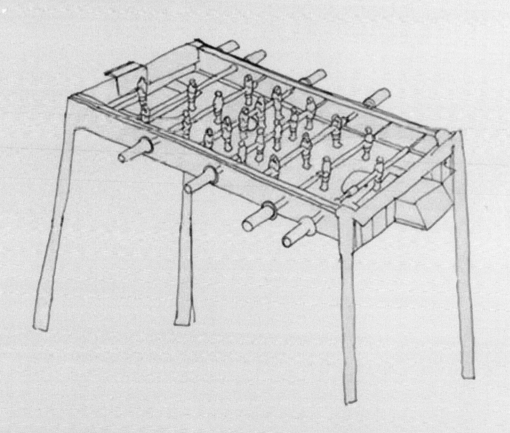

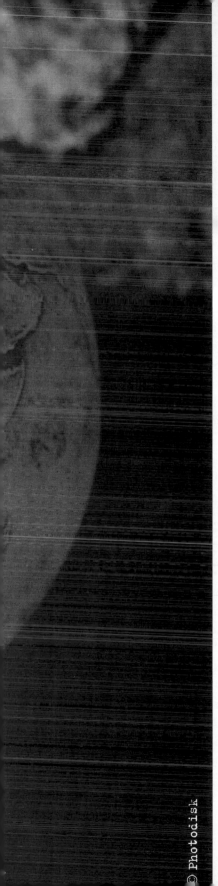

A wider world

The global game

Football was a very British game. It was also a global game in ways that the British did not realise (and for a long time would not accept). Before, say, 1914 footballers, like sportsmen in general, secure in their island home and fortified by the inspiration of the public school athletic ethos, looked to the wider world as a *tabula rasa*, a potential audience to be won over to the benefits and blessings of all things British. The reality was of course quite different.

In fact, football had indigenous roots in a

number of societies long before the British exported their version of football around the world. Football was, after a fashion, a global game long before the rise of the modern game. Indeed one factor which enabled the British to effect the process was the fact that their new, rational game (soccer) struck a chord among people already familiar with traditional folk games of football. In the pre-modern world, there were hundreds of different ball games, each with their own local rules and conventions, and each taking the local name 'football'. There was for example the ancient Florentine game of *calcio*; in France *soule*; *Lapta* in Russia; even *kalagut* among Inuit peoples.

Europe

The British spread enthusiasm for the modern game of football from the mid-19th century onwards. In Switzerland, for example, private schools adopted the game (employing British schoolmasters) as early as 1869. By the 1890s football had become an important feature of recreational life within those schools, thence in Swiss education as a whole. Swiss graduates, moving out to other European cities, took their footballing enthusiasms with them, much like graduates from English public schools and from Oxbridge colleges. The Britishness of many new European football clubs and teams was revealed in their names: 'The *Grasshoppers* of Zurich, *Old Boys* of Basle, *Young Boys* of Bern, *Young Fellows* of Zurich'. Two Dutch football clubs had even more curious names: *Go Ahead Eagles* and *Be Quick*. Football clubs in Genoa, Naples, Antwerp, Milan and Vienna adopted the English spelling of those cities, and not the obvious local version, for their club name. The Britishness of such clubs was also reflected in the clothes they wore and the contemporary styles they affected, often attracting ridicule from critics who were unimpressed by such imported pretensions.

These early European football clubs sprang from a privileged world, and many were anxious to maintain their social tone by excluding working men and openly appealing to the wealthy. Aristocrats for example were prominent in the early days of leading football clubs in both Italy and Belgium. Founded by prosperous and educated men, these early European football teams often drew their players from a range of nationalities, and were genuinely cosmopolitan. Clubs often flaunted their international membership. Fifteen of the 25 founders of Torino FC in 1906 were Swiss. The new club in Milan in 1908 was so cosmopolitan that it took the name *Internaztionale*. Barcelona was home to a range of clubs whose members' names reflected their diverse national and regional origins. They were often men directly influenced by British education and by British commercial and industrial life. In addition, there were large numbers of Britons living and working in Europe who were keen to play their favourite games and to establish or join local sporting clubs. Time and again, across Europe, football clubs emerged from among migrants and outsiders – educated men of business and commerce who brought to their adopted homes a zest for football and a determination to pursue the game.

Football rapidly took root across western Europe. It was firmly established in Switzerland by the 1880s. The Danish FA was established in 1889. In Holland the game was established in Enschede by textile workers from Lancashire. Scottish shipyard workers planted football in Gothenburg, from where the game spread to other Scandinavian cities. Football in Germany spread initially via schools and colleges, until the 1890s. Thereafter it thrived in the North Sea trading ports, and in Berlin. In Russia the game took root in major ports and in industrial regions, and the Russian FA was formed in 1912. Often, the presence of a local Briton (a businessman, a cleric, perhaps) proved crucial in encouraging the local game. Sometimes football encountered local opposition from critics who did not like the game's Britishness, and who felt that local recreations offered a more 'patriotic' activity for young men. But wherever objections were raised, they were simply swept aside by the rising tide of enthusiasm for football; the game's simplicity and easy appeal overcame most objections.

The cities which dominated European football until the 1930s were Vienna, Budapest and Prague. In each case, the British influence had been important in establishing the game. The first official football match in Vienna, for example, was played between the Vienna Cricket and Football Club, and the Scottish gardeners of Baron Rothschild. In the decaying Russian and Ottoman empires however, the imperial authorities sought to prevent or control the emergence of football among their minorities, especially in the Balkans where tensions and frictions were ubiquitous. But football continued to splutter into life, among students, schoolboys and working men, all influenced by players and enthusiasts from abroad. Imperial authorities faced enormous difficulties in containing the footballing virus.

As football became more international, as teams and players moved around Europe to play each other (or in search of work), the game needed international regulation. Thus in 1904 FIFA was created in Paris by seven nations, keen to organise international fixtures and regulate the transfers of players. By 1914 24 nations had joined, including Argentina, Chile, the US and South Africa. But from the first, the English stand-offishness riled and irritated the Europeans, who went out of their way to welcome and incorporate them. Yet the English pioneers, and the expansive popularity of the game at home, ensured that English football was thought to be the unquestioned epicentre of football. Before 1914, a visit by an English football team – a university team, a professional club, an amateur team, a national team – was invariably regarded as the highlight of the local footballing calendar across large areas of Europe. Huge crowds turned out to watch the English effortlessly rack up comprehensive victories. The English FA was not altogether comfortable about trips abroad, though they were keen that such matches should form part of the English duty to woo other people to the game of football. In time however, and as more and more Europeans wanted to beat visiting English teams, the English began to taste footballing defeat. Long before the First World War the modern game of football had taken root in every European country, from Iceland to Greece.

> **Huge crowds turned out to watch the English effortlessly rack up comprehensive victories.**

South America

Even more remarkable was the development of the game in South America. Throughout South America's major towns and cities football took root between the 1860s and 1880s. Initially the British influence was paramount, if only because South America was an important region for British investment and for the associated migration and settlement of British skilled workers and businessmen. Teams in Argentina, Chile and Uruguay (sometimes adopting British names), played visiting British teams (*ad hoc* teams from British warships, for example). Schools were the most important starting point for the South American game, especially under the influence of expatriate British schoolteachers, anxious to promote their own sporting passions among their pupils. What today seems an obvious reflection of local social life (teams with deep roots in local communities) often began their

South American life in very British circumstances. The library of the Argentine FA is named after a Scottish schoolmaster, Alexander Watson Hutton. River Plate was founded by Britons. Boca Juniors was founded by an Irishman, Patrick McCarthy, though was later taken over by new waves of Italian immigrants and their offspring. The first soccer club in Uruguay was founded by a pupil from a British college and was named the Central Uruguayan Railway Cricket Club, though its first game was soccer. Of its first 118 members, 72 were British, one was German, and the rest were local. Later they changed their name to Peñarol (1913) by which time they had been taken over by Italian immigrants.

Brazilian football had similar origins. Wealthy sporting clubs had begun to provide footballing facilities by the turn of the century in Brazil's major cities, and football clubs were spin-offs from those clubs. As the game developed (with British founders and players to the fore) football drifted away from its wealthy origins (though the wealthy dominated the game until the 1920s) and began to find a passionate following among the urban poor. When Charles Miller (British father, Brazilian mother) returned home to Sao Paulo in 1894 from education in England, he took with him two footballs – but had no one to play with. He soon formed a team in his workplace (in the Railway Company) encouraging other companies (the English Gas Company and the London and Brazilian Bank) to do the same. Miller also persuaded local sports clubs to add football to their facilities. By 1901 Miller was able to found a Sao Paulo championship for five teams. A year later, between 60 and 70 local teams had been established. The game retained its British associations (toasting the monarch, singing British songs) but it was inevitable that it would spread beyond the circle of expatriate Britons, and find an increasingly popular following in working-class communities.

From the first, Brazilian football was bedevilled not just by issues of class but also of race. It is almost impossible to believe, today, but in 1921 the Brazilian President had banned black players from representing the country in the South American Championship, played in Argentina. Meanwhile, the Brazilian poor – including the black poor – began to turn to the game in their thousands. One famous player,

the Brazilian poor ... began to turn to the game in their thousands.

Carlos Alberto, of mixed race, lightened his colour before matches by rubbing rice-powder on his face. Elsewhere, nine players quit FC America in protest when the club signed a black player. In the 1920s, some teams refused to play Vasco da Gama when they fielded a number of black players. Clubs tried to mask the racism within Brazilian football by a number of ploys: by insisting for example that players were literate (knowing of course that most black players came from uneducated communities). After all, slavery in Brazil had been ended as recently as 1888. But the growing enthusiasm for football in Brazil, and the realisation among black footballers that the game offered a possible escape route from poverty, conspired to erode the games' racist barriers. By the 1930s, some Brazilian teams even sported 11 black players. There was a drive to take the game into the poorest of black communities, often using music (samba) to encourage passionate support for the game.

Before 1914, the centre of South American footballing excellence was not Brazil, but Argentina and Uruguay, where the fierce national rivalries were periodically fuelled by international football matches. Indeed the first formal international match outside Britain (where England–Scotland games had been regular events since 1872) took place in May 1901 in Montevideo, when Uruguay beat Argentina. The winners of the regular Argentina–Uruguay games received trophies donated by the tea magnate Thomas Lipton and another named after Robert Newton. Gradually South American footballing nations began to compete regularly against each other, and from 1916 onwards there was an annual competition, played on a league basis, in the capital city of the host nation. By then football was firmly rooted in South America; transplanted by British influence, generating a passionate local fol-lowing, and taken over by new communities of other European immigrants it broke out from the exclusive social world of its pioneering days to become hugely popular among people of all social groups across the continent.

English teams had begun to travel to South America as early as 1905, when Southampton had won all five of its tour games. Nottingham Forest followed that same year, again, winning all their games. Swindon played in Argentina in 1912 (bringing back an order for 5000 footballs) and even Exeter played there in 1914. More remarkable still were the regular tours by the amateurs, Corinthians (1910, 1913 and 1914), in which they won most of their matches. More and more English teams were happy to undertake the arduous sea jour-ney out of season; they made money and attracted big crowds. South American football also began to lure British coaches and players. Just as the game in Europe had benefited from a migration of British players and expertise, by 1914 the British footballing influence was making itself felt throughout South America. At the same time other immigrant groups were adding their own, often fanatical zeal to the local footballing chemistry.

Europeans began to take serious notice of South American football in the 1920s, firstly at the Olympics, where the Uruguayans proved a startling revelation (they won Olympic gold both in Paris in 1924 and Amsterdam in 1928). They drew huge crowds and astonished the Europeans with their footballing skills. Not surprisingly, they went on to win the first World Cup, staged in Uruguay in 1930. The English (even when they won) usually complained about the behaviour both of the players and the crowds, though much of the problem was caused by the more robust style of English teams. The English game had traditionally been a very physical game. Football in South America had developed other qualities, and the physical aggression of the visiting English prompted reactions on the pitch and among the fans. Nor did the English like the quality and nature of local refereeing; they were alarmed at the way crowds were pinned back by

> **They drew huge crowds and astonished the Europeans with their footballing skills.**

barbed wire (though that did not always prevent fans rushing onto the field to kiss goalscorers). Such complaints came back from Chelsea's exhausting tour of 1929 (when they played in Argentina, Uruguay and Brazil in two weeks). There were bonuses however; they also experienced night-time, flood-lit football, and liked the excellent, modern training facilities at some of the major clubs.

International competition

Professional English clubs sought to make the most of this foreign interest in the game, though the FA also sought to control and minimise such 'mercenary' enterprises, and the national administration of football remained suspicious of the game abroad. Though English teams had little trouble in beating their foreign opponents easily, there were signs of change even before 1914. British coaches, a growing local sense of professionalism, and a determination to compete on equal terms with the British pioneers, all prompted major improvements in football in Europe and South America. Ultimately, however, the game was improved by the rise of competition. As men competed for their place within a team or a club, as clubs competed against local rivals in one-off games or, more importantly, in leagues and knock-out trophies, football everywhere emerged as a seriously competitive game. Contrary to the popular public school verse, it *did* matter who won and who lost. It mattered to players, it mattered to coaches, to the clubs, and, perhaps above all, it mattered to their fans, who were growing in numbers wherever the game took root.

> ## Contrary to the popular public school verse, it did matter who won and who lost.

The pattern was the same everywhere. Cup Finals, international matches, local derbies, all attracted large crowds from Berlin to Montevideo. Much like Britain twenty years earlier, the key restraint on the size of crowds at major games was the capacity of the local football stadium. For their part, the British had more custom-built grounds designed to absorb tens of thousands; both in Europe and South America that process had to wait until the 1920s and 1930s. The football craze really made itself felt across urban Europe and South America between the wars, but the formula which underpinned that passion was clearly in place in 1914, and it was a formula already tried and tested in Britain.

In 1914 English football could feel confident about its influence and dominance. The numbers of players, of clubs, of crowds was unrivalled. Their organisational systems were more refined and efficient than any other. Their competitive game was better, more popular, more professional, than in any other country. English teams and individual players were much sought-after. Moreover the English game was distinctive, characterised by its insistence on 'fair play', one aspect of its public school legacy. But looking back it seems obvious enough that English football (like so many other pioneering industries and commercial activities) was bound to see its primacy slip as the game rapidly took hold in other countries.

Being pioneers, however, had a long-term debilitating effect on English football, serving to blinker the English to the rapid developments in football around the world. It was understandable that the men who ran football in

1914 took pride in their game. They had, after all, seen football transformed, in their lifetime, from an *ad hoc*, informal and often ill-disciplined free-for-all, into a highly disciplined game, followed by millions and with a huge commercial potential. In all this, the English and Scots were the leaders, and felt superior. A sense of superiority was part of the British identity – part cause, part result of that extraordinary story of British imperial and industrial dominance in the 19th century – and football was all of a piece with that. The British were the best; they knew they were the best – and they felt little need to worry about competitors. It was a national self-confidence which was soon to be fissured and then undermined. This was as true of British football as it was of British industry. The day of reckoning was at hand.

> It was a national self-confidence which was soon to be fissured and then undermined.

Professionalism abroad

The post-war passion for retribution ensured that Germany was initially banned from both the Olympics and from FIFA. When that ban was lifted, the English, objecting, removed themselves from FIFA in 1920, returning in 1946. This was the very moment when football was entering a period of remarkable expansion and global popularity. Crowds at football matches were increasing dramatically across western Europe. Major club games and internationals were drawing huge crowds, from Bolshevik Russia, to Weimar Germany and beyond. In Spain, football was beginning to push bull-fighting to one side. The numbers of footballers was increasing: Germany had one million registered players by 1932; in France, there were 3983 registered football clubs by 1924. A year later, in Poland, there were 510 clubs and 17,558 registered players. The best of amateur footballers were able to demand wages and fees, and it was inevitable, as it had been earlier in Britain, that professionalism would creep into the game, paid for by money taken at the gate and by the support of local benefactors and sponsors.

This rapid growth of football in the 1920s and 1930s was marked by bitter disputes about professionalism. The founding fathers everywhere were men of 'the old school', who valued the amateur ideals above all else. They

Vittorio Pozzo carried by his victorious team. Italy 2 v
Czechoslovakia 1, Rome, 1934 © Popperfoto

viewed the amateur as the *true* sportsman. To give or receive money for playing was corrosive to more than the amateur spirit; it was the very antithesis of the most valued social qualities. Yet wherever football took root (in Britain, South America or western Europe) the pattern was the same: the game's rise to popularity was paralleled and driven forward by the rise of professionalism. The two seemed to go together.

To give or receive money for playing was corrosive to more than the amateur spirit.

There was thus a fundamental tension within the game. Founding players and organisers saw 'their' game slipping from their grasp, and saw it cuddling up to commercial, popular forces. In places the struggle between middle-class amateurism and a plebeian professionalism was protracted, and reflected the harsher social tensions in contemporary society. In Germany the process is best seen in the emergence of the club Schalke 04, in the industrialised region of the Rhineland. The team was supported by working men, including large numbers of immigrants from the east and from Poland. Stadiums in the Ruhr multiplied, crowds grew, and the old amateur authorities gradually lost the battle against the rise of professional football. But, like everything else, that was completely changed by the rise of the Nazis in 1933 and by their ban on most professional sports. Similarly, in communist Russia, football fell victim to the ideological quirks of the new regime, with the invention of workers' teams (as opposed to the 'bourgeois' teams of pre-revolutionary days). Football 'stars' were repudiated, and players were encouraged to promote collective team play rather than goal scoring. It was one of the curious ironies of the inter-war history of football that regimes which took an initial and fundamental dislike to the professional game of football were quick to incorporate the game, using it, along with other sports, to promote their own brands of nationalism.

The global game

In the inter-war years, football slipped easily into all corners of the globe. It took root in Central America and Mexico, mainly through the modernisation of local societies, again with British encouragement, or helped by men who had been influenced by the British footballing tradition. Of course football did not become a popular game everywhere. There were countries – whole continents even – which proved unreceptive. There were moments however, especially in the 1920s, when football seemed poised to spread everywhere. Even the USA seemed football friendly, but the initial enthusiasm, stemming in the main by immigrants and professionals from Europe, simply succumbed to the rising popularity of American football. Nonetheless there were enough good footballers in the USA to sustain teams in the Olympics, and in the World Cup after 1930. Much the same story was true in Canada and Australia. Immigrant groups often clung to the games of their homelands, and large crowds could be attracted to special football matches. It was local variants of football which took root, however, leaving soccer as a minority game which did not 'take-off' until the late 20th century. Football also remained insecure in Asia although it had a growing popularity in China, and was played in Japan and Korea. But on the eve of the Second World War, the real heartland of football was undoubtedly Europe.

The English, so influential in disseminating football worldwide, ought to have been at the heart of the world game. Yet at the very time the game was spreading abroad, the English displayed an indifference, at worst a hostility, towards this expansion. When football took off as a major international phenomenon – when national teams began seriously to play against each other, and when football's administrators began to band together in useful international organisations to regulate and advance the game – the English were notable for their absence. From their island retreat, they looked at the rest of the world from a position of splendid isolation. Throughout the first half of the 20th century, English football was characterised by what one recent historian has described as 'an almost arrogant self-obsession and introversion'.

In 1928, this attitude was summed up by the words of Charles Sutcliffe, who sat on both FA and the Football League.

> I don't care a brass farthing about the improvement of the game in France, Belgium, Austria or Germany. The FIFA does not appeal to me. An organisation where such football associations as those of Uruguay and Paraguay, Brazil and Egypt, Bohemia and Pan Russia, are co-equal with England, Scotland, Wales and Ireland seems to me be a case of magnifying the midgets. If central Europe or any other district want to govern football let them confine their powers and authority to themselves, and we can look after our own affairs.

It is true that exhibition games and club tours became more frequent and widespread in the inter-war years, enabling the English game to maintain contact with the thriving world game. But English football suffered from an institutional sclerosis which was to cost the game dear in the long run. Like any people kept in isolation, the English were later to be overwhelmed when they renewed their footballing contact after 1945. As football developed a distinctive global culture in the inter-war years, the English aloofness led to seriously damaging consequences for the long-term well-being of the domestic game.

At the time there were certain features of the world game which warranted serious hostility. Communist and fascist regimes alike adopted and manipulated football. In the 1930s as football established itself as the global game, attracting capacity crowds in major urban centres throughout Europe and South America, it also proved an ideal tool for creating those populist national identities so basic to the totalitarian regimes of contemporary Europe. The politicisation of football was first seen in Italy. Mussolini constructed new football stadiums forcing clubs to change their names, and ordered that the fascist salute be given before games. Major Italian clubs (notably Turin, financed by the Agnellis and their Fiat empire) bought foreign players, especially Italian immigrants from Argentina. The national Italian team was greatly influenced by the management of Vittorio Pozzo, who had learned his passion and tactical skills in England, especially at Old Trafford before the First World War. But at the 1934 World Cup in Italy, the Italian national team, prompted by Mussolini's offers of personal riches and influenced by the regime's fundamental violence, battered their way to victory.

That World Cup showed something other than fascist-inspired brutality on the sports field, however. It drew crowds, as never before, from great distances – it proved itself a major tourist attraction with 7000 fans travelling from Holland, 10,000 from Switzerland and armies of fans pouring south from Germany, waving the swastika. Many more were able to follow the games through their national newspapers and via the radio. For the first time, the game was followed by millions confined to home; young, old, sick, women with children. What happened in Britain under the BBC took place throughout the western world as the radio set infiltrated domestic life. This was a striking transformation among the poorer groups, for whom home had rarely been a location for leisure or entertainment; now, courtesy of hire-purchase, low income groups could acquire wireless sets. Important games were

Germany 3 v England 6, Berlin, 1938 © Popperfoto

even broadcast live to crowds who gathered to listen in public places. Thus even people unable to afford a radio could listen to an important game by wandering down to the nearest broadcasting venue: a bar, a square, a park or a local stadium.

Football's popularity in the 1930s was unparalleled. Crowds mobbed teams travelling to important games; crowds gathered in unprecedented numbers to watch the major games or listen to live broadcasts. The same story unfolded in both urban Europe and in South America. Inevitably the game's popularity was used by fascist regimes for their own ends; Jews were removed from their posts within the game, fascist leaders paraded before football crowds – and, of course, the fascist salute became a feature of major games. The England team, playing in Berlin in 1936, were obliged to give the fascist salute before the game. Travelling German teams flaunted the regime's trademarks whenever they played abroad. The political tensions which were to lead to war in 1939 were given a horrible dress rehearsal in Spain from 1936 and with Europe so seriously divided it was increasingly difficult to pretend that international football was a forum for harmless international sporting rivalry. With the prospect (in Spain, the reality) of war overshadowing everything from the mid-1930s, football, like other sports, was riven by political frictions. Few doubted that the 1938 World Cup in France (won by a deeply unpopular Italian team) would be the last for some time.

English national teams had periodically played against European opponents, and were on the whole successful. England lost only eight games in Europe before 1940; at home they were even more successful. English players were famous for their fitness – and their physical toughness. What was missing from the English game, however, was the tactical preparation and skills which had become the hallmark of major European teams and their coaches. English footballers were treated by their employers as little more than working men with a special skill (one that faded with age). Whatever their public fame, however idolised by armies of fans, they hardly fared better than most working people at the hands of employers who viewed single-minded toughness and resolute refusal as the main ingredients of contemporary business management. To such men, what happened abroad seemed a matter of great indifference. There were, of course, major figures (notably Herbert Chapman at Arsenal) who *were* influenced by the football they saw abroad, especially in Europe, but on the whole, the English game continued in its isolationist mode. It felt secure in its sense of pioneering importance, felt no need of inspiration from elsewhere, and was happy to thrive on its own patch, where crowds were vast, the game buoyant and uniquely popular. The men who ran the game continued to be troubled by issues which had plagued them since the early days: gambling (notably the football pools), players' wages and contract demands, women's football – and a string of other minor issues which irritated the old guard. It was not a global but a distinctly British affair.

What happened abroad seemed a matter of great indifference.

If anything confirmed football's massive hold over young men throughout Europe, it was the war itself between 1939 and 1945. Football was played wherever the armies settled and rested. Even in the midst of the most terrible privations, the game popped up to please and entertain. The relief of Stalingrad, for example, was celebrated by a scratch game – attended by 10,000 spectators. Soldiers on all sides of the conflict played their own impromptu games of football whenever circumstances allowed, in European prison camps and in the western desert. At home and away, the British remained addicted to what they regarded as their 'national' game. But football was no longer simply British. Football's universal simplicity, its ease of play and organisation (the qualities which had helped its rise to popularity in Britain in the late 19th century) had been replicated throughout the major urban and industrial areas of Europe and South America. It was a truly global game. The British however had not fully accepted that fact by 1939, and it was to be some years more before reality dawned: the British the founders of the modern game – were no longer the best. It proved a hard lesson to recognise, and still harder to learn (and even then, only from harsh experience). Not until the 1950s did British football really begin to emerge into the world arena from a hibernation which has lasted throughout the first half of the 20th century. And like most people rising from their slumbers, British football was sluggish to rouse itself.

Reality dawned: the British were no longer the best.

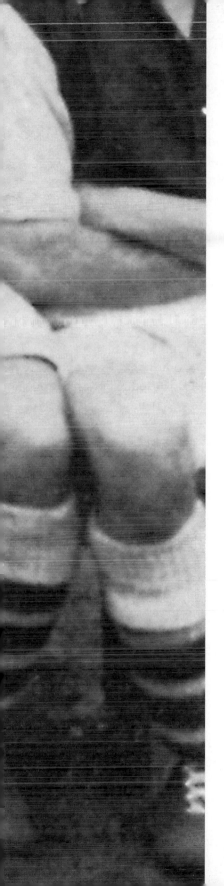

05

War and peace
1939–1958

The story of football during the Second World War might seem a mere triviality set against the epic struggles of those years. But the game remained important – and useful – throughout the war. Professional football was immediately suspended at the outbreak of war, but the mass entertainment offered by the game was too important to curtail completely. Football was quickly 'enlisted for the Home Front' but with a fundamental reorganisation. England was divided into north and south, and leagues were organised on a local basis because of travel and crowd restrictions, though the latter were eased towards the end of the war. Players could appear for any team they were selected for, not solely for the team holding their registration. Football even authorised referees with spectacles (thus removing one of the football's standard abusive insults at an erring referee). Most professional players were drafted into the armed forces and many were put to good use as physical training instructors. When the war ended, those same men emerged as managers and coaches, men who had learned the basic skills of physical training and man-management in the armed forces, and who brought that experience to the task of reviving the post-war professional game.

Though professional teams were denuded of their playing staff, the game itself stumbled through the war. Games were often *ad hoc* collections of former professionals and volunteers plucked from the terraces to make up the numbers (the size of available boots sometimes determining who played). On one memorable occasion 'Little Hallam' was drafted from the ranks of spectators to play for Blackburn Rovers against Manchester United at Stockport; he was hopeless, could not kick the ball properly and was regularly flattened by the opponents. But for him, it was a memorable game – 'It was something to have worn the colours of one of the most famous clubs in football history for an afternoon.'

Military postings and travels scattered players across the country and local fans often had the unexpected pleasure of seeing the game's greatest players turn out for the local team. There was of course a host of practical difficulties (apart from fielding a full team); travel was difficult and equipment scarce. Yet overall football survived, raising money for various causes and providing entertainment for people who badly needed some colour and cheer in their lives. Players seemed to play non-stop, for scratch teams, for military teams (which were often very good because they consisted of professional players), for local professional clubs. Even the football pools continued, admittedly in a much-changed fashion. Despite the turmoil of the war years, in football, as in social life at large, a great deal of effort went to persuade people that it was 'business as usual' – even when that was clearly not the case.

Most people agreed that civilians, and the armed services, needed to be entertained, and the government put a great deal of effort into providing a semblance of normal recreational life. As millions of troops poured into

Britain from all corners of the globe, they brought with them their own sporting interests, adding the most unusual sports to local fare. There were West Indian cricketers and American baseball players, and legions of foreign troops keen to play their own games under the curious gaze of the locals. In addition tens of thousands of European troops based in Britain displayed their own zeal for football.

Both sides in the European war tried to maintain their footballing interests. Football in Germany continued, in a much transformed form, until brought to an end by the air raids and by the approach of allied troops in November 1944. The Germans also took football to all their conquered territories; they played wartime national games against neutral countries, and fascist allies as well. It was a similar story in Russia. Football continued even in Leningrad in front of crowds of thousands and games were broadcast across the country in the hope of raising Russian morale. Football was even played, on an artificial surface, in Red Square itself in 1942 and 1943. But Russian football was not immune to the murderous impulses of Stalin's regime. Beria, infamous chief of the secret police, was an avid football fan (and a modest player in his youth for Dynamo Tblisi). He took his revenge on his footballing enemies, notably officials from Moscow Spartak, whom he consigned first to the Lubianka, later to the gulag – where they escaped death solely because of their footballing reputation.

The Germans also took football to all their conquered territories.

Throughout the war, the national games of football and cricket were viewed as important aspects of maintaining high morale. This was a significant difference from the last war, when sport and entertainment had been seen as trivial interruptions to the main task of fighting. Attitudes had clearly changed: what had once seemed unimportant was now viewed as vital, a clear sign that sport had come of age. It was becoming increasingly obvious that people gave of their best not by being kept hard at unrelenting tasks – whether military or industrial – but by being allowed moments of relief, breaks for pleasure and enjoyment. At the first post-war FA Annual Meeting, the chairman, Lord Athlone (until recently Governor-General of Canada) was fulsome in his praise of the role football had played in the war. He paid 'a glowing tribute to the work accomplished by Soccer during the war years ... Association Football had been a strong link in combining the forces that brought victory.' However exaggerated this stance, it conveyed the sense of pride which the game's formal organisation took in their contribution to the war effort.

The rush for pleasure

The British people celebrated the return of peace by an unprecedented resurgence of their old leisure patterns. Notwithstanding the restrictions of the post-war world (shortages of almost every basic kind, rationing, restrictions on all sides) people rushed back to their old pleasures in vast numbers, filling every place of entertainment. Football and cricket grounds, cinemas and seaside resorts, all brimmed with people desperate for a return to life's familiar pleasures. All the major seaside resorts enjoyed their boom years in the late 1940s. In 1946 cinema attendances reached 1635 million (the record) and queues circled the building waiting for seats at the next showing. One third of the British population went to the cinema at least once a week. The British addiction for the cinema was even greater than in the USA. Indeed in 1950 the British accounted for 10 per cent of the entire world's cinema attendances.

Post-war newspaper sales similarly reached new heights. In 1950 five national newspapers had readerships of more than 10 million. Another four had readerships in excess of five million. *The Radio Times* attracted a staggering 20 million weekly readers. All liked to devote a great deal of space to football and other sports, often adopting a pseudo-American slang devised by the US press for major boxing matches but oddly inappropriate for football reporting.

I've a hunch Chelsea are gonna kick history right in the pants.

Not surprisingly then, football was at the forefront of the post-war leisure boom. The 35.5 million spectators in the first season, 1946–47, rose to a record of 41.25 million in 1948–49. These were football's golden years; 500 clubs employed 7000 professionals and there were approximately 30,000 amateur football clubs. The Amateur Cup, switched to Wembley, attracted 90,000 spectators in 1949. Money poured back into the football pools, quickly outstripping the £20 million invested in 1938. Eight million people had a regular flutter on the pools, and the government reaped vast amounts from taxation. By the 1950s the football pools had become Britain's seventh largest industry. Such a massive post-war expansion in the old forms of leisure, which

Football:
the fo...
the post-w...
leisure boom.

had been well-established as national institutions in 1939, clearly could not continue at such a giddy pace. But, for that short period between the end of the war and 1950, the British enjoyed themselves *en masse*, and with a communal fizz, as never before.

Unprecedented numbers flocked to football matches up to 1949, when more than 41.25 million spectators passed through the turnstiles. Thereafter a marked decline set in, continuing throughout the 1950s. Armies of people were locked *out* of the packed stadiums and crowds would clearly have been bigger had the stadiums' capacity been bigger. A preview of what was in store was displayed immediately at the end of the war, when a visiting Russian team, Moscow Dynamo, played a series of exhibition games throughout Britain. The Russians completely bamboozled the FA. The players were neither professional nor amateur, and the demands of their minders, honed in the peculiar circumstances of Stalinist Russia, seemed utterly unreasonable. Nor did British officials much like their refereeing system. Nonetheless they proved a very attractive attacking team, and the British were struck by

> the impressively high standard of the Russians' attacking play. In positional work and crisp, ground combination, they were captivating ... the Russians – an unknown force, coming from behind the veil – revealed themselves as high-class footballers.

The Russian visit was just one instance that demonstrated that the game had progressed abroad beyond the ken and the notice of the insular English game. Fans flocked to the Russian games in huge numbers: 82,000 at Stamford Bridge, 90,000 at Ibrox, 45,000 in Cardiff (where Dynamo won 10–1). Thirty-four other clubs pleaded with the FA for a game with the Russians. Today, looking at the photographs of those ranks of sturdy Russians, bizarrely clutching bunches of flowers as a gift for the bemused home players, it is

Chelsea v Dynamo, Stamford Bridge, 1945 © Hulton Getty

hard to capture the excitement felt by contemporary fans. Here were exotic footballers – good ones too – the likes of which had never been seen in England.

Experienced football critics were amazed by the Russians' single-mindedness, and by their obviously careful preparation for the games. They played fluid, attacking football, yet had a clear retreating defensive plan, all of which suggested, to one critic at least, a 'quality of ruthlessness that characterised both training and playing methods'. It was clear that if football was to be taken so seriously, the English would have to rethink their approach to the game.

The seriousness of the Russians' visit was not without its moments of comic relief. The game against Arsenal (for whom Stanley Matthews and Stanley Mortenson were guest players) was played in dense fog at White Hart Lane. The match should never have been played. Visibility was between 3–6 feet – and the Russians were accused of adding a twelfth man without removing the substituted player. Fouls were frequent (players realised that the referee could not possibly see them) and the Russians hindered Matthews by simply hanging onto his shirt for much of the match. Those who actually saw Moscow's last two goals (they won 4–3) agreed that both were offside. It was only marginally better than the legendary (and abandoned) fog-bound match at Charlton, when the team were already in the bath when they realised their goalkeeper was still on the pitch.

For all that, the Moscow Dynamo visit has proved a revelation. The Russians returned home to be made Heroes of the Soviet Union. Before long other teams were to arrive, with even more devastating results and consequences for the English. The Russians were the first of many visitors who, by the end of the 20th century, were to utterly revolutionise the English game.

English football stadiums were ill equipped to cope with the massive post-war football crowds. In retrospect, a major disaster seemed inevitable. It happened at Bolton on 6 March 1946; 33 people killed and 4000 injured, from a crowd of 50,000 at a Cup Tie against Stoke. The subsequent enquiry demanded new regulations to monitor the safety of football grounds. But the Bolton disaster quickly faded from memory. Over the next half century, a litany of crowd disasters at British grounds would suggest a persistent indifference to safety by the game's authorities and by the clubs. Across industrial

Britain, vast numbers of working men headed straight from the workplace and into the grounds at Saturday lunchtime; the average at Newcastle in 1947–48 was over 56,000, 'crammed into rickety wooden stands'. Like the stadiums (and like the country as a whole) the game was badly in need of reconstruction. The task facing football was not merely a matter of patching up and painting over. Professional football was in need of a serious re-think. But the game's problems were masked by the sheer buoyancy of attendances until the 1950s.

Time to rethink

During the war serious thought had been given to how best to reform and reshape the structure of post-war sport – how to raise money, how the state should help, and how to modernise the sporting nation's infrastructure. In all this, Stanley Rous was a central figure. An ex-schoolmaster from Watford Grammar School, Rous was to become a major force in world football in the second half of the century. Naturally enough, however, sport was low on the list of governmental post-war priorities. Yet the war, with its need to ensure physical well-being and fitness, if only for military purposes, had put the political spotlight on sport as never before. Recreation and leisure pursuits were clearly important for national well-being, a fact underlined by the 1944 Education Act which raised the leaving age to 15 and obliged all education authorities to make school provision for physical recreation.

The war had put the political spotlight on sport as never before.

There was a flurry of post-war training, by qualified coaches, in a range of British sports, though much depended on the devotion of part-time volunteers. There were men both in the FA and in the League (operating from a small office in Preston) eager to change the game by establishing formal training, for example, but they invariably faced resistance from older members who simply fell back on tried and tested habits from the past.

What was wrong [said a Football League representative from Liverpool] with the Football League before the war ... were the public dissatisfied?

The men who ran the League delivered a simple thumbs-down to most reform measures (on the question of Sunday football, liaisons with the Pools, for example). Stanley Rous, Secretary at the FA, was a man of a different mould. Anxious to modernise the game, Rous wanted to bring it more in step with football abroad, and was keen to bring the sport into the mainstream of British cultural life. He was also determined to see football overcome the traditional antipathy of teachers in the public schools and grammar schools who disliked its professionalism and its social tone. Rous began to use the FA to promote the game through coaching schemes and by taking the game to the nation's youth clubs. He had broader visions too, hoping to see football develop as an international game, by encouraging the rebuilding of the game in Europe, and to promote its spread around the world. He sought to establish links with FIFA (which the English had quit in 1920). Rous also wanted a better football press (less sensational, more factual and restrained) and his ideas prompted a range of formal FA publications. This vision for the game was not, of course, shared by everyone within the FA. But Rous was right. His ideas were designed, cumulatively, to shake off that parochialism which had dominated and characterised English football from its early days, and which looked on football elsewhere with aloof superiority. He was in a minority, however, and most preferred to look to the game's domestic strength, and to its immediate post-war boom. Football was a game at the height of its popularity. Why change something that seemed to work so well? All was to change in the 1950s.

Never had it so good?

When the tide of post-war austerity began to recede, when more and more people found themselves in better material circumstances, the leisure patterns of the British people began to change. Attendance at football matches began to decline from 1949 onwards, gathering speed throughout the 1950s. By 1962, crowds had dropped by 11.25 million from their 1948–49 peak. Other popular leisures fared even worse, notably the cinema. Yet within football's declining figures there were some peculiarities. Bigger clubs seemed better able to keep their fans than smaller clubs: fans were perhaps being more discriminating about the *quality* they sought in their entertainment, no longer so easily satisfied. Throughout the 1950s, discussions about football concentrated on 'the missing millions'. The English game was inward-looking, and many sought an explanation for the game's decline within the game itself (tactical changes, goals scored, players' skills etc.). Such views overlooked the central fact that *all* forms of leisure were undergoing massive change. Rugby League, for example, suffered a much more dramatic fall in attendance figures.

The widening prosperity which transformed life in the 1950s inevitably affected the way the British took their pleasures but certain sectors of society remained unaffected by these improvements, and for them the new (and even some of the old) pleasures were costly. Football admission prices rose (from 1/3 in 1946 to 2/6 in 1960) and some low-income fans were forced from the game. More significant, however, was the rise of real wages, effectively doubling in the 1950s (and all at a time of modest inflation). People were able to indulge themselves as never before. Home improvements and electrical goods, different, more distant vacations, even private cars.

Television continued a process which began with radio and the BBC. In 1914 people learned of the declaration of war from their newspapers. In 1939 they heard it at home, on the family wireless set. By 1945 a very large majority of households, of all social classes, owned their own radios. In the late 1940s the BBC remained relatively uninterested in the potential of television, preferring to concentrate on what it had perfected so brilliantly – radio broadcasting.

In 1950, a television set was unusual, but by 1971 91 per cent of British families would own or rent a set. At the same time, there was a massive increase in home ownership and car ownership. These were social changes which transformed the lives of the British people. To speak about an age of affluence is to skip too lightly over those deep-seated social ailments which afflicted British life from that day to this. Nonetheless the material improvements were there for all to see, and remain a vivid memory among those who experienced them.

However, the Football League worried that radio commentaries on football matches would keep fans away from the game; they tended to see changes in society at large as a *threat* not as an opportunity. Few thought that such changes might actually prove an ally, not an opponent of football.

The growth in car ownership widened the possibilities for people's spare time. The car enhanced prospects of people travelling with their families. Football had been traditionally been a male-dominated game; men left their womenfolk behind when they went to a football match.

This broadly-based material improvement which had crept across the face of Britain by the late 1950s was summed up by Harold Macmillan's famous quip 'You've never had it so good'. There were, quite simply, millions of Britons enjoying levels of material bounty unknown by their forebears. Moreover, many of their recent acquisitions were directly related to the pursuit of leisure and many others served to transform the way the British enjoyed their spare time. Some of the older pleasures seemed, by comparison, faded and ever less appealing. How could rainy seaside resorts compete against guaranteed Mediterranean sunshine? And what was the appeal of a winter's afternoon on a crumbling football terrace, compared to a quiet afternoon, in a comfortable home, in front of the television?

There was a stark physical contrast between improvements in domestic life and the colourless unchanging football grounds. It is hard to convey the numbing physical misery of football grounds at their unreformed worst. When packed, it was difficult to see the match properly and often just as hard to dodge the streams of urine frothing down the terraces from men unable to force their way to the primitive lavatories. These grounds had been constructed with numbers, not comfort, in mind, in an age when the British people were accustomed to shoddy material conditions, at home, at work and at play. Nor were they much more appealing when sparsely attended, when games were poor or unexciting,

> It is hard to convey the numbing physical misery of football grounds at their unreformed worst.

and when it was hard to see what the fuss was all about. Fans began to stay at home, or look elsewhere for their pleasures. Football clubs began to consider improvements to their grounds *only* when the fans had begun to drift away – but the horse had already bolted.

Perhaps the most remarkable aspect of football fans at this time was their good behaviour. Admittedly, the issue itself has a very *modern* ring to it, a hint that bad behaviour *ought* to more commonplace. However, it is surely remarkable that so many people – millions every week – were herded into physical environments that were shabby at best, unpleasant and even dangerous at worst, with little protest or disruption on their part. Their passion for football did not, in general, spill over into misbehaviour or crowd disturbances. In the early flush of football's popularity, especially in the 1890s, there had been a worrying trend towards misbehaviour among the young men who formed the core of football's fans. Those after all were the days when the word 'hooligan' had been coined. Yet in the post-war years, crowd trouble was rare and not very serious. The FA had reports of only 22 incidents among the 41 million people visiting football grounds in 1948–49. Between 1946 and 1959, referees reported only 138 incidents. Even when the national press began to register alarm, from the late 1950s onwards, about the disruptive nature of 'youth culture', trouble at football matches tended to be dismissed more as good-natured banter than a serious social problem. That was soon to turn into an altogether different and nastier issue. On the whole, until the late 1950s, crowds were much as they had been before, though thinner. The communal singing of today's bigger crowds was rare, but they were nonetheless noisy, colourful demonstrations of partisan passions, where antipathy for opponents was sometimes vulgar, but more often than not funny.

> **Antipathy for opponents was sometimes vulgar, but more often than not funny.**

Fans could express their views formally through their local Supporters Clubs (whose numbers peaked in 1948) but, predictably, the clubs tended to maintain a distance between themselves and the organised fans and the clubs. Here as elsewhere football was a deeply negative institution. Its leaders, at club level and within the League, had a tendency to say 'no' to anything unfamiliar. Change was seen to be threatening, a worrying prospect of having to alter old habits. This was much less true within the FA, notably because of the towering influence of Stanley Rous. Yet, viewed overall, football was a very English institution – wedded to old habits for no better reason than that is how things were. Why change anything that was so tried and trusted? Again, the men who ran football were instinctively conservative and likely to consider change only when change was thrust upon them from outside.

Professional footballers were the first to feel football's refusal to change. By the late 1940s there were 7000 professional footballers, almost half of them full-timers. They came overwhelmingly from working-class backgrounds in the north and the Midlands. Despite the money generated by the football crowds, the players had little to show for their efforts. They were shackled to the clubs by a rigid 'retain and transfer' system, and their wages were pegged at a maximum, which slowly climbed under pressure from the players' union: £9 in 1945, £12 in 1947 rising to £20 in 1958. In fact, only a minority of all professionals were paid the maximum, and large numbers of players (even the less successful players with the major clubs) earned less than the industrial average in the early 1950s. Moreover, even the small band at the top found that their earning capacity had been equalled by workers elsewhere in the late 1950s. It was however clear enough that the bigger clubs could *easily* afford better pay and conditions. Football managers (including many of the legendary post-war figures) ran their clubs like martinets, handling and paying players with a tight-fisted meanness designed to satisfy the club's directors, without worrying too much about the feelings of the players. Many seemed to take their players' requests for more money as a personal insult and an affront to the clubs' directors. The post-war managers were creatures of their origins. Raised in the hard times of the 1920s and 1930s, they developed a personal toughness honed during wartime service (mainly as PT instructors). Footballers in the 1950s, however, could see that other celebrities elsewhere (to say nothing of foreign footballers) earned money on an unimaginable scale. Even though crowds had fallen, huge amounts of money continued to flow into football, notably into the bigger clubs. In 1957 for example, a tax change released almost £1 million back into the game and, that same year, a deal struck with the ever-lucrative football pools for a royalty on the use of the fixture lists yielded another quarter of a million pounds for the game. Players – particularly the stars – were clearly not getting their due rewards, even through many clubs might connive at a variety of scams to ignore the maximum wage and to give them more. When discovered however, football's authorities came down severely on transgressions to their code.

> **Many seemed to take their players' requests for more money as a personal insult.**

What made the players' position worse was the transfer system which held them, vice-like, at the whim and fancy of club directors. Time and again, men's careers were ruined by a club's obduracy, by a mean-spirited refusal to recognise that players naturally wanted to secure their own futures and to ensure their family's best interests. It was all of a piece with the way many directors treated the players personally. The legandary Joe Richards, chairman of Barnsley (and of the Football League), a man infamous for his flinty Yorkshireness (in which of course he took great pride), spoke to one of his club's main players only twice in 12 years. In many respects, the professional game of football was a startling example of the survival of the class system at its very worst, made all the more unacceptable because club directors were themselves often men from humble origins; classic self-made men, the Gradgrinds of the 20th century, their status asserted through a bluff rudeness to those beneath them. Their love of football could not mask the personal insult they often caused. There were of course many men quite unlike this. A small band of the best players responded to restrictions on their trade by accepting offers from foreign clubs, notably in Italy and South America, sometimes breaking their contracts to do so, with a predictably draconian response from their home authorities.

Post-war media

Football had always been promoted by the popular press. In fact sporting literature had become a distinct genre of its own. A number of journalists rose to fame as distinctive stylists devoted to particular games (notably Neville Cardus on cricket). A new breed of popular journalists, with a punchy style, and offering a literary mix of reporting and gossip about sports and sportsmen, now caught the eye, not least because they wrote for newspapers which sold in vast numbers. Football reporters often became stars in their own right.

Alan Hoby at *The People* posed as 'The Man Who Knows', but inevitably, some fans preferred to think of him as 'The Man Who Knows F*** All'. In the *News of The World*, Frank Butler adopted an even more aggressive, mid-Atlantic style of football commentary which invited angry reactions – then replied in spirit. 'Your column spoils my Sunday' complained one reader. Butler replied, 'Don't read it until Monday'. At *The Express*, Henry Rose took a similar line – controversial, opinionated, and always seeking a reaction. It was a curious contrast that newspapers which were deeply conservative spawned a populist tone and style when they discussed football.

These crusading football journalists found an easy target in the men who ran football. Persistent press criticism of the men at the top seems to have helped the players in their efforts to improve their working conditions. The press and players were in rough agreement that the game had slipped hopelessly behind in its conditions of employment, not merely with comparable games abroad, but even with employment practices elsewhere in Britain.

There was another aspect to post-war football journalism which registered a marked shift in the game's social position. A new generation of talented journalists writing for the 'quality press' brought style, flair and, above all, good writing to the reporting of football. In a way, they were merely bringing football up to the level which other sports had attained much earlier in the more serious newspapers. Led by Geoffrey Green, Brian Glanville and Hugh McIlvanney, they promoted football and knowledge about the game among a readership likely to look to other sports. They were important players in a broader cultural shift which conceded that football (and sport in general) was worthy of serious social debate; not merely a trivial sporting matter, best left to fans and players. Subsequent writers about football (especially academic writers) could not have begun their own work without the literary and intellectual ground-breaking work of those writers.

There was clear evidence that throughout the 1950s there was an increased interest in football among the middle class. This was clearly reflected in the newspapers they read. On the opening day of the 1950–51 season *The Observer* and *The Sunday Times* contained a single football report. Ten years later, they published a variety of reports, a review and a major article. Of course much more common (more widespread, better-selling, more provocative) was 'popular' journalism. Compared to what was to follow, even the popular journalism of the 1940s and 1950s, like its precursor in the inter-war years, now seems modest and restrained. Sexual scandals were covered up, had results (especially at the national level) was greeted more with disappointment than with the rabid jingoism of recent years. It was, in brief, light years removed from that populist and often rancid tone which infiltrated popular football journalism by the end of the 20th century.

Sexual scandals were covered up.

After 1945 football generated an increasing volume of print. Books spilled from the presses, new sports series were launched and footballers' autobiographies (generally ghost-written) emerged as a distinctive feature of sports literature. Star footballers (and others) secured regular columns in the press,

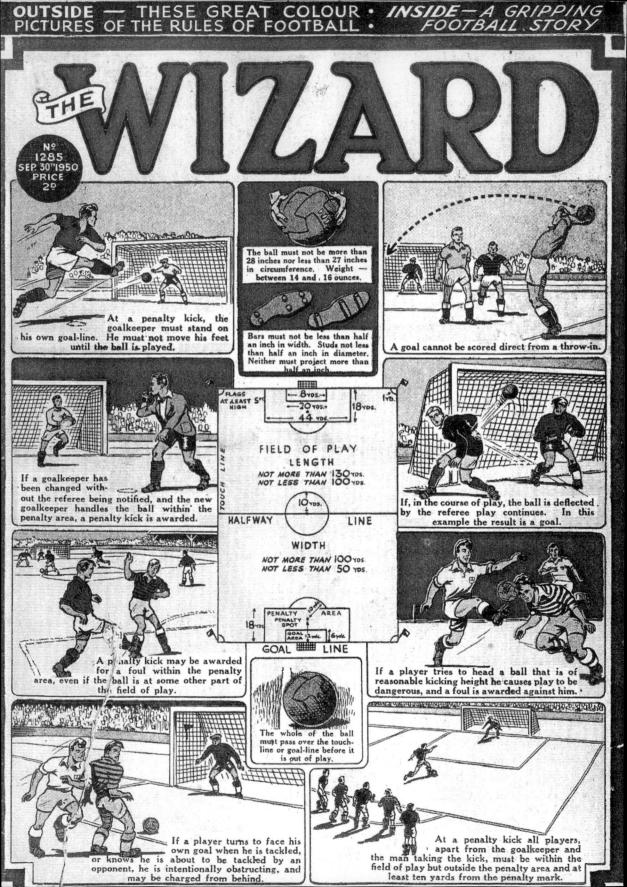

OUTSIDE — THESE GREAT COLOUR · INSIDE — A GRIPPING
PICTURES OF THE RULES OF FOOTBALL · FOOTBALL STORY

THE WIZARD

No 1285
SEP. 30TH 1950
PRICE 2D

At a penalty kick, the goalkeeper must stand on his own goal-line. He must not move his feet until the ball is played.

The ball must not be more than 28 inches nor less than 27 inches in circumference. Weight between 14 and 16 ounces.

Bars must not be less than half an inch in width. Studs not less than half an inch in diameter. Neither must project more than half an inch.

A goal cannot be scored direct from a throw-in.

If a goalkeeper has been changed without the referee being notified, and the new goalkeeper handles the ball within the penalty area, a penalty kick is awarded.

FLAGS AT LEAST 5FT HIGH
8 YDS.
20 YDS.
44 YDS.
18 YDS.
1 YD.
TOUCH LINE
FIELD OF PLAY
LENGTH
NOT MORE THAN 130 YDS.
NOT LESS THAN 100 YDS.
10 YDS.
HALFWAY LINE
WIDTH
NOT MORE THAN 100 YDS.
NOT LESS THAN 50 YDS.
18 YDS.
PENALTY AREA
PENALTY SPOT
GOAL AREA
6 YDS.
GOAL LINE

If, in the course of play, the ball is deflected by the referee play continues. In this example the result is a goal.

A penalty kick may be awarded for a foul within the penalty area, even if the ball is at some other part of the field of play.

The whole of the ball must pass over the touch-line or goal-line before it is out of play.

If a player tries to head a ball that is of reasonable kicking height he causes play to be dangerous, and a foul is awarded against him.

If a player turns to face his own goal when he is tackled, or knows he is about to be tackled by an opponent, he is intentionally obstructing, and may be charged from behind.

At a penalty kick all players, apart from the goalkeeper and the man taking the kick, must be within the field of play but outside the penalty area and at least ten yards from the penalty mark.

for as long as their sporting prowess survived. For boys, there was a plethora of post-war comics, magazines and weekly publications, keeping them abreast of the factual (and fictional) happenings in football. Much of it was fantasy football at its best: working class heroes casting aside their workaday clothes to perform heroic deeds for their chosen team. Labouring men, living under railway arches, training for big events on fish and chips, and outperforming all around them; it was pure make-believe, but it enthralled millions of school boys (including me). Annuals, and monthlies, from the FA itself, and nominally at least by star players, crowded the newsagents' counters or formed a prized Christmas gift (along with football boots and a new leather football). Throughout, most of these publications gave an unreal, sanitised impression of football, presenting their young readers with a safe image which conveyed the very best personal and communal sporting and social qualities. Often however, such images were as much fantasy as 'Roy of the Rovers'.

The attention devoted to football in print was of course paralleled, though much less influentially, by radio broadcasting. Less sensational in its coverage of the game, the BBC acted much more like the quality press, concentrating on the facts. Television, however, offered an altogether different challenge. From the mid-1950s onwards, football clubs and their governing organisations felt uneasy about allowing cameras into matches for fear of reducing attendances. There were initial agreements, but few televised league games or Cup Ties were shown to the rapidly expanding TV audiences in the 1950s. Yet the potential was clear enough, never more so than at the stunning Cup Final of 1953, won by Stanley Matthews' individual brilliance, before a TV audience of ten million people (including the author). Matthews personified the game at its best; a humble man and a dedicated athlete, nimble and sure-footed, with dazzling skills of ball-control, change of speed and direction, and an uncanny ability to cross a ball accurately. He transfixed opponents and spectators alike (and was still doing so in his 50s). Even his statue, in his home town of Hanley, evokes his mesmerising feints at speed: 'The maestro appears to be dribbling towards Milletts but could easily swerve across the street to Woolworths'.

Throughout the 1950s, Cup Finals brought home similar scenes of footballing thrills. There was the extraordinary (but reckless) bravery of Manchester City's goalkeeper, Bert Trautmann, playing for the last 15 minutes of the 1956 Final with a broken neck. A German ex-paratrooper and POW, Trautmann's arrival at Maine Road (when non-British players were rare) had caused

Stanley Matthews, 1952 © Hulton Getty

ructions, especially among Jewish fans. Trautmann persisted, and was to grace English football as one of the great post-war keepers, and a much-revered sportsman. Televised Cup Finals generally showed English football at its best: Manchester City teams, brilliantly orchestrated by Don Revie, in 1955, and 1956; Busby's fledgling teams in 1957 and 1958 – both thwarted by accidents. And always, the vast, good-natured crowds. The millions who settled down in front of the TV for the Cup Final in the 1950s converted that end-of-season game into a genuinely *national* sporting occasion. It was an example of what television might offer; a major, national sporting event beamed into millions of homes across the country. Fans who might never expect to see a Cup Final, or even watch a major game, were given a privileged seat. It was, in time, to prove an irresistibly tempting formula.

As the country slipped from that grey, post-war austerity into a contrasting mode of relative plenty, football had managed to maintain its position in the public eye as the national winter sport. In part, it was able to do so because of the extraordinarily deep roots the game had developed in British life over the previous half century and more. But football had been nourished, after the

> **Fans who might never expect to see a Cup Final were given a privileged seat.**

war, by close media attention; football was integral to the way popular newspapers were produced and sold, and the game had its own (expanding) niche on the airwaves. For all that, despite the vast numbers who continued to play the game from their earliest days, football seemed ill-at-ease with many of the changes ushered in by the days of plenty. The game's innate conservatism and its institutional rigidity (nowhere more obvious than in the chambers of the Football League) left the impression that football might simply be overwhelmed by the forces for social change transforming Britain in the 1950s. Where was the vision that might capitalise on those changes? There were some glimmers of hope among a small band of men who realised that English football must change; men who understood that football might actually *improve* itself by embracing change. The contemporary social transformation of Western Europe, for example, offered tempting prospects which began to lure a small band of footballing pioneers towards a different way of thinking about football. They looked increasingly not to the game's past, but towards Europe. A number of prominent men in the game across Europe were convinced that the future of football lay in European competitions.

© Photodisk

06

The turning point
1958

It was very seductive to feel that football was a very English game. It had its origins in England, and it had been exported overseas by enthusiastic English players. It was also easy to feel that English football was the best, because it had been the first. Yet long before the Second World War football had flourished as a major international sport, spawning international bureaucracies (based on the pioneering FA version), leagues and cups, and international competitions similar to the English prototypes.

European competition

The English, on the whole, remained indifferent to the global game, and were cool towards the emergence of international competitions. When the English FA was invited to play in the 1930 World Cup in Uruquay, the English response was curt and indifferent.

> Dear Sir,
> The letter of the 10th ultimo from the Associacion Uruguaya De Football inviting a Representative Team of the Football Association to visit Uruguay in July and August next to play in the World's Championship in Montevideo has been considered by the International Committee.
> I am instructed to express regret at our inability to accept the invitation.

Behind this refusal there lay great self-delusion. Football abroad had become a serious business. There were plenty of club sides, and national teams who could match the English in every department of the game. This became especially obvious under European fascist regimes which placed great import-ance on sporting prowess and success. There were also senior figures within the English game, notably, again, Stanley Rous, who wished to see English football become more international. Inevitably the Second World War put paid to that. Yet it was peace in 1945 which revived interest in football (and sport in general) as a means of forging peaceful international competition. The reconstruction of post-war Europe, culminating in the creation of the European Community, was driven forward in large measure by men who were determined to end Europe's divisions and to shape in their place a genuinely European community of nations with shared interests rather than bloody rivalries.

Football followed a similar route. There were men in the game who realised the importance of the burgeoning international game. By the early 1950s it had become clear that English soccer was not as good as it claimed; the most stunning evidence came in 1950, when the English, competing in their first World Cup, were beaten by the USA. It was, in the words of one historian, as if 'a representative US baseball team had been beaten by England'. That result was a freak which could happen in any game. But three years later an even more important reversal took place, when a staggeringly brilliant Hungarian team humiliated the English 6–3 at Wembley. The attack was led by the unlikely figure of Ferenc Puskas ('The Galloping Major') who, even in his prime, was a slightly tubby, muscle-bound man. His goal-scoring abilities were stunning; he went on to score 83 goals in 84 international matches. The Hungarians were a dazzling team, revealing levels of individual skill – tricks of the footballing trade – which English spectators simply had not seen before. Nor had the English players, who were simply left flat-footed. In the return match a year later in Hungary, the English were defeated 7–1. It came as little surprise when, in 1954, the English were again knocked out of the World Cup in Switzerland. The English pioneers had clearly lost their touch.

The English pioneers had clearly lost their touch.

There were some glimmers of hope however. A new breed of adventurous managers, though few in number, were keen to expose their teams, and their fans, to the best of European football. In a series of friendly matches, some of the greatest teams in Europe were introduced to the English footballing public, and all courtesy of air travel, new floodlights at the grounds and a national viewing on TV. The key innovator was Stan Cullis, manager of Wolves from 1947 who, like Matt Busby of Manchester United, belonged to that post-war generation of 'track-suit' managers – men who worked not from an office, but on the training ground with the players. They and others had spent the war working as PT instructors with trainee conscripts, and after the war brought that direct approach to players at their clubs. It seems strange, today, to talk about managers actually training and managing their players, but that had not been the practice before the war. It was a sign of the greater professionalism creeping into the game, born of men who had developed a different vision of what football could become, and how it should be conducted, both in preparation and at play.

The year after Wolves won their first Championship title under Cullis in 1954, they played a friendly against Honved, the Hungarian army team, under floodlights, with the second half televised live. It was a thrilling game which Wolves won 3–2. In an unusual moment of post-match excitement, Cullis proudly pointed to his players, exclaiming: 'They are the champions of the world!', a statement trumpeted by the popular press. Cullis's enthusiasm was a simple, off-the-cuff remark, but it prompted a remarkable reaction. Irritated by what was taken to be English effrontery, the French sporting newspaper and the journalist Gabriel Hanot launched a debate about how best to reveal the true European champions. Thus was born, in 1955–56, the

European Cup, played initially by invitation to the continent's various league champions.

There had been earlier European-wide competitions from the late 1920s, notably the Central European Cup, but all discussion about expansion of this competition assumed that the English would not join. Some voices, notably Arsenal's Herbert Chapman in the 1930s, predicted the development of European football. But the main inspiration came from France. Indeed the French were the inspiration behind *all* the most important, major international footballing changes: the creation of the World Cup and of FIFA as well as the European Cup. Moreover it seemed natural that European football should parallel the economic and political changes of the early 1950s by moving towards cross-border games on a regular basis.

Anything less European than the Football League, bunkered in Lytham St Annes, would be hard to imagine. Already worried about the proliferation of friendly matches with foreign teams, the League forbade the champions, Chelsea, from competing in the inaugural year of the European Cup. But in the following year, a new Manchester United team, under Matt Busby, brushed aside the League's objections to become the first English team to compete (though the Scots had done so from the beginning). It was the start of something utterly new, and was to transform the domestic game beyond recall. It was also to form the global mythology of Manchester United.

The professional game was being revolutionised by more than the lure of European competition. The FA had established new coaching schemes, with their own training headquarters, and a number of clubs transformed their recruitment and training of young players. All the major clubs had talent scouts scattered round the British Isles, looking for likely players, with representatives knocking on parents' doors in search of youthful signatures when the boy reached the appropriate age. Most of the great players found their way into professional ranks via this route. Duncan Edwards – widely regarded as one of the great post-war English players – had been watched as a small boy playing for school teams, before Manchester United signed him, first as an amateur. Clubs were able to 'blood' their promising young players through the new FA Youth Cup, founded in 1953–54. A galaxy of major players rose to prominence through this and similar youth schemes and competitions. But youthful promise was no guarantee of mature footballing success. Many more footballers failed rather than succeeded – fading away, returning to the amateur game or dropping out of football entirely.

By the mid-1950s it was clear that English football was slowly changing. In David Russell's words, 'inspiration from Europe, perspiration on the training grounds' had begun to transform the game. Now it all looks remarkably amateur: instruction on blackboards, players happily smoking a cigarette at the half-time break, simple training facilities, and the ubiquitous 'sponge and bucket' of cold water as the surest cure for most knocks

Now it all looks remarkably amateur: players happily smoking a cigarette at the half-time break.

or injuries on the field. Even the best of teams looked more like their forebears from the 1930s than some of their European contemporaries. Sturdy leather boots, with large studs hammered into the sole, thick knitted stockings and bulging shin-pads, voluminous shirts and baggy shorts, it all looked more like standard military equipment, dished out at random. It conveyed, again, a very English image, and formed a sharp contrast to the images conveyed by many Western European teams. Teams from Eastern Europe, however, notably the Hungarians, were less stylish in appearance, and domestic critics could brush them aside in the knowledge that they represented the very worst form of communist double-speak – superbly trained professional athletes masquerading as soldiers or other state officials. But Real Madrid were utterly different.

Real Madrid in 1958

Real Madrid dominated that first phase of European football. They captured the imagination of millions of fans, and of other players, by a level of footballing brilliance that was unparalleled. They seemed to be a different breed of footballer, and no fan who saw Real Madrid in the 1950s can forget their dramatic appearance even before they kicked the ball. Sleek, dressed in all-white kit that looked custom-made and streamlined, wearing, not football boots, but what looked, to British eyes, more like highly-polished lightweight leather carpet slippers, they were unlike any footballers we had ever seen before. When they began to play, everyone realised they were unique. It was

immediately obvious that Real Madrid played club football of a quality no one had seen before, or if they had, no one had mentioned it. They might have landed from another planet. It was a dazzling revelation.

Though they were Spanish champions, Real Madrid was also an international team, drawn from across Europe and South America. Even the very best of home-made British teams (none better than Busby's youthful team of the years to 1958) looked worthy and home-spun when pitched against the might and the athletic brilliance of Real Madrid. Even the taciturn Matt Busby (never one to praise opposing teams for fear of intimidating his own) could not contain his excitement as he described Real Madrid to his young players. Fans and professionals with long footballing memories all agreed that Madrid was the greatest club team there had ever been. Busby was confident that his own young team, still learning, was waiting to take centre stage in Europe. It was not to happen, though the tragedy which destroyed that team was to lay the basis for the mythology and the legends of Manchester United from that day to this. The Madrid team was built around a rock-like defence of large, physically tough but skilful Spaniards. But it was the attack, blended from the very best international players, which dazzled fans and opponents alike. What mattered was a man's skill, not his national origins, French, Hungarian, Argentinian or Spaniard. Today, in the debate about the balance within English teams between domestic and foreign players, we might recall that this, the greatest of all post-war club teams, was truly international, and its management looked beyond national boundaries to create that team.

> **What mattered was a man's skill, not his national origins.**

Busby's team

Manchester United had won the Championship in 1957 with a wonderful young team (and with a queue of brilliant young players, notably Bobby Charlton, fighting for a place). The proof of that team's quality was to be seen in the crowds they wooed wherever they played, especially in London, where the big stadiums heaved with fans keen to watch their youthful abilities. They were, like Madrid, an attacking team, at the heart of which was the young Duncan Edwards, one of the most complete players the English game had produced. Europe seemed the natural setting for this exciting and promising team.

At Busby's prompting, United chose to ignore the backwood dictates from League HQ (to stay out of Europe), opting instead to take on Europe's best. Busby had come to exercise an influence within the Manchester United Board that was new and quite unusual within professional football clubs. Technically Busby sat on the Board simply to offer advice, but he persuaded the directors of the benefits of regular European football. First of all (and an important factor to hard-nosed Manchester business men on the Board), Europe meant extra income, for wages and ground improvements. For his part, Busby also realised just how dramatically the centre of footballing excellence had shifted away from Britain. Busby had already watched the best European teams and, like most people who saw them, was won over to this new kind of football.

The practicalities of European football were also much more manageable. Europe no longer seemed quite as distant as it had once been: modern aircraft would allow clubs to shuttle to European venues in between domestic games. In those pre-jet days, however, air travel was often cumbersome and tiresome; on one occasion, in what proved a terrible omen, the Manchester players, returning from a wintry Bilbao, had to lend a hand in brushing snow and ice from their aircraft. United played their first home European games at Maine Road, Manchester City's ground, because there were no floodlights at Old Trafford. From the first, the team and its large body of fans quickly acquired a taste for the excitement of European games. It was, for a start, completely new and exotic. Strange teams, players with unpronounceable names, clubs from cities which Mancunians had scarcely heard of. Then there were the national anthems, most of them utterly unlike our own uplifting hymn to the revered (but, certainly from Manchester, almost invisible) monarchy. European anthems often caused collective sniggers among the Manchester fans, though that may have been more because of the sturdy, if sometimes discordant, rendition by the Beswick Prize Band responsible for all pre-match and interval musical entertainments.

The new European competition sometimes seemed easy. Manchester United beat the Belgian champions 10–0. Not even the best Hungarian teams had managed that. Moreover, United achieved it with a team of ten Englishmen and one Irishman. This was really curious, not least because English teams had, from the early days of the professional game, traditionally used a core of Scots and, to a less extent, Irish players. Manchester United had traditionally attracted Roman Catholic support from the Irish-based communities in neighbouring Salford and its local dockside communities. Busby was also a prominent Scot and a Catholic. The club also had important links to Irish football and had a reputation as a Catholic club. On match days solid wedges of priests gathered together in their favourite corners of the stadium. But this reputation never had the stark and sometimes violent sectarianism of the great Glasgow rivalries. Yet the team which began to make such an impression in Europe in 1957 was overwhelmingly English.

After a number of exciting early games, on 6 February 1957 (and the date was to be significant) United played host to Bilbao, trailing 5–3 from the Spanish leg. The game attracted 70,000-plus fans to Maine Road, in what proved an unusually thrilling and successful match, not settled until five minutes from the end, to see United head into the next round. While the Spaniards received a match fee of hundreds of pounds, the Manchester players received £5 each, and £3 as a bonus for winning. British footballing wages remained capped but teams elsewhere could pay their players what they felt the game could sustain. Every major game against European teams was prefaced by press discussion of the massive fees about to come the way of the visitors. Often, the sums were ridiculed as fantasy money; who could possibly be worth such riches for simply playing football? The United players must have felt it odd, as they flicked through their meagre pay package (a grand total of £23 for the week they won against Bilbao) to think of the vast crowd they had recently entertained, and the money which had cascaded into club coffers. They were, quite simply, grossly exploited by their club and by football's authorities. Both continued to manage the game in the spirit of that flinty corner-shop mentality which refused to countenance a fair return to the players. However glamorous the life of a successful professional footballer may have seemed, it continued to offer poor material rewards, in Britain at least. 'Abroad', of course, was a different story.

Who could possibly be worth such riches for simply playing football?

The next leg of Manchester United's first odyssey into Europe took them to the heart of Spanish success: the magnificent Bernabeu stadium in Madrid before a crowd of 125,000 – where they duly lost 3–1. The English press conveyed an impression of a game won by cynical and overly physical defence; of gamesmanship above all else. But the simple truth remains; the very best

English team (still not at their full potential) was no match for Real Madrid, a fact confirmed by the draw in the return leg in Manchester, played under United's new floodlights. Thus ended the first English club venture in Europe, halted by a Madrid team which dominated the European Cup for the first five years of its existence; an unrivalled team against which all contemporary (and subsequent) club teams sought to measure themselves (in the main, unsuccessfully). The Manchester United team, still young, still naive in the ways of European football, was a fledgling footballing force, and could feel they had acquitted themselves well against the best in the world. Yet here they were, generally recognised as one of the best teams the English game had ever seen, badly paid, and with no immediate prospects of capitalising on their extraordinary commercial appeal. English football was a wretched employer, forcing even its greatest stars to look elsewhere to supplement their earnings, and even to turn to shady activities to make the most of their footballing fame. The growing commercial prospects of the game, enhanced by the potential offered by television, stood in sharp contrast to the game's endemic meaness to the men, the players, who made it all possible. Even the most famous of players were not above bending the rules to make a decent living. And who can blame them?

> **Even the most famous of players were not above bending the rules to make a decent living.**

Players' wages had been capped since 1900, partly because of the traditional FA 'old school' distaste for professionalism, and partly from the fear of smaller clubs about rising wage bills. Clubs had formally agreeed to the wage restraints, and made public protestations of the need to restrain players' wages, but they frequently ignored the agreement when it suited them. Time and again, teams, and players, were caught out and punished for their transgressions. Officials and players were fined, suspended – sometimes banned for life – for breaking rules that were clearly inequitable and morally indefensible. The maximum wage survived until 1961 (by which time it had peaked at £20 in the season, £17 in summer). Even then only a small proportion of players received the maximum. Certain perks came the way of the best players – club housing, certain bonuses, small-scale sponsorship and commercial deals – but it rarely amounted to much more than modest extras, even for the greatest of players. Billy Meredith before the First World War (suspended for illegal payments), and Stanley Matthews before and after the Second World War, earned a fraction of their true commercial value. And so it continued, down to the early 1960s.

Many of the men who ran football in the twenty years after the Second World War had been reared in a harsher world. Born and raised in poor working-class communities of the 1920s and 1930s, tempered in all things by the experiences of the war itself, they were men to whom hard times seemed normal; men of working stock, normally of little formal education (notwith-standing their native brightness) and unsympathetic to what seemed, as the 1950s advanced, the fleshier delights which attracted their younger players. More than that, they generally saw themselves as the custodians of the clubs' interests (that is, the directors' interests), elevating the club above the demands or concerns of the players themselves. They were, almost to a man, hard on their players, even when they viewed them (as Busby clearly did) as their protégés. In money matters, the managers were the instruments of the directors' wishes and rarely took into account the central fact that players deserved a better deal. Even when they accepted this fact, in the bigger, more successful clubs, managers and clubs fell back on the time-hon-oured but dubious system of conniving in infringing the game's rules.

Managers and clubs fell back on the time-honoured but dubious system of conniving in infringing the game's rules.

It was impossible for clubs not to become involved in the double-dealing which flowed from this anachronistic restriction on trade, and which, today, looks positively Victorian. Fathers of promising footballers were paid, ostensibly for scouting for the club. As clubs developed genuine youth policies, parents realised there was money to be had from football clubs. Wiser scouts realised that the way to a good youthful prospect was via the boy's mother. Manchester United were able to beat off rivals for one of their future stars (whose parents had already been offered £4000 for the boy's signature) by trading on their already famous name – and bringing an item from Lourdes for the devout mother. A common scam at the time was the illicit use of scarce Cup Final tickets as a bonus for players. Formally, the FA decreed a small number of tickets be allocated to each player. In fact clubs liberally distributed tickets, and the players, in their turn, sought ways of capitalising on the tickets. Sometimes they made very little, the profits going instead to the touts. The game was riddled with such ploys and stratagems. Everyone involved in the game knew what was happening, and so too did large numbers of people outside the game. Fans also knew it because they were the ones having to pay ridiculous prices for scarce tickets to special games. What everyone also knew and accepted was that it was a totally unsatisfactory state of affairs, demeaning to the players who were reduced to black-marketeers and hustlers, and diminishing for the clubs. For the grand old men who ran the game, however, it represented, not a tawdry hypocrisy, but a valiant defence of traditional values in a world sliding rapidly towards commercial domination.

The example of Manchester United had begun to show how tattered the existing trading restrictions really were. Paid more like artisan workmen rather than the gifted professionals they were, the team fondly assembled by Busby, and known then and since by his name, had at the end of the 1957 season won the Championship and narrowly missed the Cup (and therefore the Double) simply by an outrageous injury to their goalkeeper. The FA was doggedly opposed to substitutes – another historical relic which made no sense whatsoever – and so the finest English team that fans could recall, which drew packed crowds wherever they played and which had already flexed their muscles against the best in Europe, were denied what they had earned. The following season, 1957–58, promised even better. In the event it was to prove the most shattering experience for English football, more profound and far-reaching, in ways no one could have predicted at the time.

6 February 1958

Busby nurtured his young players, those in the team and those waiting in the wings, with a paternal attention. But he also dropped and shuffled his stars around, buying replacements when needed, responding to results and performances and building a team that would again win the Championship and challenge for the European Cup. By the New Year 1958 his team was playing better than ever. On 1 February they won 5–4 at Highbury in what most of the 63,000 fans present accepted was a classic game, before flying to

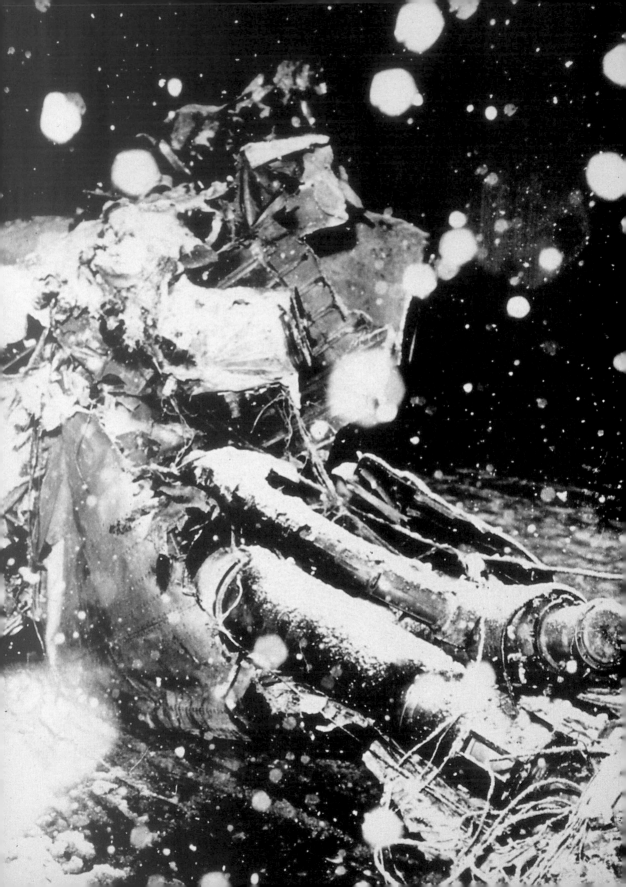

Belgrade for their next European game – another epic, a draw being enough to see United through to the semi-finals. The players endured the usual after-match banquet (and speeches) while the press struggled with the terrible Yugoslav telephone system to file their rapturous reports. The following day, 6 February, the party flew home, stopping in Munich to refuel. The plane had problems on two aborted take-offs, and the passengers disembarked in the snow and encroaching gloom. Ten minutes later they were called back to the aircraft. Just before 3 pm the plane began its third attempted take-off. Weighed down by ice on the wings, the plane ran out of runway and crashed.

Later that same afternoon, at about 4.30 pm, placards began to appear on the street corners of central Manchester. 'United plane crash. Many dead.' I saw the first, on Oxford Road, from the top of the school bus taking us to Piccadilly. Crowds had already begun to gather around the city centre news-paper vendors, as people left their place of work. Shops and offices simply emptied. There were, of course, no transistor radios and people had to rely on news from the local newspapers, which came spinning off the nearby presses in a series of special issues. Crowds snapped up the papers as the vans delivered them. The city ground to a halt, and normal life was rearranged into large knots of people, dotted across the city, waiting for the next delivery of newspapers. Looking back, it was an extraordinary experi-ence. A major industrial town, the centre of the great cotton industry, brought to a grinding halt by word of mouth and newspaper placards. Rumour was piled on snippets of news, gleaned from radio and from the fortunate few with access to TV. For those of us who had grown up as United fans, it was, at first unbelievable; a 'pinch-me-it-isn't-true' experience. Miserably, it was true. In the event, 23 people died, among them eight players.

The scale of the disaster cannot be conveyed by a simple counting of the dead. Today, after all that has been written about the Munich aircrash on 6 February 1958, it is hard to capture the mood of a major city plunged into mourning. It was as if the city of Manchester had itself died. Even people who remembered the blitz could not recall so palpable a sense of communal grief and misery. In the immediate aftermath of the Munich aircrash, that enormously proud city was a desolate place. Here was a city whose Victorian civic pride was tangible and visible; its magnificent civic buildings, the Halle orchestra (its great days under Sir John Barbarolli), its national-yet-local newspaper, *The Manchester Guardian*, and, the cause and occasion of

The death of the United team was, in a strange way, the herald of a deeper decline.

everything else, its role as the heart of the cotton industry. Then, very briefly, it had become the home of one of Europe's eye-catching football teams. 1958 was a turning point. The death of the United team was, in a strange way, the herald of a deeper decline: the dramatic collapse of cottonopolis itself, the later demise of the Halle, and the move of the *Guardian* to London, leaving its birthplace and its name – Manchester – behind, somewhere up north.

In the days that followed the accident, the collective grieving among people not given to public expressions of private feelings was staggering. Moreover it was national, though always more profound and public in Manchester. There followed successive reminders of what had happened. In the weeks immediately after the accident each new sorry twist added to the misery; the death of Duncan Edwards (possibly the greatest of that team's young players), the night the coffins were brought back to Manchester, in convoy, from the airport to the stadium, the myriad local funeral and memorial services, and then the hasty cobbling together of a new team from survivors, young boys and new signings. When the new Manchester United appeared to play its first game, it did so to a match programme which could only list eleven blank places where players' names should be. A new mood took over; a mass, sporting frenzy which was as potent and as daunting as the communal grief which nurtured it. At first, this makeshift team, gradually augmented by signings of experienced players, was swept along by the adrenalin of the moment; by that heady mix of grief for lost friends, by the infectious support of the packed stadiums (fans queued for hours to get in) and by the understandable hesitation of opponents. Inevitably too, the team faltered in the teeth of its own weaknesses. Though they managed to reach the Cup Final again – to be defeated by Bolton – they were clearly in no position to be Champions, still less pose a threat in Europe (where Real Madrid triumphed yet again). Manchester United were a broken team and a desolate club. The ringing rhetoric from club spokesmen, that the great club would rise from the disaster, seemed hopelessly implausible. When Matt Busby, recovered from his grievous injuries, returned to work later that year, the future looked impossibly daunting. Yet, he had already built two great teams (the post-war team, and the team killed at Munich). Why not a third?

The aftermath

The Munich aircrash was a defining moment in the story of English football. And not just for Manchester United – the accident also destroyed the plans and hopes of the national team. Four players, Byrne, Edwards, Taylor and Colman, would have formed the backbone of the English team hoping to play that summer in the World Cup in Sweden. In the event, that series was best remembered for the emergence of the 17-year-old Pele, and by the fact that the games could be watched live on TV. Along with games in the European competitions, the 1958 World Cup exposed British fans and a widening circle of fans watching on TV to the remarkable quality of football outside the British Isles. It was becoming indisputable that world football had changed, that the English variant was no longer the *only* way of playing football, still less was it the best.

Matt Busby at Manchester United and Stan Cullis at Wolves had been instrumental in bringing European football to English fans who were remarkably local in their allegiances and tastes. Fans followed their local teams by birth and upbringing, and supported them through displays of local loyalties which, at times, seemed to follow the contours and bound- aries of parochial divides. Sometimes it was impossible to predict *why* fans followed a particular team, though in places religion was a sure guide. Why did fans in the same city support one local team rather than another? Support was often inherited, like genetic traits across the generations. But, on the whole (and this was to change in the late century) football fans were supporters of their home-town teams. In a sense, that was one of the attrac- tions of the innovative European games; local teams, steeped in the folklore and mythology of local support, took on players from the far corners of a foreign field, hoping for an assertion of local achievement over the exotic. The problem was that the exotic often proved itself equal or superior to the local. Our Team, Our Boys, The Lads, were often no match for the foot- balling visitors who stepped off the plane at the nearest airport. What a small section of football fans had recently witnessed with their own eyes, in Manchester and Wolverhampton, became clearer to millions when they

Support was often inherited, like genetic traits across the generations.

turned on the TV sets to watch the World Cup in 1958. This projection of the game into millions of homes worldwide was to prove revolutionary for the game itself. Teams (and their stars) which had once commanded a local following, henceforth found a global audience, with all the commercial potential that entailed. Pele began 1958 as an unknown Brazilian hopeful. By the end of that summer, he had become one of the most famous sportsmen in the world.

For the English footballing fraternity, measured in their millions, 1958 marked a clear break with the past. They had become aware as never before of a wider footballing world. They learned from watching visiting teams and televised football that it was a world game and that some of the greatest teams and finest players plied their trade far beyond English shores.

This was not simply a problem which beset English football but was representative of a broadly-based British malaise. A major industrial and imperial power was now, in the late 1950s, in a state of indisputable retreat and decline on all fronts. Britain was withdrawing rapidly from its imperial possessions, rebuffed in its last great effort to be a global power (at Suez in 1956), and with its old industries beginning to buckle before the onslaught of newer, more aggressive rivals round the world. The story of football was the story of another form of isolated British superiority finally coming to terms with, and grudgingly accepting, the challenge of the wider world. Though the Munich aircrash destroyed one of the country's best teams, it served in the long run to confirm the importance of being actively involved with Europe. There was no going back.

The quest for spontaneity is fundamental in art and football expresses it best.

Eric Cantona

Into the
1960s

The 1960s has entered the realms of widespread mythology, just as it has entered the popular terminology. Perhaps no other decade of the 20th century occupies more secure a place in the popular imagination — swinging or not. In large part this was due to the popular music, unleashed especially by the Beatles, but it goes much deeper than that. For those critics looking for the origins and the dynamics of social change however, the 1960s seemed, at first, no different than any other arbitrary date. There was nothing special about the decade when it began and there were many for whom the benefits and appeal of the 1960s began late.

Popular culture

Having said that, profound social change swept across Britain and other parts of the western world in the 1960s. The British became the centre of a new form of international attention, especially for the dramatic and eye-catching qualities of its popular culture, from music to fashion. That popular culture was influential all round the globe, courtesy of new media able to send and receive images and sounds in the blink of an eye. It was, in brief, the period which witnessed the first benefits (and disadvantages) of immediate global communications. Looking back, the colourful highlights leap off the page: the Beatles and the Rolling Stones, the explosive rise of an irreverent (and often doped) youth culture, the English victory in the 1966 World Cup, the often outrageous fashions which found a narcissistic parade ground in London's Carnaby Street. There was of course a much darker side to the whole business, culminating in the disasters of the Vietnam War, and the massive and often ugly demonstrations against that war by millions who flaunted their new-found styles and music as emblems of protest against old, hawkish regimes. For millions of people in the west, memories of that war are best evoked by contemporary music, which formed a refrain to the daily horrors from South East Asia beamed to our TV screens by new satellite broadcasting systems.

Popular culture came of age in the mid and late 1960s, thanks to new electronic media, influencing the home (at least in the prosperous west) via the ubiquitous TV set and ever-cheaper music systems. And the whole process was given a global audience by orbiting satellites. The most immediate triumph of the space programmes was not so much the discoveries of other worlds but the transformation of the humdrum habits and pleasures on earth itself. Pleasures once reserved for paying spectators could henceforth be enjoyed by untold millions around the world. The impact on the ways people spent their leisure time was profound beyond measure. This globalisation of culture is, today, so obvious, so much a part of the world we live in, that it takes a leap of the imagination to recall what it was like *before* the era of modern satellite communications.

No major sport could remain uninfluenced by these changes. Some new sports were invented, and some old, marginal, sports became massively popular; who would have dreamed that snooker (once a slightly seedy pastime hiding in smoke-filled halls) would attract millions of viewers? And who could have imagined that, before the end of the 20th century, the popularity of cricket in the West Indies

No major sport could remain uninfluenced by these changes.

would find itself under threat from football, even basketball? The impact of TV was to be greater, more seismic and more universal, than its most dogged of opponents feared, even in their worst Orwellian nightmares. Yet in time TV was to bring more pleasure to more people than anything in the history of mankind. Football was, then, only *one* sport which was to be dramatically transformed by the coming of modern TV, by colour transmission and by the global reach of satellite broadcasting.

Managers, new and old

At first, football seemed to plod on much as before. Football stadiums remained grim fortresses – architectural reminders of a bygone age, affording little but a precarious perch, and that distinctive waft of footballing fragrance: a mix of disinfected urinals, warmed-over meat pies and players' linament. Not surprisingly, crowds continued to fall. The 28-plus million spectators of 1960–61 would slump to 16-plus million by 1985–86. Whenever proposals for changes in league football surfaced they invariably hit the buffers formed by the serried ranks of football club chairmen. There were other institutional reasons (notably the voting procedures needed for constitutional change) which made it hard to change football. It had long been obvious to the bigger, more famous clubs that change would come only by breaking away. The League system was far too constitutionally unbending to be able to reform itself, a fact confirmed by the rejection of the reforms proposed by Sir Norman Chester in 1968 and 1983. As the Football League approached its centenary, it proved about as nimble and alert as most other

Footballing fragrance: a mix of disinfected urinals, warmed-over meat pies and players' linament.

centenarians trying to cope, on their own, with the world at large. The game of professional football was regulated and monitored by an arthritic and immobile organisation which had become institutionally incapable of distinguishing the broader interests of the game from its own narrow, sectional and outdated concerns. As fans turned away from the game, the Football League responded by devising more of the same; more games and new competitions. But the arithmetic simply did not add up; a falling fan base being chased by more and more football matches.

At every level English football, like so many other institutions, had been shackled for years by a paternalism which resisted the rise of professionalism. Managers at club and international level found themselves countermanded by directors and administrators. Men with no footballing expertise, but esconced in football's boardrooms, felt no qualms about selecting teams, conducting transfers of players, and offering tactical instructions. By the early 1960s this old system (comparable to other areas of British management – and with similar results) was under strain. Younger managers chafed at the old restrictions; these 'track-suit' managers worked closely with players on the training ground and often identified more with the players than with the directors. They were anxious to see football change; the more prominent, especially in the bigger clubs, looked enviously at the European game. European football had *already* shown what could be achieved by freeing management from outdated controls The English game needed to cut free from its institutional and ideological baggage, from the historical clutter which was so burdensome and which was a prime cause of the game's insularity. Not until English football turned to other ways of organising itself would the game begin to change. Football needed to modernise its stadiums, its management, its relations with players, its links to international football and, of course, the way the game was played.

The English game needed to cut free from its institutional and ideological baggage.

There were prominent men in the game who tried to change things – up to a point. Alan Hardaker, in charge of the League since 1957, wanted to put the game on a sound financial basis. But he, like many around him, remained wedded to old ideals. True to his clerical background, Hardaker defended the Sabbath, disliked gambling and its associated wealth, and sought to equalise income and power between the bigger and smaller clubs. Here was a management fired by an admirable egalitarianism, but it had the disastrous effect of maintaining the mediocre. This was most striking in football's dealings with the players. The insistence on maximum wages meant that the best were paid little more than the worst. There was no truck with the ideal that rewards should follow ability, or that excellence should be rewarded above the mundane. Yet what possible sense did that make in professional sport – for which the very rationale was winning, success and victory? Competition was the very heart of the game, in the leagues and in the knock-out cups. Players, teams and clubs all played *to win*, ideally to prove themselves the best. Yet football's management sought to squeeze the game's natural drive towards excellence into a egalitarian straitjacket. Looking back, the game looks more like a corner Co-op shop than a major industry facing ever more serious international competition. Again, this was also true of many other institutions. What ailed English football was a local variant of a widespread social problem.

Hardaker was however responsible for a major financial breakthrough in 1959, by forcing the football pools to pay a reasonable fee for the use of the League fixtures. It was a small beginning of a process (the tapping of football's commercial potential) which, by the end of the century, was to transform the game utterly. In the meantime, however, the game remained weighed down by old restrictions. Players' wages were low, and seemed worse as real wages increased more widely in the late 1950s. Again, Europe showed that football could be organised differently. The most successful teams and the finest players were paid enormous sums. English football

Europe showed that football could be organised differently.

meanwhile remained wedded to its flat-cap financial ideals: maximum wages and restrictions on the players' movements.

The professional footballers' cause had been fought with an abrasive (though often counter-productive) vigour throughout the 1950s by their union led by Jimmy Guthrie. His removal in 1958 enabled Jimmy Hill to emerge as the

players' most effective, successful spokesman and leader. People found it easy to poke fun at Hill. But he was a profound force for the good of the game, to whom modern players owe a debt of gratitude. His articulate advocacy, his clever use of the media (he proved himself a master of TV), and his dogged persistence in the players' cause, transformed the whole debate about players' wages. The story of the shabby treatment of professional footballers had long been familiar, mainly via ghost-written books by the stars, and through an endless litany of newspaper articles. Despite a contrary, minority voice, professional footballers had clearly had enough of their outdated conditions of employment, and Jimmy Hill tapped into that widespread disatisfaction.The most famous footballer of his generation was Stanley Matthews, the stuff of footballing legends in a career spanning the 1930s and 1960s. But even he, though financially secure (largely from outside earnings), was paid the same as the men around him. Even Matthews raised his hand for the footballers' strike, due to start 21 January 1961, but two days before the strike was due to start, the League capitulated and abandoned the maximum wage.

Football clubs tried to renege on the deal in a variety of ways (agreeing among themselves, for example, to fix informal wage limits). They also clung to the highly restrictive transfer system. In the event, that system lasted another two years and was destroyed partly by the union, partly by the law case, brought by George Eastham (with union support) against his old club Newcastle United. In July 1963, the player's case, marshalled for Eastham and presented to court by the union, was accepted by Mr Justice Wilberforce as 'an unjustifiable restraint of trade'.

Some of the game's backwoodsmen wanted to fight a rearguard action, but they had been comprehensively trounced by the players union (now the PFA), and by their leader Cliff Lloyd. The 1964 season began with a new, fair transfer system in place (made completely free in 1978). By

The 1964 season began with a new, fair transfer system in place.

1963, professional footballers had secured their major demands; an end both to the maximum wage and an end to the restrictions on their movement between clubs. Throughout the whole, protracted business, the management of English football showed itself in its true light. The game was run by older men who were doggedly resistant to change, contemptuously ill-disposed towards the players and truculent about any shift in their own form of management and labour relations. They wanted to run football clubs the way they had run local businesses (not very well). But what was the alternative?

If club directors and league management had cared to raise their vision to look beyond their parochial boundaries, they would have been able to see a different way of running (and playing) football. The visiting Europeans teams which graced British stadiums in the late 1950s and early 1960s, in friendlies and in the European Cup, were not accidental freaks of sporting nature. Many of them had emerged from an utterly new footballing culture. Spain and Italy, with their lavish new stadiums, successful teams and well-paid players were light years removed from the Edwardian footballing culture which continued to cling to the English game. Moreover the European game began to attract some of the best British players, keen to make the most of their short careers, but unable to capitalise on their abilities at home.

Professional football was not, it is true, fully developed across the whole of Europe. Professionalism came late to Belgium and Germany – in the early 60s – and there were oddities about the game in Sweden, the Netherlands and Portugal. But when change was needed, it tended to come quickly. In large measure, a major catalyst was the rapid political and economic movement towards the European Common Market – with the British, of course, on the outside.

There were of course contrary voices – contrary visions – in all this, in football as in politics. There were demands that coaching should change, and that English football should seek to produce players and teams to compete with the best in Europe. Much hinged on formal, professional coaching – initially viewed as a European oddity. Long before the First World War, football training had been established as a leisurely affair, beginning at mid-morning with a regime of skipping, walking, running and some ball practice – until lunchtime. Some clubs trained in the afternoon, though many did not, and much depended on a club's conventions. It was often claimed that the most important aspect of training caricatured by contemporary writers, was to keep footballers as far away as possible from

Much hinged on formal, professional coaching – initially viewed as a European oddity.

a public house. Before the war (at Huddersfield and Arsenal) Chapman had placed great emphasis on the development of ball skills, but this seems to have been unusual. After 1945 there had been a greater emphasis on careful training and tactical preparation, especially under the influence of the first English manager, Walter Winterbottom, and FA-sponsored training schemes. But even that fell short of the training regimes revealed from European encounters. Not surprisingly, then, demand increased that English football should change its attitude towards training methods – and towards the general physical well-being of professional footballers. Yet even at the end of the 20th century, foreign footballers continued to be surprised by the poor facilities and systems they found scattered throughout the English game.

By the early 1960s, the genesis of modern football coaching had taken root in the English game. Yet English training remained remarkably unimaginative: a three- or four-week, pre-season regime, of what Holt and Mason describe as 'lapping, running and physical jerks followed by a nine month slog of training sessions for five days every week'. The actual amount of time put in varied from club to club. Many players found the whole business boring and those who wanted to practise outside their clubs' formal regime were generally discouraged. Few clubs made serious attempts to plan for forthcoming games. Some coaches even refused to allow players to train with a football.

In England and Europe, much of the tactical imagination in the 1960s was invested in defensive play, with the consequent tedium of unattractive defensive games, with players marshalled into defensive battalions. Little thought was given to the game's appeal to paying spectators. The most attractive of teams of the late 1950s (Wolves, the pre-Munich Manchester United), and Bill Nicholson's Double-Winning Spurs team of 1961, all played lavishly attacking games, and scored remarkable tallies of goals. Not surprisingly, they played to packed grounds wherever they appeared. They were also managed by men who were as remarkable for the inspiration and loyalty they inspired as much as for their tactical nous. Like all the revered football managers of the second half of the 20th century, they were men with great but indefinable man-management skills.

Yet it was still the case that prominent football coaches who had proved themselves in various European countries often found themselves unwelcome in English football. The English game tended to look no further than Scotland for its best managers. It was also true that many famous players, well into the 1960s, resisted formal coaching, feeling that their skills (and experience) were more valuable than formal instruction. Such men, players and management alike, tended to share that widespread suspicion of formal instruction, an instinctive distrust of education, and a tendency to feel that footballing skills were natural and innate, and required no formal cultivation. It was, again, a very British disease. But it was being put to the test by progress in other parts of the footballing world.

The tactical approaches to football had differed throughout the history of the game but had generally been in the charge of the Board of Directors. Powerful managers – Chapman and Allison at Arsenal in the 1930s – insisted on keeping tactical decisions and training in their hands, a trend advanced after 1945 by the influence of Winterbottom, and by the emergence of the 'track-suit' managers of the 1950s. The ability to spot players' strengths and weakness – to know how to arrange and change team formation, who to play in specific roles and positions, and how best to allow individual talent and leadership on the field to find its own level – was, in addition to overall inspiration and man-management regarded as the key to good management. And always, of course, the really great teams needed the indefinable qualities of a master-craftsman; the playmaker and leader on the pitch.

The emphasis on defensive play in the 1960s meant that teams scored fewer goals, in all leagues, a trend that was maintained until the mid-1970s. Clubs had come to realise that success came from not conceding, rather than scoring goals. And that realisation bought about a change in tactical arrangements on the field, all designed to cut off and stifle opponents' attacking options. Football in the late 1960s and 1970s became a game which showed all the signs of detailed planning and training. It was the beginning of a new professional approach to football, an approach which embraced qualities many older observers did not like. Even the word 'professional' was now used differently. Henceforth, it conveyed a sense of steering close to the professional wind; getting away with anything the rules allowed – just. Gamesmanship, time-wasting, a cynical robustness – all and more presented an image of teams willing to use almost any available tactic and ploy to gain advantage. That approach also included physical intimidation, challenges (sometimes menaces) to officials and, off the pitch, the use of the media to plant mischievous or disruptive stories about opponents. All this is familiar because it is basic to the way the game of professional (and later even amateur) football is played and understood. The defensive spirit ushered in during the 1960s was in effect the dramatic curtailing, possibly the death knell, of old 'gentlemanly' footballing habits and the culture of 'fair play'.

The hard men

In England it was perfected by Don Revie's Leeds team (ironically garbed in all white, imitative of the magical Real Madrid team), with their mantra (repeated by old Leeds players to this day), 'Get your retaliation in first'. They were in many respects a great team with many fine players. But, to their intense irritation, they remained unloved outside the city of Leeds. From the mid-1960s through to the 1970s, few top teams could hope to succeed without their 'hard men', who were often talented players but whose daunting physical presence and natural aggression intimidated opponents as much as it excited their followers. Bremner and Hunter at Leeds, Stiles at Manchester United, Smith, later Souness, at Liverpool, Harris at Chelsea. More recently it reached its nadir in the lumbering figure of Vinny Jones. Jones was to make a post-football career out of his physical menace, suitable perhaps, because his most memorable achievements as a footballer had been to grab Paul Gascoigne by the testicles and to bite a reporter's nose. A similar litany of physical players could be recited for contemporary European and South American club and national teams. The importance of such men was only diminished by the authorities' determination to curb the worst excesses, and to prevent the havoc and injury wreaked on better players by the games' hard men.

> **Jones was to make a post-football career out of his physical menace.**

To confuse the matter further, some of those men were also wonderful footballers; talented sportsmen whose abilities sometimes disappeared into the infamous 'red mist' when they lost control and struck out viciously at players (and even, in the much later case of Eric Cantona, at fans). For all this, there were many who felt that the game was less physical, less tough, than it had been in the 1930s, though this may have been a generational issue. Much the same is said today – that modern players are more protected than they were a generation ago. In part this is largely the nostalgia of old men, and old players, looking back to what they regard as better times; when men were men and attackers were terrified. Nor do the statistics help much, because the

Don Revie and Jack Charlton of Leeds, 1970 © Hulton Deutsch

index of bookings and dismissals was a function as much of changing refereeing policy as player behaviour. What *is* clear however is that from the late 1960s football, like all other sports, was increasingly subject

From the late 1960s football was increasingly subject to detailed and instantaneous scrutiny.

to detailed and instantaneous scrutiny. The intrusion of television cameras enabled games to be analysed carefully. Before the advent of TV, matches – and misbehaviour in those games – were merely recorded by word of mouth, and in writing, and sometimes, if the cameraman was lucky, in photographs. From the 1960s onwards TV cameras caught the action and replayed it. Film enabled critics and armchair fans to make up their own minds about players' behaviour. Often what they saw was unpleasant or unnecessary. In effect TV put football's hard men on the spot, and generated a growing demand for change, for tighter control, and for protection for threatened players.

The impact of widening TV coverage of football, plus ever more sophisticated TV technology, transformed the game not merely by widening the audience but by providing unprecedented and detailed analysis of the game and its flaws. The evidence of TV cameras was generally unambiguous, leaving little room for argument. Rough play and dirty players could be spotted and singled out. This detailed scrutiny of the game pinpointed the game's hard men and their tricks. By and large, they were disliked by football's authorities (and by a sporting press eager to moralise about football's shortcomings and to demand action). TV coverage clearly reshaped what was deemed to be acceptable behaviour on the pitch.

A gulf apart

Whatever the hidden consequences of TV, its prime purpose was to entertain. TV brought football to vast new audiences in the 1960s and 1970s. For their part, football fans could measure their footballing passions against the best teams in the world. Televised football quickly had massive consequences. The English World Cup victory at Wembley in 1966 (its TV highlights rerun *ad nauseam* to this day) was watched by a majority of people living in Britain. The tournament was eagerly awaited, promoted by an increasingly

Pele celebrating Brazil 4 v Italy 1, Mexico City, 1970 © Popperfoto jingoist popular press, with expectations sharpened by the emergence of a promising England team under a shrewd manager, Alf Ramsay. (In the event – of course – winning the World Cup did not guarantee Ramsay his job afterwards.) The tournament was a great success – well-attended, well-organised and well-behaved, with some memorable teams and games – and the added spice of the trophy itself being stolen, and found (by a dog). England, led by a flawless Bobby Moore – perhaps the greatest ever English defender and play-maker (opponents claimed he knew where the ball was heading twenty minutes before anyone else) – had the advantage of playing all their games at Wembley. Moore and Bobby Charlton proved themselves players of outstanding flair and skill, as good as any. The England team had its share of luck, beating strong opponents (Portugal and Argentina) *en route* before finding itself in the final against Germany. Their luck held again. The Germans were a strong, well-organised team orchestrated by the magnificent young Beckenbauer whose cool, calculating presence was to dominate the German midfield for years to come. After an even, tense game, it seemed that England would win by a very dubious goal – argued about to this day. Geoff Hurst completed a unique hat-trick by scoring *that* memorable last-minute goal which has been rerun thousands of times ever since. Curiously Hurst was knighted – 32 years later. The game quickly entered popular memory as a peak of England's footballing achievement, and a talisman against which all subsequent English teams have been compared – unfavourably. England came to a halt to watch that game. The match also prompted that array of absurd attitudes towards the Germans and Germany which simply refuse to die, not least because they are used so frequently by the popular press.

Few serious observers doubt that, for all the unquestioned qualities of the England team of 1966, the best national team in the years up to 1970 was Brazil, and the best player was Pele. It is hard to imagine a team bettering the performance of the Brazilians when they won the Mexico World Cup in 1970; their victory over Italy that year in the Aztec stadium was a peerless football match. The Brazilians offered a rare blend of individual brilliance and flawless team-play, simply transfixing millions of viewers worldwide who watched the game on TV. At the heart of the team was Pele in his prime.

By 1970 Pele was magic and unstoppable.

At the 1958 World Cup, Pele had been the boy wonder. In 1966 in England was battered, match after match, retreating from the tournament too injured to continue. But by 1970 he would be magical and unstoppable. He was also a humble man who carried his gifts with affecting modesty. In a game where lesser players proclaim their own virtues with vulgar self-promotion, Pele stands out as the greatest player of the 20th century.

Despite the England 1966 World Cup victory, it was obvious that English football was slipping behind. Television served to emphasise the gulf between the best and the also-rans, and much of the footballing fare on offer at English grounds was mediocre. But the story was uneven. The English (and Scottish) game continued to produce a series of brilliant and successful teams which made an impact in Europe.

> **Television served to emphasise the gulf between the best and the also-rans.**

Spurs had won the European Cup Winners Cup in 1963. Celtic (1967) and Manchester United (1968) won the Holy Grail of the European Cup. At the heart of all those teams were a number of exceptional players. Spurs were blessed with Danny Blanchflower – a fiercely independent and articulate figure, always his own man throughout a distinguished career – whose graceful orchestration of a talented Spurs team was critical for its success. Blanchflower always conveyed the impression that he was *lucky*; lucky to be blessed with footballing and leadership skills, and that he was, after all, only a sportsman. But he was a great footballer and sportsman whose achievements never diminished his personal modesty.

In Bobby Charlton, Manchester United had a star of comparable mettle. A youthful survivor of the Munich aircrash, Charlton rapidly developed into one of English football's greatest players – for club and country. He accumulated records, attainments and plaudits on an unprecedented scale and was, throughout, an exemplary sportsman, apparently unaffected by the adulation which rightly came his way.

Charlton helped his club win the 1968 European Cup, against a formidable Benfica team (doubtless inspired by my own voice from the Wembley seats). That cup was later won twice by a much less glamorous club, Nottingham Forest, under Brian Clough who, for all his undoubted managerial abilities, was immodesty personified, and whose absurd pronouncements served to diminish his very considerable attainments. Clough was a football 'character' (the word so often used to add a favourable gloss to some unattractive characteristics) who could, by turns, inspire players or alienate them utterly. Clough became a caricature of himself, always on hand with a quotable quip for waiting press men ('even my grandchildren don't like me'). But he was a great manager, denied elevation to the England position by his openly admitted personal foibles.

English football, clearly, could compete with the best (though rarely without the help of prominent Scots and Irishmen as players and managers). The English game occasionally produced players of world class – Bobby Moore, Bobby Charlton, and George Best, whose career was as brief as it was dazzling. Best was in effect the first major casualty of the new age of major footballing celebrity; a footballer whose name and good looks proved irresistible to the marketing men. No one – club, manager, the player himself – seemed to know how to cope with fame and fortune, or how to remain focused on the game which made it all possible. Like a shooting star, Best briefly dazzled all who watched him, before burning out in a series of misadventures and in a confusion of alcohol. He was to be the first (and best) of many modern foot ballers in the TV age whose celebrity and wealth brought little but long-term trouble. But for those who watched him in his prime, Best remained the most unforgettable of footballers, one of those rare players who left spectators speechless. It was all the more brilliant to behold for the pathetic contrast which was to follow.

> Like a shooting star, Best briefly dazzled all who watched him, before burning out.

From the late 1960s there were, then, a series of major English teams who were as good as any in Europe. With the exceptions of Nottingham, they were part of a broader visible trend in English football – the successful clubs came from the major cities. Though southern clubs had become more prominent in football's top flight in the years after the Second World War, the centre of footballing gravity continued to be the north and Midlands, much as it had been before 1914. But the most striking feature of the game in the second half of the century was the dominance of teams from major cities, Liverpool,

London, Manchester, followed — a long way behind — by the Birmingham region. Many clubs which had been the backbone of the English game in its early days, indeed many of the game's major pioneers, slid into the lower divisions, financially straitened, their best players lured away by the big clubs, their fans melting away, along the new motorway systems, to watch bigger clubs nearby. Preston, Blackpool, Burnley, Blackburn (though briefly revived by a multimillionaire local patron) slid out of football's limelight, which was now dominated by their bigger, more prosperous and infinitely more glamorous neighbours down the road.

Being a big city team did not of course guarantee success. There were plenty of such teams which struggled to get out from under the shadow of their major local rivals. For their part, the successful major clubs were also notable for their managerial stability. Like the dominant clubs in the interwar years, those of recent years had been steered by powerful men able to combine man management with tactical nous. Liverpool under Shankly was perhaps the most famous, his legacy inherited by men reared in the club's own distinctive culture. But a change of manager, especially after a dominant successful manager, could break a successful cycle. Footballing success was never guaranteed and even the mightiest of footballing empires could quickly be brought to an end. This was not always obvious, for as clubs became ever more successful, they proved able to attract the best players. Success begat success, and success generated still more money. For the great majority of professional teams, however, life was an altogether more precarious existence; a struggle to survive on declining attendances, rising costs, and permanent reminders of the difference between themselves and the best clubs in the land.

The impact of TV

For anyone in doubt about the huge differences in football, the evidence was available on television. By the late 1960s a TV set had become a central feature of domestic furniture and was basic to the way the British people lived. By the end of the 20th century a majority of British people switched on television to watch major international sporting events. The crucial breakthrough for televised football was the introduction of *Match of the Day* in 1964 which quickly became a Saturday night ritual. Thanks to new technology (and later colour), games were cleverly edited and soon attracted a regular late evening audience of between 10 and 12 million viewers. Not only star footballers but even TV's football presenters became celebrities. To millions of viewers, interested in football though never visiting a football ground, TV presenters (like other sports commentators) became the interpreters of the game itself.

Televised football had been pioneered and developed by the BBC. But as commercial TV became ever more powerful and wealthy, televised football became a much sought-after prize. Football occasioned a major conflict between the BBC and commercial TV, as later it would between terrestrial and satellite broadcasters. The deciding factor was finance – who could offer the best deal. Both sides sparred for access to football; to league games, cup matches and international coverage. It was already clear that football and TV needed each other. Football persuaded viewers to switch on their TV sets and the consequent viewing figures enhanced the power of the broadcasters. Both sides found themselves locked in an ungainly embrace (whilst trying to keep a careful eye on their respective wallets).

The end result was ever more televised football, though even the massive audiences of the late 1960s and early 1970s paled into significance when satellite TV began to flex its considerable commercial muscles from 1988 onwards.

Football and TV needed each other.

The figures tell their own tale. The first televised football match in 1964 was watched by a mere 75,000. By the early 1970s, *Match of the Day* attracted upwards of 13 million viewers. Armchair football fans outnumbered fans in the stadiums by 10 to 15 times. By the end of the 20th century, negotiators for televised football were tossing offers of hundreds of millions of pounds onto the negotiating table. By then the game had entered a heady, glitzy period where the best footballers were millionaires, where clubs floated on the stock exchange and where fans found themselves paying lavish admission prices. What had happened to the people's game?

The profound changes which swept across football from the late 1960s onwards were not simply those initiated by TV. Football began to reflect a number of troubling and deeply unpleasant social problems. Indeed for the last thirty years of the century, English football was better known for its problems than it was for its footballing triumphs.

Masked hooligan © Mark Thompson/Allsport/Hulton Deutsch

Racism and hooligans

The English disease

English football from about 1970 to the mid-1980s tends not to be remembered for great teams or epic matches, but for the social problems which came to dominate the game. Yet these were the years of some remarkable teams, whose achievements have been buried under the rubble of football's troubles. It is true that the England team continued to disappoint, never able to win a major international trophy, rarely coming close to threatening the dominant national teams of the period (Holland, France, Argentina and Germany). It was in these years that the tabloid press began that taunting of England players, managers and teams which reached a frenzy of personal, vindictive abuse in the 1990s.

English club football on the other hand fared better than ever, and the period was dominated by some of its finest ever teams. Though Revie's great Leeds team broke up without really achieving its full potential, this failure went largely unmourned elsewhere. In 1971, Arsenal became the second club to achieve the Double in the 20th century. Clough's Nottingham Forest won the European Cup twice (1978–1980), but rarely received the plaudits its success warranted. Above all else, this was a period dominated by Liverpool, who remorselessly accumulated domestic and European trophies. Launched by the legendary Bill Shankly, Liverpool's unparalleled success was really clinched by his successor Bob Paisley – who won an astonishing 20 trophies between 1974–1983. Paisley masterminded a string of brilliant teams, carefully blending home-grown talent with shrewd purchases – none more crucial than Kenny Dalglish (who went on to manage the club's Double-winning run in 1986). Year after year, Liverpool's succession of entertaining teams swept others aside with a ruthless attacking style which dominated English football. But even Liverpool, with four European Cups to their credit, found their unparalleled success overshadowed by events off the field. It was as if the best was dragged down by the worst.

Racism

English football had reflected the changing features of English society throughout the game's history. In the last thirty years of the 20th century, however, it began to reveal a number of the more unpleasant aspects of English life. Major social problems inexplicably found a home on the football terraces in those years, and were so troublesome, so threatening and disruptive, that football *itself* was transformed from the simple pleasure of millions into one of the country's leading social problems. In the mid-1960s football was the national game; by the mid-1980s it had become a national problem.

In the 1970s a series of ugly noises began to appear at football matches. Insults, chants, animal grunts, a grotesque verbal battery (often accompanied by bananas) was directed at the first generation of British black footballers. The problem became increasingly severe over the next generation – loud and inescapable. Eventually such racist outbursts at football were banned in 1991 by an Act of Parliament. Such overt racism was a sore trial to the growing number of black players in English football. A small number of black players had been professional footballers in the past. Arthur Wharton, a West African, had played for Preston in the 1887 Cup Final, and other Africans and West Indians had followed his trail. Black players had become noticeable, though still unusual, in the 1960s, but the early 1970s saw the first generation of players born to West Indian immigrant parents. In 1978 Viv Anderson became the first black footballer to play for England. Today, the English (and French and Dutch) national teams invariably contain a number of black players; some African-born (notably in the French team), but most from Afro-Caribbean families who had migrated to Europe. By 1995 an estimated 15 per cent of all English professional footballers were black, mainly drawn from Caribbean families in London and the Midlands. It was an inevitable reflection of the changing demography of Britain, and indeed of western Europe, though similar patterns have not emerged from Britain's Asian communities.

The growth of Britain's immigrant communities, especially from the Indian subcontinent and from the West Indies, was the context for the ebb and flow of Britain's politics of race. British racial attitudes have a long and complex history, reaching back to the days of Britain's imperial and slaving past. But the racism which emerged on the football terraces in the 1970s was new. Not all racial abuse came from the extreme fringes of the hooligan fraternity though hooliganism and racism clearly enjoyed each other's company. Moreover the neo-fascist groups who had infiltrated the game were able to use racial tensions (and to distribute racist literature) in order to strike a sympathetic note among fans who shared their racial prejudices. Racism was an inescapable feature of British social life by the 1970s; picked up by radio and TV broadcasts, the vocabulary and rhythms of orchestrated racial abuse, with their distinctive sounds and offensive language, rippled across the nation's football grounds and settled into millions of sitting rooms via the TV set.

The end result was that, at times, British football grounds seemed to provide outdoor relief for the nation's misfits and antisocials. It was difficult to attend a game without feeling somehow tainted by the company. Who needed it? Getting into the grounds involved running a gauntlet of an increasingly sinister police presence. The good-natured banter of the bigger crowds was replaced by a cacophony of racial abuse. The climate at football grounds had become uncomfortable and deeply offensive. Unprepared to tolerate the unpleasantness lapping around the football ground, I followed the lead of

The good-natured banter of the bigger crowds was replaced by a cacophony of racial abuse.

many others and vacated the spot on the terraces where I had stood, one way or another, throughout my teens and adult life. Like millions more, I had had enough of the people's game.

What made matters worse was football's inability to combat the problems which were clearly corroding the game itself. One man, to his very great credit, took a brave, personal stand against racism at his own ground. Armed with a bull-horn, Brian Clough – characteristically the loner – marched towards the sound of baying fans, ordered them to stop, and threatened to ban them from the ground. In the main, however, there was an uncomfortable silence. Indeed the problem was made worse in many respects by football's complicity in racism towards black players. A number of managers and men in footballing authority regularly trotted out a stream of racial stereotypes about black footballers. Even broadcasters resolutely refused to acknowledge their own role in transmitting racial abuse into millions of homes. It was as if there was a conspiracy of silence; a refusal to admit, to discuss or to tackle the problem. Thus, week after week, black players became accustomed to the cascades of bananas and the barracking of animal grunts and racial animosity. It was to take a full twenty years before English football came to grips with racism and only then after years of pressure from outside bodies (notably the CRE) and the growing resolve and influence of black players and later black officials. In 2001 the FA openly admitted that they had done little to tackle the problem when help was needed.

Racism at football grounds was not, of course, a uniquely English phenomenon. Racist troubles of all kinds erupted across European football grounds from the 1970s onwards, sometimes copying the English, sometimes drawing on older local traditions of social discord and unpleasantness. Confrontations between rival fans in Holland, political links between certain teams and the far right in both Germany and Italy, and the eruption of violent nationalist instincts at international games, all became commonplace and predictable.

Italy saw some of the worst examples, notably the rivalries between Lazio and Roma, and the flourishing of racist groups with their own insignia and banners paraded at a number of Italian stadiums. In Hungary, anti-semitism surfaced in the orchestrated chants at Ferencvaros. Real Madrid fans gestured about the glory days under Franco. Supporters of Marseilles made similar postures towards the right, adopting an often bizarre blend of historical myths and catchphrases. Even behind the Iron Curtain, fans began to display signs of that footballing deviance which, by the early 1980s, formed a wound on the face of European football.

Racism blurred into the politics of the far right – and found a comfortable home at football matches across Europe. It found succour among groups who caused mayhem in the game from the 1970s onwards. Slowly, the major clubs brought it to heel – but again, only under pressure from outside. Left to their own devices, the football authorities remained pathetically incapable of handling the social problems which lapped around the country's football grounds. Even today, despite a campaign to eradicate racism from the game, despite an Act of Parliament in 1991, racism continues to lurk below the surface of the game (just as it does in English life itself) especially in a number of smaller clubs and in the following for the national England team.

> **Racism blurred into the politics of the far right – and found a comfortable home at football matches.**

Early hooligans

Some of the most vicious forms of racism stemmed from organised gangs, which themselves became a feature of the English game from the 1970s onwards. English football quickly developed a reputation for the behaviour of some of its followers. Within a decade, what had seemed at first to be mere rowdyism had erupted into a new and disruptive form of hooliganism. Critics comforted themselves initially; football had traditionally been boisterous. But this was different.

The history of football has been frequently punctuated by crowd troubles. Indeed large crowds of people, especially of young men, had long been a worry to men in authority and was one of the reasons why folk football was brought under control in the early 19th century. From the 1870s onwards, the modern game of football had experienced periodic crowd troubles, sometimes caused by overcrowding or drink, but often by fans' anger (about decisions, goals and events on and around the pitch). In a game which attracted huge crowds and where partisan passions ran high, it was inevitable that trouble would periodically surface. League football registered crowd troubles from its earliest days in the 1890s, and clubs were urged to erect railings, rather than ropes, between the fans and the pitch. Some grounds were closed because of crowd disturbances. The police were always prepared on match days to deal with trouble among football fans. But none of this, from the 1890s to the 1950s, *remotely* approximates to the troubles in living memory: mass arrests, pitch invasions, the use of mounted police to drive back fighting fans, special police and government units to track fans as they criss-cross Europe. What happened from the 1960s onwards was utterly different in substance and scale from anything the game had experienced before. To argue otherwise is to misconstrue both the present and the past. It is certainly the case that hooliganism is hard to define. But anyone who has been caught up in it, at football matches or elsewhere, has no difficulty in recognising it.

Crowd disturbances at early football matches, although small-scale, were more common than earlier historians recognised. It also seems that official football records under-reported the number of incidents. Most common of all such incidents were verbal abuse and encroachments onto the playing pitch. There were also attacks on players, and fights in the crowd. But both before 1914 and in the interwar years there is *no* evidence of an organised youthful culture among football fans. It is inconceivable that troubles simply went unnoticed. There was a hostile late 19th-century press, ready and keen to expose and lambast the shortcomings of contemporary youth in British cities. Moreover the police never showed themselves reluctant to crack down on social 'problems' in the cities, from drunkenness to street games. Yet the police simply did not register football as a major social problem. Most telling of all perhaps, the men who ran football grounds made no effort even to recognise that there was a social problem among fans (for example by segregating them). There was no suggestion that mixing together opposing fans might cause trouble. The phenomenon we have recently grown accustomed to at football matches in Britain and abroad (where trouble has been exported by travelling fans), of strictly segregated groups of supporters, was not a fea-

THE CAPTAIN

SEPTEMBER

1/- NET

SPLENDID SCHOOL TALES
FINE ADVENTURE STORIES
BRILLIANT SPORTING ARTICLES

Ronaldo © Ross Kinnaird/Allsport

LIVERPOOL
LIVERPOOL
LIVERPOOL
LIVERPOOL
LIVERPOOL FC
LIVERPOOL
LIVERPOOL
LIVERPOOL
LIVERPOOL F.C.
LIVERPOOL

Liverpool v Man Utd, 1994 © Clive Brunskill/Allsport

World Cup Final 1966 © Hulton Deutsch Collection Ltd

ROY OF THE ROVERS

7th JANUARY, 1978
EVERY MONDAY

8p

WIN A FOOTBALL!

30 TO BE WON IN OUR FREE COMPETITION!
PLUS 100 T-SHIRTS!

£2 VOUCHER! EVERY ENTRANT GETS A DISCOUNT OFF THE COST OF A FORWARD PEGASUS FOOTBALL!

(Just enclose a stamped, addressed envelope)

ture of football until the 1960s. The antisocial behaviour among fans which sociologists have located and analysed in the earlier history of the game was quite different in kind, scale and tone from the troubles which have disfigured the game since the 1960s. After reading the historical and sociological analysis of hooliganism written over the past thirty years, it is tempting to feel that the hooligans of the 1890s would have been alarmed to find themselves in the company of the hooligans of the 1990s.

There was no suggestion that mixing together opposing fans might cause trouble.

It is true that football matches had rarely been noted for their reserved, pensive spectators. Fans had long been infamous for their noise, their passionate partisan support and for all their varied but harmless exuberance, especially at major games; for their songs, their dress and for their fancy, colourful favours. Football seemed to bring out the zany streak in its followers. At the 1920 Cup Final, Blackburn Rovers' mascot was 70-year-old Mrs Catterall carrying a blue-and-white canary in a blue and white cage. This was far removed from York City's one-legged fan, arrested for cartwheeling down the aircraft aisle en route to the 1970 World Cup in Mexico City; he got only as far as the FBI at Houston. Big games, and excursion trains to those games, echoed to favourite songs and chants. But all this, familiar to anyone who has taken an interest in football, was generally harmless fun. Rivalries tended to be benign, with some obvious big city and religious exceptions; chants of 'F*** the Pope' have always mystified visitors to the 'Old Firm' games in Glasgow. Antagonisms tended to be vocal, occasionally crude, and major games were heralded and concluded by armies of fans swirling back and forth, peaceably, between the stadium and the trams and trains. Of course it is easy to romanticise these images of the past. Yet, to repeat a simple point, the labours of many scholars over a generation, scrutinising the history of football hooliganism, have failed to change the broad outlines of this picture. What happened from the 1960s on was totally different from anything the game had experienced previously.

An alien world

There had been flurries of crowd trouble in the late 1950s and early 1960s. As a schoolboy in the 1950s I was hit by a hot meat-and-potato pie thrown by an Evertonian at visiting Manchester United fans, my injuries compounded by an angry slap from my mother when she discovered the grease stains on my school raincoat. The FA expressed concern about crowd behaviour in 1961; two years later, Everton erected fences behind their goals – to the surprise of many in the press. By the late 1960s, however, there was no doubting the changing behaviour of some football fans.

At first glance the emergence of crowd trouble seemed odd, for it came immediately after the England World Cup win of 1966 had heralded a brief revival in football's fortunes. Crowds returned to the professional game, and the English national team seemed, for a short while, as good as any. When Celtic won the European Cup in 1967 and a rebuilt Manchester United repeated that performance a year later (ten years after the Munich crash), the English game seemed in a healthy, vibrant state. This optimism proved short-lived, and by the turn of the decade football was being discussed as a rising social problem. By the early 1970s the game was the forum for a host of major social tensions which seemed to find a perfect breeding ground. Football became the occasion (if not the cause) of violence, of group/gang hostilities, of foul abusive language and, increasingly, of a rancid and demoralising racism directed against black footballers. All this proved too much for many fans. Most simply wanted to watch a football match without running the gauntlet of threatening behaviour on the one hand, or a heavily marshalled and increasingly intrusive police presence on the other. At its worst, walking to a major game was like entering an alien world, where the fan was scrutinised by ranks of policemen, captured on their cameras, detained and penned into the stadium long after the game was over (in order to allow the crowd to disperse), and all the time serenaded by a shaming chorus of filth and racism. Why bother?

All this is familiar because so much of it survives, especially the heavy-handed policing (and the recent stewarding, by armies of club officials drafted in to relieve the police inside the stadiums). The present-day level of crowd control and scrutiny emerged slowly, however, and is the result of a whole generation of gradual adaptation to the persistent (though changing) challenges of football hooliganism. Hooliganism was a new and unknown virus, understandably catching authorities (of all kinds) totally bemused and unprepared. The clubs, the League, the FA (later, football's international organisations), the police, public transport – indeed anyone or any institutions caught in the slipstream – were baffled by what erupted. And not knowing what constituted hooliganism, they found it hard to contain, and impossible to cure. Even today it is hard to *define* hooliganism – but who needs a definition when caught in the middle of a dizzying confusion of threatening tension and physical intimidation? The problem, from the late 1960s onwards, was not so much finding a definition to satisfy scholars, but to find a solution to satisfy the public. Football clearly needed to *do* something, not least because fans, repelled by hooliganism, began a major exodus from the professional game. Attendances had declined before 1966, and the new troubles were, clearly, only one element in alienating many fans. But those deserting the game singled out hooliganism as a main cause of their disenchantment, and there is no reason to doubt their word. Conversely, once the problem of hooliganism had been contained, fans began to return to the game.

> # Fans, repelled by hooliganism, began a major exodus from the professional game.

A number of the major clubs developed an early reputation for their unpleasant fans and their unruliness and abusive language, especially when travelling to away games. The perpetrators were young men, hence older fans began to stay away. It is hard to be precise, but it seems that such groups of young fans were, in effect, clearing the terraces of all but their own type. Left to their own devices, en route to the grounds, and in their favourite section of terracing, they became a law unto themselves. Freed of any moderating presence, and caught up in the heady toxin of their own misbehaviour, they easily swarmed over local stewards inside the grounds, and over ill-prepared policemen outside. No less important, they were able to play out their antics before an ever-more curious TV presence, and, of course, before the critical gaze of the press. They caught the eye and, true to form, the media became involved. In effect the media (especially TV) played their own role, sometimes unconsciously, sometimes deliberately, in providing the publicity which hooliganism enjoyed.

Pitch invasion, 1984 © Topham Picturepoint

What emerged was an obscene weekly ritual of an aggressive youth culture. Visiting fans arrived in loosely organised bands of young men, passing through the city centre to the accompaniment of obscene chants, aggressive behaviour (especially towards other young men) before establishing themselves in the football ground. There, the show continued with more acts of bravado, the hurling of objects, ritualised chants (generally filthy), and physical attacks on opposing fans. At its worst it took the form of 'invasions' of their opponents' space inside the ground, with running scuffles and fights breaking out like bush-fires around the stadium. Among the fans themselves, there emerged weird conventions and practices; how to dress and behave, who to target, how to rank and reward each other by degrees of toughness and acts of violence. Those who studied it recognised familiar patterns of youth gangs. But why football?

What emerged was an obscene weekly ritual of an aggressive youth culture.

Many of the old explanations did not fit. Hooliganism flourished at a time of economic buoyancy, and in any case most of the young men involved seemed to have plenty of money to spend on their activities. Moreover, the game had traditionally thrived in communities where social hardship was commonplace; hardship alone could not explain what happened. Hooliganism did not seem to emerge from, or thrive in, deprived social circumstances or unemployment. The young men involved were, it is true, largely from working-class communities, and many of those communities had changed dramatically in the course of the 1950s. Knocked down, rehoused, relocated, their traditional industries decayed or closed, many working-class communities were unrecognisable by the late 1960s. These had, of course, been the traditional breeding grounds of football supporters (and players too). Many of the social and economic certainties, even the geography, of an older generation of working men had simply vanished by the time a new generation entered early manhood by the late 1960s. For growing numbers of young men, older rituals about territory and about displays of masculinity were now transferred to the world of football, to the stadiums and to the travelling parades of fans flowing to and from the games.

Though hooliganism attached itself to football, it was, in essence, utterly removed from the game itself. As critics said at the time, and since, it had nothing to do with football. Many of the ideals which underpin modern sports had no place in the hooligan's vocabulary. The idea of fair play, of abiding by rules devised by others, the whole package of sporting conventions which grew up with modern sports, and which traced their roots to the 19th century public schools were utterly alien to football hooligans. Instead, the young men who formed the core of football's gangs developed their own rules and conventions, an etiquette of misbehaviour. Much revolved around battles for territory: territory lost in the social upheavals of community displacement and regained on the football terraces.

> **Many of the ideals which underpin modern sports had no place in the hooligan's vocabulary.**

To make matters even worse, a racial edge was added to the whole noxious brew. New immigrants, notably Pakistanis and Bengalis, became one of the targets of the hooligan gangs. Football gangs thus became a fertile breeding ground for a range of neo-fascist groups. Fascist publications, organisations and prominent members circulated comfortably in the company of football's hooligans. They clearly felt at home in such company and football hooligans seemed at ease with such grotesque bedfellows. Much the same pattern evolved in other parts of Europe, notably among the fans of particular Italian teams. To this day, racist and fascist insignia disfigure Italian football.

Hooliganism to date

There were of course different *kinds* of hooligans, even though most of them might band together, on match days, to try to damage their opponents and create mayhem in and around the grounds. The young men of violence and the neo-fascists formed a minority, always in search of trouble, and were able, under the cover of large crowds, to slip in and out of violent activity like marauding guerrilla bands. Later, small well-organised groups of well-dressed young men came to the fore, travelling openly to games, and initially able to avoid police attention by appearing more 'respectable'. Their

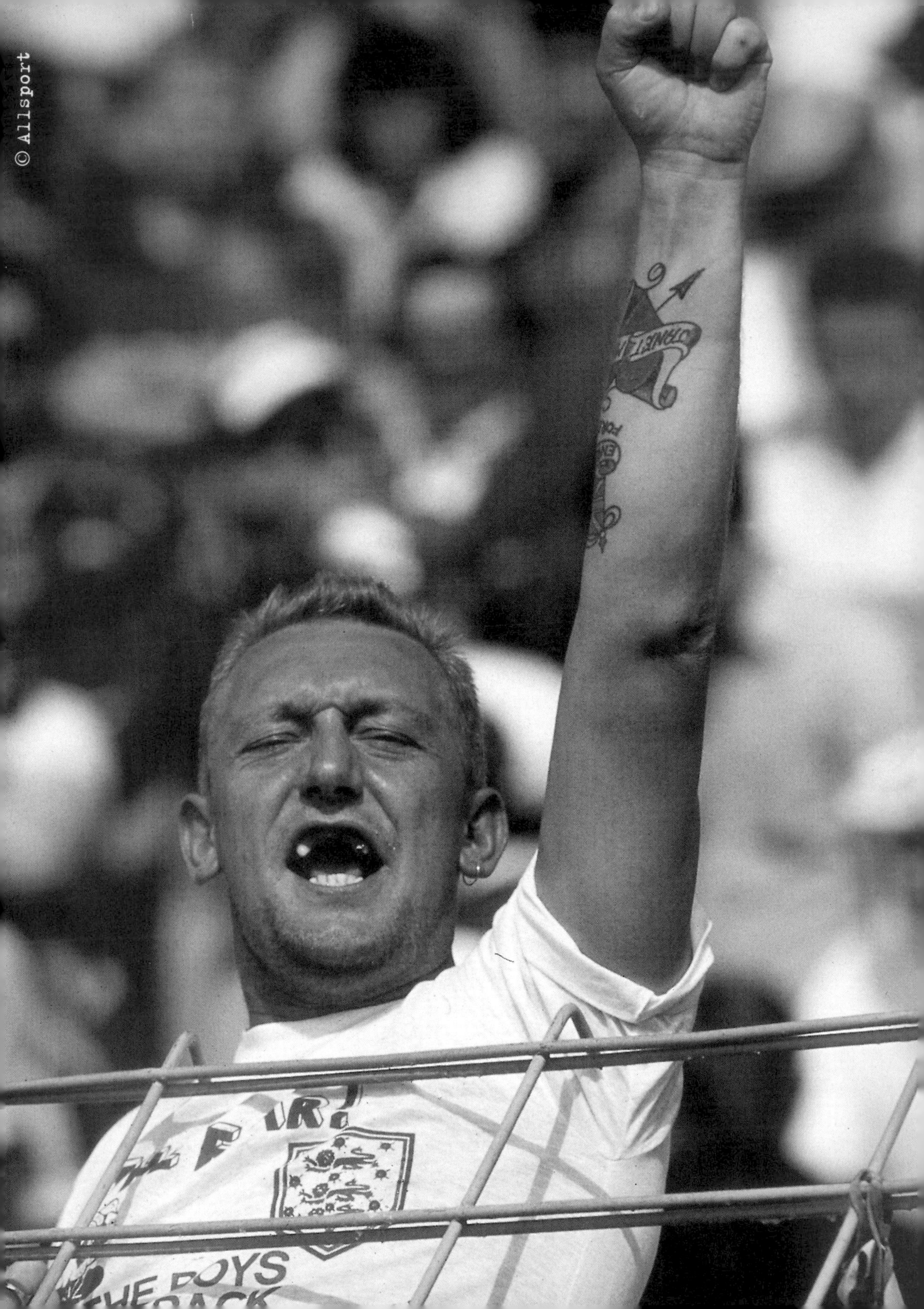
THE BOYS

anonymity was eventually challenged by the development of video cameras, and by the widespread use of police surveillance units. In their turn, by the 1990s hooligans began to use mobile phones to rally support, to spot and target potential opponents. Both sides – hooligans and police – became adept at the use of new technologies, each using the latest innovation to promote violence or to anticipate it and contain it. Many of the hooligan groups, notably from the London teams, adopted flashy names, and carefully planned their weekend assaults. It was this hooligan elite which attracted the keenest interest of the police and their new intelligence units (who increasingly co-operated with European colleagues as such troubles spilled into Europe).

Most football hooliganism was, however, much less sinister than this; more humdrum, though no less worrying. Large gangs of young men and boys, charging through a town or racing from one end of a stadium to another, though worrying, was not of the same order as the neo-fascist infiltration of football. Gradually, policing developed effective responses. This was also part of a much broader intrusion of policing into everyday life, mainly in response to the rise of IRA terrorism. Such troubles spawned a new investigative industry among researchers and academics, in the Home Office and police forces, to say nothing of a debate in the press, which often spun off into the realms of fantasy. Most observers were left utterly bemused. This was as true for those most immediately bruised by these new forms of hooliganism, as it was for the rest of the nation watching events unfold on TV, or reading about in their newspapers. What people witnessed seemed completely alien; it had no historical reference point, no rhyme or reason, and seemed totally foreign both to the game of football and to the way the English behaved. Very quickly however hooliganism established itself as a English social disease: a virulent form of misbehaviour which shaped a new national reputation. Henceforth the English football fans became known for their thuggish tendencies, especially on their excursions abroad. In preparation for the visit of English fans, police forces from Amsterdam to Istanbul flexed their defensive muscles. The end result was predictable; broken heads, arrests, mass confusion and innocent bystanders harmed and arrested in the running battles as police tried to retaliate first. The last thirty years of the century were disfigured by football 'incidents', at home and abroad, some of them fatal, as violent incidents and an inescapable chorus of foul language and racial abuse drifted around most major football grounds and tournaments.

The 1998 World Cup in France, won by a wonderful French team, was heralded by remarkable cross-border police preparations to prevent crowd violence. It was not entirely successful in keeping suspected hooligans out of France, mainly because of the ease of movement between countries in contemporary Europe, and partly because much of the trouble came from men who were *not* on the police list of known hooligans. In the event, 286 English fans were arrested in France, but 82 per cent of them were previously *unknown* to the police. Those intent on trouble had their weird moment of glory, surging through French towns, scattering bypassers and tables, pursued by French police, and receiving global TV coverage, and the predictable denunciation of politicians and footballing authorities. There was however another issue at stake. The English were seeking the nomination to host the 2006 World Cup in England, and everyone concerned (football, government and the media) was anxious *not* to overdramatise English hooligan behaviour. They all knew that too much discussion or coverage of hooligan outbursts was bound to damage the English bid. In the event, the English came nowhere close to being successful, though not because of the hooligans. What England had to offer was simply not as good as their German competitors.

> # Those intent on trouble had their weird moment of glory.

What was clear in France in 1998 was that English football continued to attract some strange and often unpredictable bedfellows; young men, often fuelled with alcohol, who were prepared to fling themselves into running battles with local police. Better still, they liked to play cat and mouse with the police, racing through an urban area, trashing bars, cafes and public places in lightning raids which might erupt, like bush fires, without any warning. These small bands of English football fans were behaving differently from earlier hooligans.

In the last years of the 20th century, English football experienced a number of incidents which suggested that hooliganism was far from dead. At times, it seemed scarcely under control. Fights broke out between rival fans at a number of major games (including the 1998 English Cup Final). And there was trouble among fans hundreds of miles distant from the games themselves. Serious troubles erupted abroad, where local police forces, braced for the arrival of the English, sometimes used excessively violent tactics, which then set in train subsequent fan disturbances. At home, on the other hand,

English police forces had perfected a different tactical approach which, though girded with all the terrifying apparatus of modern riot police, has managed for a number of years to prevent the outbreak of major footballing disturbances.

Politicians were forced to adopt a stand on the question of football, and Parliament passed a series of Acts to control football's worst problems. Those Acts (in conjunction with other legislation not directly aimed at football), gave the police enormous powers. Restriction orders could be slapped on potential trouble makers, effectively preventing them from attending a football match. Magistrates could restrict fans from travelling abroad. Supporters could also be prosecuted for throwing objects onto the pitch (there had been a phase when the goal area was festooned with lavatory rolls hurled by supporters towards the goal). They could also be arrested and prosecuted for running onto the pitch, and for shouting racial abuse. Alcohol was limited at games (and on the way to games). Cars, coaches and trains carrying fans to games could be searched by the police. The unauthorised sale of tickets was declared illegal. A fan could even be arrested if the police deemed a banner likely to cause offence. All this greatly expanded the powers of the police; in effect giving police and sentencing authorities wide powers to prevent and punish the behaviour which had troubled football for so long. The cumulative effect however was also to threaten civil liberties to an alarming degree, not least because many of these restrictions were not aimed uniquely at football, but could be applied to many other walks of life.

Lord Justice Taylor and West Midlands Chief Constable Geoffrey Dear,
April 1989 © Topham Picturepoint

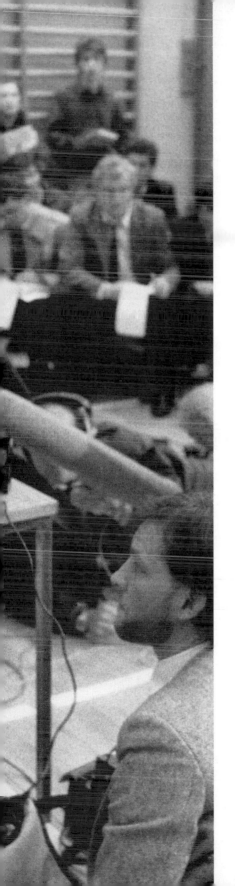

09

Disasters
Tragedy
and
reform

The story of football hooliganism was bedevilled by the involvement of the media. A number of newspapers, locked into circulation wars and keen to advance their sales by appearing more populist than their rivals, used the issue of football hooliganism to take a stand against national shortcomings, and to demand political change. There was a strident demand for 'firm action', for the smack of firm government, to deal with the problem of football. Such voices found their patron saint in Margaret Thatcher, who emerged, handbag at the ready, primed to smite her enemies hip and thigh. After 1979 British life slid into a period of social confrontation, under a Prime Minister fizzing with righteous indignation, and keen to use whatever power the state could muster to confront her political and social enemies. Given the power of the modern British state and Thatcher's political dominance, there was never any doubt as to who would win. Thatcher was given no option but to act when two disasters profoundly rocked the game of football and society at large.

More and more English football fans had begun to follow their club and national teams to European games in the 1970s. They were helped of course by the ease (and cheapness) of international travel in Europe. But they also took with them many of the features of the domestic game which their hosts dreaded; those noisy swarms of young males who were increasingly unpleasant and who began to replicate in European cities what they had already perfected in England (and to a degree, Scotland). Hooliganism began to spill out from its English homeland and to affect European football.

Despite the European-wide nature of such problems, few doubted that the inspiration and root cause lay in England. As if to prove the point, two major footballing disasters took place in the early summer of 1985. At an end-of-season match at Bradford's stadium, where the home fans were celebrating promotion, a fire broke out in rubbish underneath a highly combustible old wooden stand. Within minutes, the fire had ripped through the stand with devastating speed, killing 56 spectators and injuring many more, the whole spectacle broadcast by TV cameras, present to record the club's celebrations. The root cause of that disaster was an inadequate stadium, poor maintenance and fire prevention, and a club financially unable to modernise its facilities. Everyone in the game, especially the fans obliged to endure such conditions, knew that the Bradford stadium was not alone. There were dozens of grounds up and down the country which were survivors of a bygone age, long out-dated and manifestly unsafe. Indeed there had been a number of serious, earlier accidents (notably at Bolton and Glasgow) which had illustrated the widespread dangers of football stadium design and structure. The surprise was that more accidents had not taken place.

Only weeks after the Bradford fire, and as the customary judicial enquiry began its work, another major footballing disaster took place, this time in Brussels, but involving fans from Liverpool and Turin. Just before the start of the European Cup Final between Juventus and Liverpool, at the 55-year-old

Heysel Stadium in Brussels, crowd disturbances (a stampede, prompted by Liverpool fans assaulting their opponents) led to a crush of people against a wall. The wall collapsed and in the resulting mayhem 39 lives were lost (most of them Italians) and more than 350 were injured. Once again, the stadium was clearly inadequate and outdated, though this is not to deny the role played by the hooligan fringe among the Liverpool fans. Crumbling stadiums, marauding fans, death and injury – and all instantly accessible on the TV set at home. Football was plunged into a major crisis, and no one doubted that the English were at the heart of it. English teams were promptly banned from European competitions (and not allowed back until 1990). The English were given the opportunity to reflect on the crisis which afflicted their national game, and which had brought such suffering to so many people.

The Bradford and Brussels disasters were, first and foremost, a terrible human tragedy. But they also formed a deep humiliation for the country at large. The Scots carefully distanced themselves from these troubles, claiming with some justification that, despite periodic violence in Glasgow, this was an *English* disease which stopped at the border. FIFA and UEFA doled out the punishment to the *English* game. Few who had watched the course of English football since the late 1960s could feel that football had been harshly punished. But for millions who loved the game, what happened in 1985 was a distressing reminder of how far the game had fallen. The country which prided itself in giving football to the world, now found itself a footballing outcast. Thus, a mere twenty years after England won the World Cup, English football was cut off from its European neighbours, and

> **Few could feel that football had been harshly punished.**

allowed only to play on its small offshore island. Here was humiliation heaped on disaster. It also effectively brought to an end the era of Liverpool's footballing dominance. A string of wonderful teams, stretching back twenty years, under three managers, had dominated the domestic and European game. Now, in 1985, the club's name was associated with disaster. And worse was to come.

Football was now a major political issue, a social problem demanding prompt and effective government intervention. Quibbles about the precise nature of hooliganism, analyses of who and what constituted the gangs at the heart of the troubles, disputes about who, exactly, was to blame, all were swept aside in the political insistence for solutions. After the disasters of May 1985 (on the day of the Bradford fire, another fan had been killed in an incident at a game in Birmingham) there was no doubt that the game itself was on trial. The establishment of the Popplewell inquiry seemed, at first, merely the latest in a long line of formal commissions into football's many problems. This time however, it was ordered by a Prime Minister of a different stripe. A woman who had taken on, and destroyed, the coal miners was unlikely to bend before the resistance of football's arthritic management. Popplewell's report spelled out what any football fan (and even a casual visitor) could have spotted: English football grounds were hopelessly (and lethally) outdated.

Some clubs had tried to control the problems of hooligans in their grounds, though the solutions were sometimes bizarre. Luton Town had devised a membership scheme which excluded visiting fans. But the idea that football should

The idea that football should become an exclusive club ran counter to everything the game stood for.

become an exclusive club ran counter to everything the game stood for. The Prime Minister, however, who saw the world in black and white, liked the idea. Not surprisingly, Thatcher was deeply unimpressed by much of what she learned about football, and by the men who ran it. Prompted by Popplewell's findings, she demanded tough policing systems inside and outside football grounds. She also insisted on a new identity card system to gain admission to football grounds. It was a barmy idea, opposed by the police, by almost everyone within the game, and by the civil liberties movement. Thatcher's identity card bill (The Football Spectators Bill) would have caused more harm to the game than the disasters themselves. It was, in a supreme irony, deflected from the statute books by yet another, even more terrible, football disaster,

In April 1989, at the FA Cup Semi-Final between Liverpool and Nottingham Forest at Hillsborough, serious overcrowding at one end of the ground led to a massive, unmanageable surge of people. Ninety-six fans died in the crush

Hillsborough, 1989 © Pascal Rondeau/Allsport

against the perimeter fencing (fencing erected to pen in fans who might otherwise invade the pitch or cause similar upheavals). The political and legal consequences of that disaster, to say nothing of the widespread grief, survive to this day.

Liverpool FC had been present at two of the disasters of the 1980s, and the experience clearly had a profound effect on everyone at the club. It clearly marked a turning point in the affairs at Liverpool, and though the club seemed to bounce back, the disasters took a toll on players and management alike. It took years for the club to overcome those events and though further winning teams and successful managers emerged, in the short term Liverpool's great days had passed, brought to an end by a catastrophic loss of life.

The reforms

Major disasters had become far too common in Britain in the 1980s. There had been major rail crashes, an horrendous London underground fire and a major disaster at sea. Public safety seemed seriously compromised. In the space of four years, almost two hundred fans had been killed at football grounds. It was utterly unacceptable and clearly something had to change. Not surprisingly, Hillsborough prompted a massive political (and media) debate. Thatcher commissioned Lord Justice Taylor, a level-headed senior judge who had both sympathy for football and a sharp critical eye for its shortcomings. He proved the ideal man for the job of reviewing safety at Britain's outdated football grounds. Lord Taylor published an interim report by August 1989, his full report emerging in January 1990. He outlined in detail the unfolding of events at Sheffield, proposed restrictions on crowd capacity at grounds, and demanded new safety features. The final report took a broader view, looking at football in the context of sports grounds as a whole. Most of Taylor's 76 recommendations were accepted. They were to alter completely the physical face of British football, and to usher in the game as we know it today.

To deal with the pitch invasions of the past decade, football clubs had erected perimeter fencing. At Sheffield those fences prevented people escaping the crush building up behind them. Taylor recommended the removal of all such fencing. More fundamental still, he proposed an end to all standing space at all grounds of the major leagues in England and Scotland. Taylor demanded that by the beginning of the 1994–95 season all major grounds should be all-seater stadiums. A new, statutory body was proposed to license ground safety, and all clubs were expected to have fully trained safety officers, with many more stewards to help them. Taylor also sided with the critics of Thatcher's membership card scheme, which was quietly dropped.

Looking back, a mere ten years on, it seems almost unbelievable that it had taken so long to reform football. Now, thanks to Taylor, the reform of football came in a rush, scattering the physical remnants of the old professional game and reassembling it in something like modern order. A game which had been utterly loath to change its ways, which had, throughout the 20th century, placed the interests and the well-being of its fans at the lowest rung of Edwardian expectations, suddenly found the will to transform itself. More money was invested in football grounds in the years between 1990–94 than throughout the whole of the 20th century. The physical upheaval in the game was astonishing. Old grounds were ripped apart and converted into major building sites, emerging from their chrysalis of cranes and scaffolding as handsome, lean and stylish modern stadiums. Many old grounds were abandoned altogether and clubs started all over again on new sites. In all this a small band of commercially

> A game which had been utterly loath to change its ways suddenly found the will to transform itself.

minded hackers and entrepreneurs showed how rapidly football could be reformed and revitalised. And all with an eye to its commercial potential.

Whether any of this could have been achieved without the terrible loss of life of the 1980s is a moot point. What *is* abundantly clear, however, is that the physical restructuring of the game would not have taken place without outside pressure. Football itself was too unbending, too arthritic in structure and outlook, to have dreamed-up, still less effected, so massive a programme of modernisation. Here, once again, was yet another illustration of English football's inability to recognise its own best interests, and especially the interests of its supporters. The late 20th-century story of professional football was of a lazy (in many respects moribund) leviathan, brought to face the realities of the changing world only by outside insistence. Of course, football was not the only old English institution which was pulled up short, and forced (reluctantly) to reform by outside pressures. The same was true of London Zoo and English universities.

The 1980s had been a terrible decade for English football. Yet the disasters which punctuated those years have overshadowed some extraordinary footballing attainments. Liverpool had dominated the domestic game with a string of aggressive, attacking teams, and had won the European Cup four times. Liverpool's ground, and especially the Kop, had become the stuff of footballing legends. But like most legends, it was as much mythical as it was real. The image (repeated time and again in the media) emerged of the good-natured, witty and vocal Scouse fan, at full voice in the company of swaying armies of other fans, connoisseurs of good football, and always ready to applaud skilful opponents (unless they played for Manchester United). But Liverpool came to be remembered as the team and the fans at the centre of two of the game's greatest disasters. The loss of life among Liverpool fans at Hillsborough was catastrophic, and if any good emerged from that terrible day it was surely the dignified way in which the club marshalled its players and staff to deal with the bereavement which swept through the city of Liverpool in the wake of the disaster. Whatever else Liverpool Football Club won in the 1980s, they (and especially their manager Kenny Dalgleish) won the admiration of a grieving city.

Liverpool's famous Kop went the way of all the terraces at major grounds; bulldozed and transformed into neat ranks of plastic seating. It is important to recall *why* the terraces were destroyed. They were doomed not merely by their own antique inadequacies, by the sheer crudity of their arrangements, but by their inherent dangers. Crowds of excited fans and old football terraces had long proved to be a volatile mix. Whatever criticisms might be levelled against the new arrangements (lack of 'atmosphere', the example of peaceable standing sections at German grounds), it is curious how quickly critics have forgotten the most stunning of recent events in English football: the deaths of large num-

Crowds of excited fans and old football terraces had long proved to be a volatile mix.

bers of football fans in crude physical arrangements utterly ill-suited to modern enjoyment and crowd control.

Lord Taylor's reforms, eagerly accepted by a government anxious to end football's troublesome problems, ushered in a new era in the story of English football. The game had clearly been crying out for change for a long time, but football's management and ownership had long shown themselves incapable of any useful reform. Politicians too seemed baffled by what to do about football, save for demanding ever more effective policing, which was the hallmark of Thatcher's regime. In the end, Lord Taylor's reforms were a triumph of shrewd judgement and common sense. The exact chemistry of what happened at the beginning of the 1990s in the wake of the Taylor report remains elusive. The timing was perfect, the proposals were exactly what was required, and the social/political climate just right for the consequent massive changes. It could however have gone horribly wrong; a different man, a different set of suggestions, and the game of football might have continued its gormless slide towards — who knows what? Lord Taylor's name should be commemorated not so much for enabling the game to be transformed, but for rescuing it from what many critics regarded as a terminal decline. Yet, even now, a decade on, sections of football fans demand a return to the old system, especially of standing at football matches. Football's conservatism, its periodic longing for the 'good old days', is not restricted to men in the boardroom. Football fans need to recall the horrors which football's refusal to change had visited on so many innocent people.

10

In the front room

The media revolution

The disasters of the 1980s were all filmed and broadcast by television — though in much-edited form. There was no escape from television. Cameras were present at most professional games. But a mere generation ago, the amount of football on TV was tiny. The Cup Final, selected internationals, major European ties — and a selection of other important games — formed a meagre diet for the housebound fan. Today, televised football is inescapable. Major networks plan their schedules around football, and they readily delay and postpone programmes to make way for football. Professional football can be seen on most days of the week, most weeks of the year.

From the late 1980s to the present, most people recall football as seen on TV. Even ardent football fans are more likely to recall televised games rather than matches they attended. I am no exception. Virtually all my footballing recollections over the past 15 years have been from television. Maradona's 'hand of God' goal (and his spell-binding second goal against England); England's various shoot-out defeats; Arsenal's last-gasp goal at Anfield to snatch the championship from Liverpool. And of course the domination of Manchester United in the Premiership for much of the 1990s – and their May 1999 victory in extra time in Barcelona. I have visited most of the great stadiums and watched live football from the Azteca to the Olympic in Munich – but all via TV. When my friends ask 'Did you watch the match?' they invariably mean the match on telly.

The excited crowds that pack the country's main football grounds for major matches are the lucky minority, able to afford and to get their hands on tickets which, on the black market, change hands for ridiculous sums. Yet for many, many more – measured in their millions – such games are seen in the comfort of the home, brought into the front room (or the local pub) by a mere flick of a television switch. Televised coverage of European football keeps football fans entertained from Helsinki to Athens. Every four years national teams, after lengthy international qualifying competitions, line up for the World Cup, its location (like the Olympics) a cause of protracted international debate and horse trading, and its exact programme determined by negotiations with the television companies prepared to pay millions to beam the games to a global audience. Football is now ubiquitous because television has become unavoidable. To escape from football involves escaping from television. Today that is hard to do, even in the most isolated of communities: Tibetan monks and remote African villagers clamour to get a ringside seat for football's major games. The public school men of a mere century ago, anxious to promote their games around the world, could never have imagined the global popularity and importance attained by modern football.

Football is of course only one of a myriad institutions utterly transformed by modern television and the modern media in general. People in the public eye, however fleetingly, find the attention of the media pervasive and often

intrusive. The telephoto lens, banks of cameramen hiding in bushes or perched on ladders, journalists booked into the next room at holiday hotels, or occupying a nearby seat on planes, bugs on telephone lines, high-speed chases by pursuing paparazzi – all form a familiar part of the modern media circus. Most of us tend simply to see the end result: the film and pictures of the famous in the most mundane or compromising circumstances. But those involved, celebrities of all sorts and conditions, find themselves caught in a web of their own creation. They emerge and thrive as commercial entities courtesy of media coverage, their fame and wealth calibrated by public recognition, and the public recognise their faces thanks to the intrusive media. They live in a 'frenzy of renown', sometimes famous only for being famous. Today, the very best footballers are well known beyond the world of football, sought-after by the media and by commercial backers seeking valuable names to promote their products. They become celebrities far beyond the ranks of the fans who adore them, at least for as long as their footballing skills endure. Like the beauty and strength of youth, such athleticism quickly fades.

The global fame of football now is completely different from anything the game has known before. There were of course earlier patterns of footballing fame and commercialism, but they were vastly different, minuscule and low cost, as to be completely incomparable. Footballers on cigarette cards, ghosted newspaper articles and autobiographies, footballers' photographs used to promote this product or that – the commercial value of footballers was low key and marginal. Most players, even the more famous, could live a public life generally unrecognised and untroubled by people around them. Even when they were recognised (travelling for example on public transport alongside the fans who watched them), they remained largely unpestered. I once stood in a bus queue after a match alongside my boyhood hero, Duncan Edwards. The likelihood of seeing David Beckham waiting for a Manchester tram is extremely remote. Beckham is a footballing millionaire. For that, he can thank television.

The likelihood of seeing David Beckham waiting for a Manchester tram is extremely remote.

Broadcasting football is almost as old as the radio itself. To listen to, or to watch old English sports broadcasts is to be transported back to an almost mythical past, where deference, social snobberies and 'posh' accents positively oozed from the loudspeakers. Sports broadcasting was pioneered and perfected by the BBC, first on the radio and then, from the 1950s onwards, on television. Broadcasters enunciated 'BBC English', in a style which conveyed authority and correctness. They sounded more like wartime bulletins masquerading as sports reports. Today, those early broadcasting voices seem almost strangulated by their clipped, blimpish tones. But at the time they conveyed unimpeachable authority to millions of people long accustomed to the rich tones of their educated 'betters'. Not until the cultural changes of the 1960s were the wonderfully rich and varied regional accents of the English people allowed to break free of this BBC linguistic grip. As sports broadcasting entered a new, more popular, more widely disseminated phase from the 1960s onwards, the very tone of sports broadcasting changed.

They sounded more like wartime bulletins masquerading as sports reports.

The post-war football boom was further titillated by the rapid spread of radio broadcasts. Radio had of course come of age during the Second World War, and the radio was securely established as a vital feature in domestic entertainment (to say nothing of government propaganda). From the first, the best (most sophisticated, varied and informed) form of sports radio was cricket, with a BBC team that was to make an easy transition to TV coverage. In large part this was because the informed but amiable chat of educated men provided soothing background to the inevitable *longeurs* of a cricket match. The cult of cricket commentary quickly emerged as a quintessential English tradition which the BBC found hard to tamper with. Changes brought howls of complaint, from the House of Commons, and from across the English shires.

Football, by comparison swift, fast-moving and lasting only for 90 minutes, required different verbal skills, but in the early days its coverage still acquired those unmistakable BBC tones and voices. From 1948, football results (vital for people checking their football pools) were broadcast on *Sports Report,* its famous introductory music ('Out of the blue') remaining its signature tune to this day, surviving the switch from one BBC programme to another. Radio coverage of football gradually increased, notably after 1970, finally filling the whole of Saturday afternoon. In recent years, in order to keep its audiences BBC radio has been forced to compete both with new commercial radio stations and with television. New technology allowed radio to bring instant coverage from grounds throughout the country, with highlights and latest scores from dozens of games spliced effortlessly into the fast-running commentary of a chosen game. All this is followed by prompt and instantaneous reports, from Aberdeen to Exeter, spiced by the comments of footballers and managers. Now, thanks to 'talk-in' programmes, football is debated endlessly by anyone who cares to make a call to the studio. The babble of footballing gossip fills the airwaves, much of it, of course, in the varied accents of a cross-section of the British people as a whole. It is as far removed from Raymond Glendenning as could be imagined. The end result is that football on the radio has created and, by and large, maintained its own special niche.

That niche is, however, minuscule compared to the massive cultural and commercial importance of televised football, whose enormous potential was first revealed at the 1953 (Stanley Matthews) Cup Final. Even the Queen turned up to a game with an estimated ten million people gathered round a TV set. The royal presence (in Coronation year) was the seal of approval, bestowing respectability of a kind on football. Two years later, the launch of commercial television created that competitive edge which forced the monopolistic BBC, for the first time, to look to its laurels. Both sides, BBC and commercial TV, began to wrestle for the rights to broadcast football. Football itself however (especially the Football League) saw television as a *threat*, even though it might yield extra income for the game. Yet whenever major games were shown (especially the best, most gripping European matches – particularly when they involved a British team) millions of people turned on their sets. Broadcasters realised, even if football's old guard refused to accept the fact, that football was *the* key to unlocking massive television audiences, and thus tapping into an unparalleled commercial potential.

The process began in earnest in 1964 with the advent of *Match of the Day*. The programme was launched at the very time English football had some

fabulous players and teams. The rebuilt Manchester United, with Best, Charlton and Law, was perhaps the most eye-catching, especially when Best's real genius flowered. TV and that Manchester United team seemed ideally suited to each other; an attractive attacking team, resurrecting the name and memory of the team killed in 1958, and promoted, by regular televised coverage, to an audience of millions. Other great teams and players also filled the screen. Shankly's early Liverpool teams, Bobby Moore's West Ham, and the raw power of Don Revie's Leeds United, all showed some of English football's most compelling qualities. Between 1964 and 1968 television was well placed to promote the national game. In 1966 England won the World Cup, and in 1967 and 1968 the European Cup went first to Celtic and then Manchester United. TV audiences were enormous and laid the basis for what was to follow, even at a time, from the late 1960s, when attendance at football began to decline and when the game seemed to attract a host of unfathomable social problems. Like all sports, football was hugely enhanced and made more visually attractive by the perfection of colour transmission in the early 1970s.

The BBC had secured rights to and perfected sports broadcasting almost by default. In the early years there had been no rivals. It seemed theirs by right, and many British people certainly thought of it that way. The BBC was in effect the voice of sport, admittedly a rather plummy voice, but a recognisable, distinctive voice which always spoke with authority on the sport in question. Commercial television was, from the first, naturally attracted to football. But ITV was managed and presented by men of a different type; aggressive, commercially-minded entrepreneurs keen to prise open the BBC monopoly, especially in sport. ITV began to broadcast recorded football on Sunday afternoons in the early 1970s. In 1978 Michael Grade almost succeeded in snatching league football coverage from the BBC by offering to the League three times the value of the BBC fee. The two sides came to a compromise, sharing transmissions on alternate years. This agreement increased the annual income for the

The BBC was a recognisable, distinctive voice which always spoke with authority on the sport in question.

clubs from £5000 to £25,000 each. Fans were deserting the terraces, but ever more people were becoming aware that TV might be the game's financial saviour.

All this needs to be set alongside broader changes in sports broadcasting. Televised coverage of a range of major sports had become more important, more real even, than the sports themselves. This was especially true of tennis from Wimbledon. The annual TV coverage, with reassuring expert commentary, colour TV and the latest replay technology, brought the thrills and excitement of the Centre Court to millions who could never have dreamed of (or afforded) a trip to south west London. Tennis on TV established itself as ritual of the English summer, a tournament which was, in the words of a recent study, 'English and international, pastoral and suburban, middle class and monarchical'. Presiding over this annual event through rain and shine, was Dan Maskell with his unmistakably English tones, his measured commentary and his cautious observations. Much the same was true of horse racing, where Peter O'Sullevan racing voice-overs had long epitomised the BBC coverage of the Sport of Kings (but on which millions had the occasional flutter). Nowhere however was this more striking than with cricket, where the voices of John Arlott, Brian Johnson and E.W. Swanton managed, year after year, to capture the English summer (even when damp and miserable) for millions of viewers. Much the same happened with golf. It was a curious phenomenon: a televised calendar of major sporting events unfolding with predictable regularity – and all in the comfort of the home.

Here was a very *visual* experience – sport – transmitted for the *viewing* pleasure of millions around the country but its credentials substantially established through the *voices* of unseen commentators. True, many sports spiced their commentary teams with the regional or foreign accents of ex-players, the casual bluntness of Lancastrians and Yorkshiremen, and the democratic twang of Australians. Certain voices became inextricably associated with certain sports: hearing a particular voice on televised commentary was enough to indicate which sport was being broadcast. But the men whose voices came to dominate TV coverage of football – Kenneth

Certain voices became inextricably associated with certain sports.

Wolstenholme, David Coleman, John Motson, Brian Moore – were voices from a very different England. Turn the formula round: it would be inconceivable that Arlott, Johnson or Swanton could have made careers commenting on football, or that Motson could have commanded the affection of cricket fans.

The BBC had held sway in sports broadcasting by the simple fact of being first in the field. But its dominance was maintained by the assumptions of men in high places that the BBC was the natural – the only – institution which *ought* to have access to the nation's major national sporting events. It was hardly surprising that the All England Club and the MCC saw eye to eye with the BBC, nor did it seem unusual that the Conservative party and their governments were happy to abandon their ideological attachment to free markets, and tolerate (sometimes insist on) a closed shop between sport and the BBC. It was a cosy arrangement between old friends.

Commercial broadcasting

Commercial TV was circling round the much-prized showpieces of BBC sports coverage. The BBC claims to public service broadcasting (i.e. that the Cup Final, Test Matches, Wimbledon and others were part of the nation's *cultural* heritage, and ought therefore to belong to the BBC by right) were set against the free-market claims of commercial TV. Commercial TV argued a much simpler case, namely the virtues of competition, which they asserted by offering money on a scale the BBC simply could not contemplate. To hard-pressed chairmen of football clubs, looking at the gaps on the terraces where fans once stood, and glancing at the escalation in players' wages, extra income from television proved irresistible. Their decisions were complicated by government intervention to ensure that the BBC did not lose out completely in sports broadcasting. Even Thatcher felt unable to allow a completely free market in sports broadcasting. Eventually however, even the rearguard defence of the BBC was to buckle before the rising power of satellite TV and the global power of Rupert Murdoch.

Recorded highlights of football did not generate the viewing figures (and therefore the advertising revenue) the commercial TV companies really wanted. Above all they wanted live football. Finally (through deals struck in 1983 and 1986) they persuaded the Football League (desperate in the face of falling attendances) to agree. From the late 1980s onwards, the story of football is intimately linked to the story of television.

Football's choice of broadcaster hinged largely on finance. Whoever had most money stood the best chance of securing rights to live football – and other sports. Throughout the 1980s and 1990s sports and recreations of the most varied kind came to the television screen, each hoping to secure a niche market and to expand the commercial opportunities afforded by large viewing figures. Who could have predicted that darts would become a popular game – with its own professional players?

Reach for the Sky

The arrival of satellite TV in 1988 transformed football as never before. British Satellite Broadcasting, formed in 1988, viewed sport as the key *entrée* to a mass audience; a means of quickly building up a broadly based viewing. When British Satellite Broadcasting merged, in 1990, with Murdoch's Sky to form BSkyB the scene was set for the most fundamental upheaval in the history of the game. Football changed more quickly, and more fundamentally, in the ten years of the 1990s than it had throughout the previous century. Again, the timing was perfect, for the game was already experiencing the upheavals set in train by the Taylor report. Grounds were ripped apart and rebuilt, and the old standing arrangements on the terraces disappeared. Football began to show a new, more modern and altogether more sympathetic face to its viewing public. These two revolutions – the physical reconstruction of football and satellite broadcasting – came together to wrench football free from its late 19th-century roots and to create what was, in many respects, a new game.

In the 1970s and 1980s, the broadcasting monopoly of the BBC had effectively given way to a duopoly between ITV and the BBC. Throughout, the sums offered and accepted for televised football were relatively low. Football's four-year deal with the BBC in 1978 had cost £9.8 million. The deal in 1983 to screen live league football had yielded a mere £2.6 million. When BSkyB entered the ring, backed by Murdoch's global News Corporation, such sums were made to look like petty cash.

The crisis in which English professional football found itself after the Heysel disaster (the ban on games in Europe, falling attendances, confusion about broadcasting rights and income) had rekindled debate among the bigger clubs about the very structure of the game itself. They felt shackled to a footballing culture in the Football League which was constitutionally incapable of change. At the same time, they felt that their own earning power was being held back by smaller clubs, who tended to vote against proposals for reform. There had long been talk about a 'super league' of the major clubs, a debate heightened by the progress of the various European competitions. Should the bigger, wealthier clubs break away from the 100-year-old League, and strike out on their own, in a potentially lucrative market, always with an eye on Europe – leaving the rest to fend for themselves? In the event, the threat of a break-away proved enough to force the smaller League clubs to agree, in 1986, to reform the League's voting system and to accept a distribution of income from broadcasting. The bigger clubs got a greater share of the money. This arrangement was brief, however, for in 1988 ITV, in its increasingly bitter battle against satellite broadcasting, offered to finance a break-away league. Football was the prize scalp all broadcasters wanted to claim; televised football was universally viewed as the key to survival and prosperity in the ever more ruthless world of television. The result, again, was an agreement to give still more money to the bigger clubs. Television had in effect become Robin Hood in reverse, ensuring, year by year, that a *decreasing* proportion of football's income went to the poorer clubs.

> **Football was the prize scalp all broadcasters wanted to claim.**

Lord Taylor's report had brought matters to a head. The order that the game rip down its ugly habitat, and rethink how it should treat its paying spectators, set in train a massive programme of reconstruction. The cost of rebuilding English football grounds was clearly enormous. The £100 million set aside by the Football Trust (the money derived from a reduction in the government's football betting levy) covered only a fraction of the total cost. Money had to be found from other sources. Some clubs simply sold their old grounds to developers, using the money to move to a cheaper site elsewhere. Others were lucky in having wealthy backers able to siphon millions of pounds into the new footballing palaces. Some clubs attracted (or already had in place on the board) a breed of hungry young entrepreneurs anxious to transform the club into an aggressive and commercially successful business.

It was hardly surprising that money seemed to be the main topic of conversation in the football world by the early 1990s. Forced to invest millions in ground redevelopment, the bigger clubs found themselves at the same time seduced by offers of mind-boggling sums of money for television rights to the game. In 1992 the top clubs broke away from the Football League, which had been their bread and butter for a century, to form the Premiership – striking a deal with BSkyB for £304 million over five years. The BBC bought the rights for recorded highlights to be shown on Saturday nights. The Premiership deal involved a major act of footballing duplicity, for it had been orchestrated by the FA, behind the back of the Football League, working in conjunction with club chairmen, to strike a deal with BSkyB. When the deal was renewed, a new four-year agreement brought £670 million from BSkyB and £73 million from the BBC. In June 2000, the latest deal (excluding the BBC) pumped about two *billion* pounds into the game. BSkyB hoped to recoup its money not simply via advertising but from the new pay-per-view arrangements it was able to demand of the millions of viewers *already* hooked into its system. The sums involved were beyond the dreams of avarice, and they flooded the game, or at least the elite teams, with unprecedented volumes of money. New-found riches whetted the clubs' appetite; more and more football clubs turned to stock market flotations. The major clubs had come to realise that, in the world of global television, they had one asset that was worth even more than their real estate – their name.

The sums involved were beyond the dreams of avarice.

None of this would have been possible without the satellite TV coverage which beamed football into the far corners of the globe. The story of Manchester United provides a glimpse into this whole complex process. The club had, it is true, already created a mythology for itself in the wake of the Munich disaster, and through the eye-catching flair of the rebuilt Busby team of the 1960s. But the commercial triumph of Manchester United can only be explained by the fact that they were the most successful team of the 1990s. Their past history would have counted for nothing had they not, year after year in the first decade of the Premiership and in the full glare of TV cameras, won most trophies on offer. They, more than any other English team, were able to ride the commercial tide of that decade because they were more widely broadcast (to the irritation of their opponents) than any other team. Television wanted to show the best teams and the best games. And as Manchester United dominated the Premiership, Sky followed their progress with regular and detailed scrutiny. The club was also at the forefront of the game's marketing revolution, capitalising on its TV fame, equipping itself with a mega-store, its own marketing departments (later, on-line facilities). Manchester United became a money-making machine the likes of which had never been seen anywhere in the footballing world – a model for any aspiring merchandisers of football, admired by city investors and commercial strategists. Their tactics and roaring success did not always please their fans, however. It was one thing to watch attractive football; it was quite another to feel exploited by the club you followed so avidly.

> **It was one thing to watch attractive football; it was quite another to feel exploited.**

It was football's television audience, via advertising, which dictated the game's commercial clout. BSkyB attracts upwards of two million viewers for its televised matches, *Match of the Day* attracts between six and ten million viewers. When Manchester United won the Champions League Cup in Barcelona in May 1999, the TV audience in Britain peaked at 18.8 million. Television had, by the turn of the century, conquered football – and most other sports too.

In all this, BBC, the pioneer and pacemaker of broadcast sports, had become the poor relative. Its limited income, derived primarily from the licence fee, was simply inadequate to secure football coverage. More than that, the Corporation was battling satellite TV on a much broader front. Murdoch's television (BSkyB made profits of £314 million in 1997) was also supported by the apparently bottomless pockets of News International. Sky had clearly made major inroads into TV viewing, their dishes now dotting the British skyline and their programmes and wares were promoted, often shamelessly, by Murdoch's newspapers. It is of course hard to unscramble football from this broader media story. But without football it is inconceivable that Murdoch could have made so massive and so successful a commercial breakthrough into British television. Thereafter, televised football was used to open up new markets, notably in Asia. It was – and remains – a dizzying, global race of unimaginable wealth chasing and creating still more wealth.

Throughout the 1990s each new injection of television money into football outstripped the last deal by a massive amount. The deals struck by ITV and BBC between 1983 and 1988 had brought £2.6 million and £3.1 million to the game. That rose (from ITV) to £11 million for 1988–92. In 1992 BSkyB paid the Premier League £38 million for 60 live games. What trickled down into the ancillary but vital schemes of the professional game (youth development, school football, various trusts) was derisory. Clubs did not share this money equally however. Even within the Premier League, a small band of giants managed to grab the lion's share for themselves. Five clubs, Manchester United, Arsenal, Liverpool, Chelsea and Leeds secured 30 per cent of television income for themselves. Though this had a certain logic (more people wanted to watch their games), it conveyed a growing sense that football was now dominated by a clique of footballing robber barons, enriching their coffers left and right, not caring a damn about the smaller fry.

Each new injection of television money into football outstripped the last deal by a massive amount.

For most of the Premier League clubs, but especially the smaller ones, television income made up a substantial proportion of their overall income. The one team that bucked the trend was Manchester United. A mere 7 per cent of their income came from television (Arsenal's for example was 20.9 per cent). The reason was simple enough. Manchester United had, far and away, the largest overall revenue of all the nation's football clubs. In the 1996–97 season £80 million rolled into its already well-lined coffers, twice the volume of its nearest financial rival (Newcastle United). A great majority of all the clubs in the Premiership attracted a mere fraction of Manchester United's earning power. In the space of a decade, the club had established itself as a financial behemoth.

It was hardly surprising, then, that Murdoch tried to buy the club (for £623 million) in 1998. An adulterous liaison between Manchester United and Murdoch's News Corporation, via their regular weekend trysts on BSkyB, was one thing, but a formalised marriage was quite another. It would have placed unparalleled commercial and broadcasting power in Murdoch's hands. Even the most avid of United fans, generally content to see their club become the one of the most vaunted of world club sides (more so even than clubs with greater attainments) felt queasy at the prospects of a deal with

Murdoch. Objections from fans and alarm within government blocked the move through the Competition Commission. Even so, by the end of the century Manchester United was not simply the richest English football club, it was one of the wealthiest sports clubs in the world. People had already forgotten that, as recently as 1989, the club's directors had been willing to sell control of the club for a mere £10 million. That deal collapsed largely because of the absurd antics of the would-be purchaser. Yet here they were, a mere decade on, the wealthiest sports machine the country had ever seen. Even for so famous a club, this was a stunning rise. And none of it could have been remotely possible without television and the commercial power it placed in the club's hands – by transmitting their name, their team, their star players and their dizzying changes of costly kit (yours for a mere £45 a shirt) to all corners of the world. One third of the club's income now came from merchandising.

Though Manchester United sits at the top of football's financial league, it is just one of a coterie of major self-interested clubs, fierce rivals on the field, but single-minded in advancing their collective well-being, often against the better interests of smaller clubs. In the process, the gap between the rich and poor has widened year on year. The top handful of Premier League clubs have a combined financial turnover greater than *all* other 72 Football League clubs combined. On the surface, it seems that there is a natural, commercially-driven drift towards a 'super league'. Many in the game (fans and officials among the smaller clubs) would be happy to see a Super League; they would be pleased to see the giants drift away into a small clique of super clubs, with a regular cycle of competition among themselves, and all with an eye to playing in Europe. That would leave the others to play each other, and not be dominated by teams with the largest financial reserves. Who is to say that might not happen?

> The top handful of Premier League clubs have a combined financial turnover greater than all other 72 Football League clubs combined.

European Championships, 2000 © Ben Radford/Allsport

The relationship which has developed between football and TV could not have been predicted by either side (though some had prayed for it). Football initially proved the saviour of satellite TV, providing an expanding audience when the whole system seemed, at first, to be floundering. Once secure, once the dishes had begun to flourish, satellite TV thrived, amassing profits, diversifying into a huge range of channels beamed round the world and always poised to open and develop new TV markets in other parts of the world. The TV moguls courted nations' leaders and even chopped and changed their offerings so as not to cause local political offence.

It was of course part of a much wider, global broadcasting revolution. American companies created their own television dominance. The news coverage of CNN, despite its bland snippets of information, forced the BBC and other major European broadcasters to follow suit. The television revolution rushed forward at a giddying pace, spitting forth cable and satellite channels, using and sponsoring remarkable technical changes, and anchoring ever more people in front of a TV set. Television coverage was everywhere. It had even become available in aircraft. It made accessible major events, disasters, deaths, politics but above all sports for hundreds of millions of people. It also had the side effect of creating new celebrities; for the world's best sportsmen (though very few women), television in the 1990s transformed their earning power. No longer famous merely within their own particular game or sport, sportsmen saw their skills projected to national then international audiences on a stunning scale. In league with their agents (a key element in the escalation of footballers' wages), star players became valuable commercial commodities. A small elite became millionaires. Though there was a general inflation of professional players' salaries, the gap between the best paid and the majority remained enormous. Star footballers came to enjoy the life style previously restricted to pop stars and pools winners. Theirs was, in fact, a subspecies of show biz, with all its rewards, absurdities – and pitfalls.

None of this could have happened without the new culture of television which found in football its perfect commercial and social bedfellow. It had hardly been love at first sight, for football had always played hard to get. But as the 1990s advanced, and as the two sides clung ever closer to each other, each side changed perceptibly. Like many other couples, they became inseparable, an item. In time, neither could imagine life without the other. They clearly needed each other. And that feeling was accentuated when each looked at their respective bank balance. They prospered together. Yet cynics had once said it would never last . . .

Football? It's the beautiful
game.

Pele (attributed)

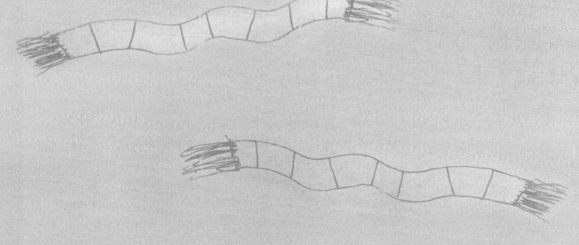

11

A land of plenty

Money and markets

In the 1930s, Arsenal players were mocked for lending their names to so many unlikely commercial ventures. Star players could capitalise on their fame, after a fashion, by sponsorship. Even Dixie Dean, the personification of a tough, physical striker, could collect £50 a week for sponsorships. Given their low wages, players jumped at whatever opportunities were available. In the 1940s, Dennis Compton, footballer and cricketer, lent his name to promote Brylcreem. Charlie Buchan published his own schoolboy football annuals, while

Stanley Matthews advocated a brand of football boot. In the 1950s, Manchester United obliged their players to wear trilby hats, made by a local company. And so it continued on a small scale, advertising items now obsolete, and more likely to prompt a smile than a sale. Today it is very different; the scale and the impact of football's merchandising is vast, and basic to the game's strength, and to the players' earnings. At first, the governing elite did not approve of advertising, but their objections were eventually swept aside, especially when TV revealed how much football could earn from TV-related sponsorship.

The first noticeable move towards more blatant commercialism was the proliferation of advertising hoardings carefully angled at the TV. It was clear that television would dictate and even define football's commercial potential. Bit by bit, advertisements crept across the face of the game; around the stadiums, onto the players' shirts, marketing products via the teams and their star players. Indeed marketing football, then individual footballers, became a major industry itself. Clubs and elite players scrambled to secure ever more lucrative deals. In 1996 Manchester United's ten-year deal with Umbro was worth £10 million annually (though a similar deal between the Brazilian national team and Nike netted £250 million). But it was the marriage of the game's leading clubs and satellite TV which unleashed a marketing and commercial revolution which sent money cascading into the clubs' coffers and the players' accounts.

A small group of men at the helm of the major clubs had long realised the hidden commercial potential of football clubs, but even they did not realise how *vast* it might be; some had tried to sell their stake long before that full potential was realised. Scholar and Sugar at Spurs, Edwards at Manchester United and Dein at Arsenal were all men who had made a great deal of money elsewhere. They were acutely aware of the market and keen to spot a commercial niche for their clubs. A number of them had also watched commercial developments in sports in the USA. American baseball and football clubs had long since developed a profitable sideline in club kit and regalia: shirts, baseballs, bats and caps, each and every item emblazoned with a club's name and logo. And all, of course, paraded before television cameras. Football's entrepreneurs thought it odd that their very own fans sometimes turned up to a football match wearing the favours of an American sports team.

Thus was born the decision to launch into the lucrative merchandising of football kit and equipment, and anything else that might sell, providing it bore the club name and colours. The whole transformation began in the wake of Lord Taylor's report, and the modernisation of English football. As the 1990s advanced, tens of thousands of fans settled into their seats wearing their team's shirt, with their favourite player's name on the back. Official team shirts quickly became a necessary clothes item among millions of children, to the groans of their hard-pressed parents. It soon proved a marketing dream; tens of thousands of adults and children donning the (costly) merchandise available only from the clubs – though there also developed a booming industry in coun-

> **Tens of thousands of fans settled into their seats wearing their team's shirt.**

terfeit items. Moreover the football marketing virus quickly spread round the world, proving itself not so much a triumph for English football but for the marketing men behind the major English clubs. How did it all come about?

High finance

The post-Hillsborough rebuilding of the fabric of the game forced the FA to look to its financial laurels. The obvious first need was to market football to generate an annual income of £112 million, to be added to the £200 million provided by the Football Trust over four years for rebuilding the stadiums. There was also a pressing need to reform both the FA and the League. There was however good reason to suppose this would never happen. The FA distrusted the businessmen who ran the major clubs. It was a divide as old as the game itself, but accentuated in the 1990s by the financial stakes involved. For a brief moment, after Hillsborough, the FA had it within its power to galvanise and revitalise the game. As usual, they proved themselves as inept as their forebears over the past century. It would have been amazing, and contrary to its historical pedigree, had the FA seized the reform initiative. The events after Hillsborough illustrated not merely the moribund condition of English football grounds but also of the administrations which controlled the national game.

On the other side were the club chairmen, entrenched in their own baili-wicks within the clubs and within the Football League. They were the same men who had supervised the physical decay of English football stadiums, and who, in response to the game's troubles, had converted the grounds into sporting prisons, ringed with fences and marshalled by a massive police presence. What could *they* have to say, collectively, that was of any possible use or inspiration? However, those individuals who realised both the need for change, and the commercial potential the game offered, only had to look to the bigger clubs in Europe or to sport in North America to see what could be done with commercial imagination and a will to change. It was clear enough that the League clubs would never agree to a major structural reform of the game. Thus it was, in the confusion after Hillsborough, that a small coterie of men in the country's leading clubs were able to seize their opportunity. They used the aimless FA as their collaborators against an intransigent Football League, to force the Premiership on the rest of the game.

The chairmen of the breakaway clubs involved in the Premiership were a varied bunch, but they formed a team of aggressive entrepreneurs whose various businesses had prospered in the Thatcher years, and who preached money-making as a civic virtue. They brought the same approach to football. They naturally attracted money men, and financiers and advisors began to swarm around the country's leading football clubs. Football became a hot financial topic, and was regularly discussed in the *Financial Times* and *The Economist*. Analysts pored over the game's finances. In 1992 the accountants Deloitte and Touche began to produce an annual survey of football's finances. In the process, the very language used to discuss football changed. Gone were the game's familiar terms and phrases, their place taken by the analysis and vocabulary of the City and of the financial markets. Supporters became 'captive customers', the clubs were 'brands', support was known as 'brand loyalty' which was 'inelastic'. The game itself was reduced to mere 'entertainment product'. The game which had for a century been the people's game was now discussed as 'an investment vehicle'. Most fans reading this City guff (even those, like myself, obliged to spend my professional life partly in the unsympathetic company of economists), found it hard to stomach. Where, in all this, was the excitement of the game; the passion of the play and of the fans, and that sapping pleasure (and misery) of watching games swing this way or that?

> **Financiers and advisors began to swarm around the country's leading football clubs.**

In every single case, the top English clubs required major financial help. A few of the major clubs had directors with considerable sums to invest in ground redevelopment. Most clubs, however, had to look elsewhere for the capital to rebuild. In every single case, the top English clubs required major financial help. The market was waiting for them with open arms. The clubs turned to the serious task of making money, steered by directors and marketing advisors anxious to shake off football's cloth cap approach to economics. The first task was to rebuild. But once again English football reverted to type, for the new stadiums which began to sprout across the country betrayed a narrow-minded functionalism, with little thought given to style or flair, let alone eye-catching beauty. It was as if football's bosses had never visited a major European ground. English football once again found it impossible to accommodate aesthetic taste, preferring a crude, sometimes brutal stadium design. There were exceptions of course, all the more appealing because of their rarity. In general, though, England quickly acquired 'some of the safest but ugliest stadia in the world'.

> **It was as if football's bosses had never visited a major European ground.**

Clubs began to increase their income by the most obvious method: higher entrance fees. They also diversified the accommodation on offer. There was a proliferation of 'executive suites' and boxes, and entertainment facilities of the most lavish and comfortable kind, creating a cocooned viewing environment for the prosperous and the corporate clients. Catering staff at beck and call, TV sets blinking in the corner, and windowed facilities maintaining an insulated distance from the games the privileged viewers had come to see. The major English clubs transformed themselves in the 1990s, developing a host of facilities never before seen at football grounds; restaurants, museums, supermarkets even hotels – all clung to the stadiums like lucrative barnacles. Without the game itself, however, they were lifeless and valueless. Hospitality, catering, football tourism; shares and share-holders, city analysts and marketing – football had become an alien land for its own supporters. For those with money invested in the major football clubs, however, 1990s England proved to be a land of plenty.

'Ordinary' fans were henceforth called on to pay increasingly usurious admission prices – if they could get their hands on a ticket. Lord Taylor's report had demanded that low income fans should be protected; it was one recommendation that clubs universally ignored. Entrance charges rose profusely year after year. A seat at Manchester United which in 1988 cost £3.30 would seven years later command £15; by 2001 the same seat cost £25. At the time of writing, to take my grandson to watch Manchester United (a short drive from my home in York) will cost me about £100 for the day's enjoyment. There are, clearly, millions of people for whom such sums are out of reach.

For all that, Old Trafford was filled, week after week, and there was no shortage of people anxious to snap up available tickets, and even to pay well above the official price for the chance to visit the ludicrously self-styled 'Theatre of Dreams'. As the Premiership boomed some clubs even floated bonds (for £1000–£1500) which merely secured a guaranteed place in the *queue* to buy a season ticket. Flotation brought enormous sums to the clubs, allegedly for development, though also to profit existing directors. Inevitably major investors (especially leisure groups) moved into professional football, buying whole clubs, or a stake in them. By the mid-1990s, this massive investment in the game had begun to yield rich returns to its backers. The value of Manchester United's shares increased sixfold from 1994–97. Directors were able to sell blocks of shares and become instant millionaires. Some had the best of both worlds, making millions and yet clinging to substantial blocks of shares. The whole process was much vaunted as a means of enhancing the power and the voice of ordinary fans; buy shares and your views would find their way to the board. Quite the reverse happened. What the football clubs heeded was the City, and their major institutional shareholders – not the fans. What flotation *actually* achieved was to provide cash, by the barrowload, for existing shareholders. Flotations, when successful (and not all were), enriched existing shareholders, the men on the club boards for whom football in the 1990s was a succession of financial windfalls. The football boom of the 1990s transformed a small number of rich men into multimillionaires.

The football boom of the 1990s transformed a small number of rich men into multimillionaires.

Many of the older heads in football, men who had sat in club boardrooms for years, had cautioned that football was a financial drain, a black hole, which would simply swallow investors' money. Such men had long been accustomed to gaining little for their investment save the antipathy both of fans and of the press when their team played badly. But that era rapidly disappeared, washed away by saturation TV coverage, and by the commercial largesse it generated. Younger men, nurtured and tempered by the free market years of the 1980s, saw a different commercial prospect. Shareholders, mainly directors, who had invested in big clubs *before* the boom of the 1990s, found their relatively modest incomes soar into major personal fortunes.

The figures are astonishing. David Dein's £1 million at Arsenal became £37 million. Martin Edwards at Manchester United found an investment of £600,000 turn into £64 million. At Newcastle, Sir John Hall's family investment of £3 million became £102 million. The list goes on and on; Bates at Chelsea saw £1 million become £35 million. Perhaps most spectacular of all, and that at humble Wimbledon, was Sam Hammam's £100,000 which grew into £30 million. These men, and others, could justifiably claim that they had taken commercial risks at a time when football was in dire straits, that they had been instrumental in transforming the game – of lifting it from doom to boom – and that they therefore deserved to be rewarded. But even they must have been privately staggered by the scale of their success.

Even they must have been privately staggered by the scale of their success.

The marriage between the Premiership and television created a financial structure that has rewarded the rich, yet clubs outside the Premiership mainstream have no access to the money sluicing through the coffers of football's barons. And there is no Robin Hood in sight. A game which can afford £20 million for a single footballer, and which can pay run-of-the-mill players astronomic salaries, has no way of funnelling its enormous wealth elsewhere than into the pockets of the rich. In many respects, the elite Premiership clubs form the swan song of the free marketeers of the 1980s; untrammelled by fiscal regulation, dominating a world of their own financial making, and all without a modicum of social responsibility towards others. The more successful clubs have become a heartless bunch, even towards their own fans, though their remorseless avarice is generally masked by the weasel words from their PR men. Few have pursued the ideal of self-interest more thoroughly, more successfully, than the richest clubs in the Premier League. At one level, we ought to take pride in their achievements. After all, there are not many other British industries which have proved so successful. It is however an unregulated industry. Even at the apogee of Victorian industry, when profitable British industries dispatched their produce to all corners of the globe, there were powerful forces moderating and containing the worst excesses of the Victorian free market. The Premiership is a more extreme form of free market success than even the free marketeers could have expected. In its wake has come a serious destabilising of the game itself, with huge amounts of money hoarded in one small corner of the national game. Yet at the same time, English football begs for money. The FA pleads for lottery money, or for government loans and gifts (to build a national stadium for example), at the very time the Premier elite accumulates tens of millions of pounds year after year.

Sponsorship

Football was of course not the only game to be revolutionised in the 1990s by Murdoch's television. Rugby, both League and Union, was utterly transformed; professionalism (where amateurism had once been sacrosanct), sponsorship, transfer fees, high salaries, and the whole heady mix concocted and fermented by slick TV coverage and endless studio discussion. Rugby League teams which had rarely ventured outside Lancashire or Yorkshire now found themselves criss-crossing the globe to fulfil Murdoch-inspired competitions. The bigger teams adopted marketing strategies, much like their footballing mentors, to promote themselves and to enhance their revenue. In cricket the convulsions, over a longer period, were infamous. But again, they were triggered by commercial and media interests.

Whichever major sport we care to look at in the last twenty years of the 20th century (Formula One, golf, tennis, basketball) the broad outline was similar: a sport utterly transformed by the power of television coverage and by the related commercial sponsorship both of teams and of individual sportsmen. Whenever a sport or sportsman struck commercial gold, it provided a blueprint for other marketing men in other corners of the globe. The sporting genius and success of a single sportsman (say Tiger Woods or Michael Jordan) not only generated commercial deals of unparalleled wealth, but they created marketing templates which other sports copied.

Football began its long march towards modern marketing by acquiring sponsors, initially on a very modest scale. In France, Germany and Italy it had been common for a dominant industry or its owners to sponsor a local football team. Television coverage transformed the whole process. Sponsors were much more attracted to teams which had regular TV coverage. The more successful the team, the more TV coverage they attracted, the more valuable they became to sponsors. Within twenty years, most professional sports with TV coverage succumbed to the blandishments and cash of sponsors and advertisers. Products and services struck exclusive deals to sponsor a league (Carling/Barclaycard/Nationwide), a competition (Axa), a team or a club. Each and every aspect of the game itself was hived off to promote other commercial products.

Players became athletic billboards, promoting this or that on their kit. Football managers, commenting to camera, were positioned before carefully arranged advertisements. And, of course, TV coverage of major games or competitions was itself sponsored by a range of commercial activities. The bigger clubs, with global fame and millions of viewers (rising in the middle of the night to watch the game live in Asia, for example), promote international products.

Players became athletic billboards.

Smaller clubs tend to advertise more local items. Scottish football has survived, for years (for good and ill) by a heavy reliance on beer advertisements.

The importance of football as a global marketing tool was signalled by the decision of the global sporting giant Nike to enter the football market, with a deal reported to be worth £250 million with the Brazilian national team. It was a decision born of an earlier failure. Nike had – oddly – initially believed (following the success of the US team at the Barcelona Olympics in 1992) that basketball would dislodge football as the world's most dominant game. Thereafter they looked at what the world wanted, rather than what American corporations would like them to want, and realised that football reigned supreme. Nike quickly penetrated the game, courtesy of massive investments on TV, and by securing star players and clubs. What happened is instructive for the way commercial interests have come to dominate the game of football.

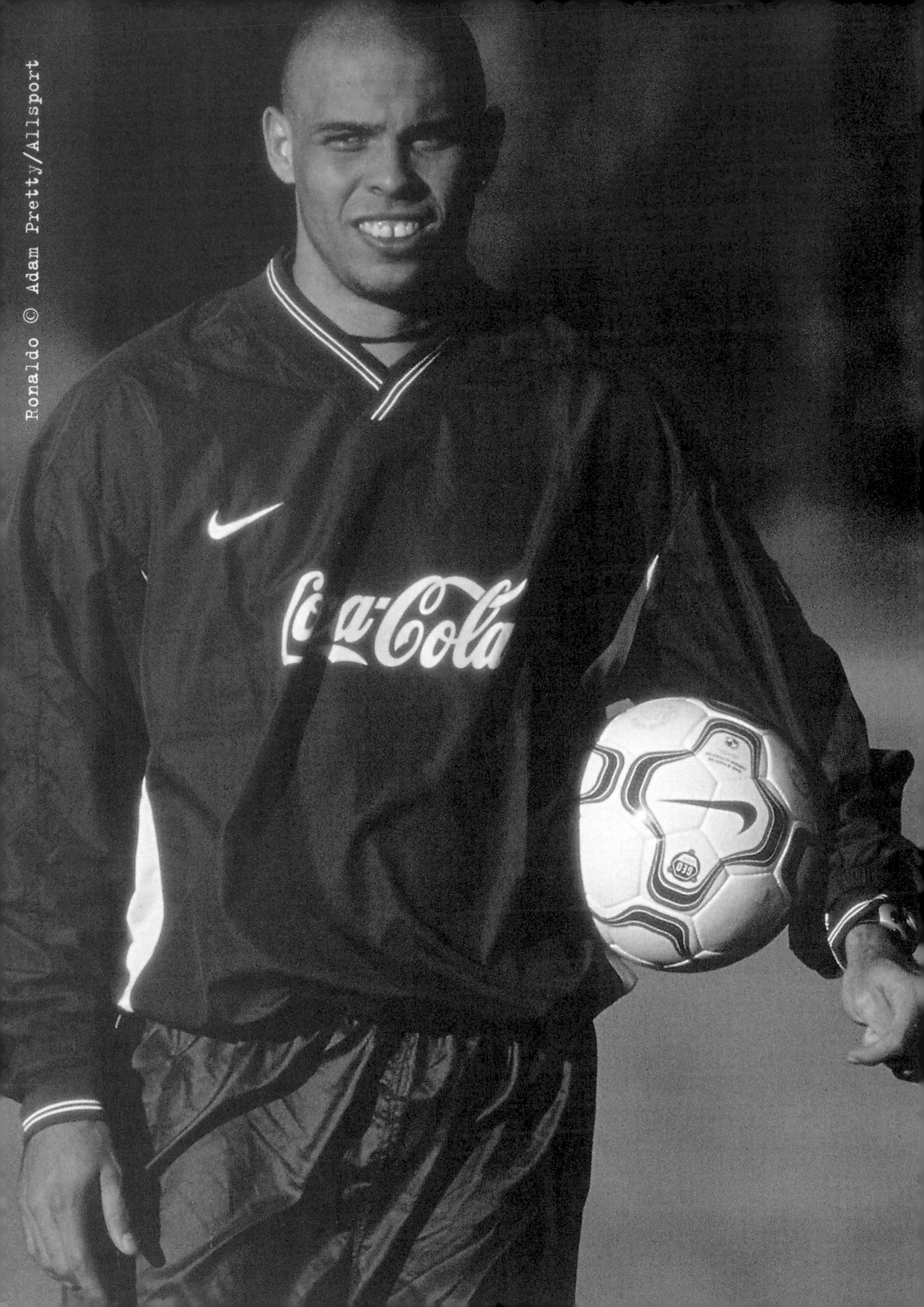

Ronaldo © Adam Pretty/Allsport

In 1996, Nike struck a deal with the Brazilian footballer Ronaldo, providing him with a lifetime's riches. But the player's commercial links with Nike clashed with the deal agreed between his club, Barcelona and Kappa. A similar clash happened when the player was sold to Lazio, whose sponsors were Umbro. When Ronaldo eventually signed for Inter, the Italian club also signed up with Nike. Inter immediately sold 35,000 Ronaldo shirts, and promptly recouped part of Ronaldo's massive transfer fee. Behind the whole affair lay unanswered questions about the power which Nike had come to exercise over the Brazilian team itself.

In the 1990s rush towards lucrative sponsorship deals in football, a series of conflicts had emerged. Individual players and their agents signed agreements with, say, a boot manufacturer, yet played in a team which had a corporate agreement with a rival. It was as if commercial interests were fighting over each and every part of the team, and of all corners of the players' dress and equipment. It may be only a matter of time before we are startled by a glimpse of the first sponsored jockstrap.

Marketing and sponsorship quickly became a vital form of income for the major English clubs. In 1996–97 Manchester United earned almost as much from merchandising as from gate receipts. Their teams could

> **It may be only a matter of time before we are startled by a glimpse of the first sponsored jockstrap.**

play in an empty stadium, and the club would *still* make millions of pounds' profit. Shirt sponsorship was the most visible of football's commercial forays, and it yielded wonderful returns for the bigger clubs. Carlsberg paid £1 million a year to have Liverpool display their name. It was a trend which swept right across the game and by the mid-1990s was worth some $256 million. But the most staggering effect of sponsorship – the most obvious, most talked-about and the most dramatic – was its impact on individual footballers. Star players earned massive wages from their employers (all made possible by the clubs' commercial success). But players were also able to multiply their wages by cashing in on their public fame through sponsorship deals.

The older managers in the Premiership (though few survive in the game to become old) had begun their playing careers under the punitive maximum wage system, yet here they were, in the late 1990s, managing young men who were multimillionaires. In 1997–98 the wage bill for the Premier League was more than £100 million (£40 million in Scotland). Annual deals of £2 million were struck with the very best players. The average wages for Premier League players in 1996–97 was £210,000. By 2000 that had risen above £400,000. By the turn of the century, more than 100 footballers earned more than £1 million a year from their clubs (not counting sponsorship). This massive inflation in players' wages was reflected right down the lower leagues. Average wages in First, Second and Third Divisions stood at £128,000, £52,000 and £37,000. In 1999, four footballers were ranked among Britain's top ten sports earners, with incomes ranging from £2.85 million to £4.75 million.

The players

The gap between footballers' wages and national earnings widened beyond reach. Indeed, footballers' wages have driven them beyond the wildest dreams of the millions who idolise them. The first English footballer to earn £100 a week received seven times the national average wage. By the mid-1990s, the Premiership's best-paid players earned sixty times the average wage. Not surprisingly, surveys showed that people widely believed that sportsmen were paid too much. Clearly, the major premier clubs could bear such costs, but it remains uncertain how well smaller clubs, with a much lower revenue, can sustain these wage levels.

The more successful players now need financial and business advice in managing their careers. The days of a friendly bank manager shuffling a few surplus pounds in and out of different savings accounts have been replaced by aggressive, international agents and advisors, each pushily advancing their clients' interests. Sport, like show business, is littered with cautionary tales of rags to riches – and back again. There are few more pathetic sights than yesterday's hero, once front and back page news, awash with cash and invariably swamped by glamorous women and showbiz associates, reduced, when his playing days are over, to anonymous penury, dependent on football's charitable funds and the help of old friends.

The astronomic wages in the Premier League made English football attractive to players from all over the world. Thanks to changes in the law, players could move more easily throughout Europe and, because of the Bosman ruling, players can simply change clubs when their contracts end. The change produced in the English game has been amazing. In 1966–67 there were only ten overseas players registered in the Football League. By 1980–81 this had risen to 57. But it was the creation of the Premier League which lured substantial numbers of foreign players to England. In 1992–93 only eleven foreign footballers played in the Premier League. By 1998–99 the figure had increased to 166. Critics of this substantial flow of footballers into England (and Scotland), worried that it might harm the prospects of local players. Few stopped to ask why there was so little movement *the other way*; major European clubs were hardly overstaffed with English players. 'Abroad', with its alien ways and languages was too threatening for many home-grown players. One famous English international, transferred to Italy for a brief unhappy spell, thought Italy 'like being in a foreign country'. Frenchmen and Danes, Swedes and Germans must have felt much the same when parachuted into the deeper recesses of decaying industrial England, but, by and large, they adapted, to the great improvement of their clubs and the English game. They were of course handsomely paid for their efforts.

European players brought much more than their playing and technical skills. Many of them also brought to the ranks of their fellow professionals a very different cultural attitude to football itself. Local footballers were steeped in a very different cultural ethos which was, at once, less educated and less sophisticated. Indeed the professional footballer has long been the object of snobbish ridicule: lots of money and thick as a plank. English football had traditionally cared little about the education of its players, and even though new licensed footballing academies have been established to develop young professional footballers, the levels of formal education among players remain depressingly low. Despite the massive expansion of higher education, footballing graduates remain a rare breed. Elsewhere in Europe, however, major clubs made strides to develop coaching which integrates football with more basic social and educational skills. Slowly the English game looked round and saw what needs to be done. Year after year there were infamous examples of English footballers exposed and ridiculed by the press as inadequate and sometimes utterly dysfunctional people, ill-prepared for the

European players brought much more than their playing and technical skills.

challenges even of normal social life. Often such failings are simply personal, or were established in early life when football seemed (to them and their parents) the surest route to material improvement. But the *pattern* in the English game is too striking to be accidental, and the game itself carries a heavy responsibility for the way it has treated its raw playing talent. Boys have traditionally been plucked from the most uneducated corners of British life and, a few years later, returned there, sometimes with a successful career to look back on (and sometimes with plenty of money), more often however with nothing but thwarted ambition, no money and no education.

In the 1990s a number of clubs, in co-operation with the monitoring FA, began to provide a better, more rounded education for their young recruits. Looking back over the whole history of the English game however, there has clearly been a persistent failure, at club level, within the leagues and in the FA, to integrate formal education with professional football training. This has, again, a distinctively English ring to it; players learn their trade by *practice*. Distrust of formal instruction and education, one of the most resistant of all English diseases, is not peculiar to the national game. But it is responsible for some of the more troublesome disadvantages bequeathed by the game to its professional players.

The contrast with what might be achieved is easily available. The French football academy at Clairefontaine, founded to spot and nurture the best French footballing talent, has dispatched a huge number of gifted and sophisticated players to adorn the game around Europe. The irony remains however that the weakness of the French club system has seen the best French players drift inexorably away to spend their careers in Italy, Spain, Germany and England. A mere glance at the Premiership in 2001 reveals the benefits which this French educational and training enterprise has unwittingly provided for the *English* game; three major coaches (Wenger, Houllier and Tagana) and at least 30 Frenchmen in the Premiership. England's gain has of course been a considerable loss to France. It was made possible by the revolution in the English game in the 1990s and by the realisation among foreign footballers worldwide that to play in England is to live in a land of plenty.

There have been any number of unsuccessful imports of foreign players, sometimes at great cost to the clubs. Overall, though, it is impossible not to feel that the English game has benefited enormously by the 'foreign legions' playing in the Premiership. True, it has, in one spectacular example (Chelsea) taken a bizarre turn, with Englishmen an unusual sight in the most cosmo-politan 'English' team ever. That apart – and Chelsea were exceptional for a number of reasons throughout the 1990s – the quality of the English game has been hugely enhanced by foreign players. It was no accident that the fortunes of Manchester United in that decade were galvanised by the arrival of a Frenchman. Cantona alone cannot explain that club's success. He proved however to be the most important element around which another great team was created. Cantona helped his last club to become the richest football club in England.

Cantona provides a remarkable example of how fans can change devotion to a player. Adored at Leeds (when he played there), he was promptly disliked at Leeds when he moved to Manchester. Mancunians, who had once disliked him, took him to their hearts (not least because he converted Manchester United into a successful team once more). In the words of one Manchester United fan:

> One minute I'm thinking, 'Who's the ugly, French, one-eyebrowed git?', then, one trip over the Pennines and suddenly there's this dark, brooding Heathcliff-type figure on the horizon. Not that I'm biased or anything.

Cantona's intellectual claims sometimes confused his adopted followers. His much-proclaimed affection for Rimbaud led to a proliferation of Rambo pic-tures among fans. He was, in an almost inexplicable way, perhaps the most loved Manchester United player of all time.

> Eric is an idol
> Eric is a star
> And if my mother had her way,
> He'd also be my Pa.

Following his infamous kung fu attack on a fan, my instinct was a frigid out-rage; he must never again play for Manchester United. Fortunately for the club and the game, Alex Ferguson was the manager not me.

The Premiership set in train a remarkable commercial revolution in English football. Footballing talent followed the money – and money was available in abundance. Some of the game's finest players migrated to England, much as they had traditionally moved to Spain and Italy. The riches which showered on English football following the launch of BSkyB and the creation of the Premiership in 1992 stand in stark contrast to what went before. Football had been notoriously purse-proud and mean. Now, in the 1990s, rich footballers and even richer clubs became a significant part of England's cultural landscape despite being a small minority. In the process football's past, even its recent history, had been unceremoniously forgotten, gone, irrelevant. Football's past is indeed a foreign country. Yet history weighs heavily on football, and beneath the glamour and the frothy dazzle of the game's undoubted riches, the old game, the old habits and instincts, remain much the same. That small minority who live in football's lap of luxury need the others, the millions of extras, fans and players alike (and armchair-based TV viewers), who continue to sustain the ubiquitous game of ordinary people.

Football and cookery are the two most important subjects in the country.

Delia Smith in *Observer* 23 February 1997

12

The grass roots

Lesser mortals

Books about football invariably concentrate on the professional game. Most tend to be preoccupied with the highly successful end of the football spectrum; the famous teams and clubs which catch the eye, which vie with each other, year after year, for awards and public acclaim, and to whom vast crowds of fans are devoted – and on whom the lion's share of income is scattered. This book has been no different. But there is another football story to tell; about ordinary, run-of-the-mill football, about boys in the park, schoolchildren driven to games by parents, older men (long past their prime) struggling on bleary-eyed Sunday mornings to recapture their footballing best, and millions more simply kicking a ball against a back wall. It is generally untold because it is so mundane, so obvious and unremarkable, that it requires no telling; it is part and parcel of the world we live in. We see it, know it, have taken part in it, as children, parents, as players or as spectators. At this level football is just another feature of life's weekly routines and scarcely warrants a passing thought. Yet it is this massive, incalculable substratum of popular football that sustains the professional game; the millions of ordinary players who nurture the national (and global) interest in the high-powered, commercially driven world of successful professional soccer. More than that, this popular attachment to the game takes us right back to the origins of the game itself. This is how football has always been; a simplicity and ease of play embedded deep in the routines and habits of ordinary people. That is why the game

> **Football remains the people's game, however lavish and absurd the antics of the wealthy minority.**

of football remains the people's game, however lavish and often absurd the antics of the wealthy minority.

The lower leagues

Once you leave the glamour of the top professional sides and begin to look at (or follow) poorer professional clubs, you step into another world, recognisably similar (it is, after all, the same game, same rules, same aims), but different in tone and environment. For a start, there are not so many people around, and the physical surroundings are much less well tended, often wedged into poor urban communities. You are back with football as it was before Lord Taylor's revolution. Here it is possible to *stand* at a football ground. You may have to jostle with others and crane your neck, juggling for a good vantage point, to watch the game. More likely than not, you can choose your spot on the large expanses of empty terraces, hoping the elements stay kind to you. There is little sign, here, in the lower leagues, of the wealth surging through the Premiership.

© Mark Leech

The departure of the major clubs left the Football League struggling to manage the poorer clubs, in generally straitened circumstances. The clubs in Division One keen to be promoted to the Premiership are generally well managed, and trim, often owned by entrepreneurs or companies similar to their Premier League peers. Financially, the gulf between Premier and First Division is vast. Those relegated from the Premiership face immediate financial hardship, for they are instantly denied millions of pounds as TV money dries up to a trickle. Beneath the upper reaches of Division One, a number of clubs struggle financially. Some, perhaps twenty at the end of the 1990s, face serious financial trouble – a backlog of debts, dwindling support and unaffordable wage bills. Such strugglers are inevitably exposed to take-overs and asset stripping. Their football may be unattractive, their coffers empty and the ground threadbare, but they sit on a prized asset: urban real estate. In the take-over merry-go-round which has characterised the story of smaller professional clubs (some with famous old names), with businessmen of all sorts moving in and out of the board room, local fans have to be alert to the danger that their club might simply disappear, swallowed by developers and regurgitated as new supermarkets or private houses, to the great profit of the developers involved.

Their football may be unattractive, but they sit on a prized asset: urban real estate.

There are of course examples to the contrary: of businessmen who have redeveloped a small club along efficient and profitable lines, trying throughout to remain faithful to the club's old image and status. Some of the more appealing new stadiums are in fact to be found in the lower leagues, where the ambition has not simply been to cram in as many people as possible into the new facilities. There have been important and successful efforts to enhance a club's standing, to improve its physical structure *and* put the whole thing on a sound financial basis. The examples of Preston North End and Crewe Alexandra spring to mind. Here are two famous old clubs (both founded in the 1870s – well before Arsenal or Manchester United) with names unlikely to strike a chord in today's global footballing fraternity. But they are typical bedrock clubs of the traditional English game, clubs which, year after year, have exemplified the appeal of football for local supporters.

These two clubs, under very different but stringent control, developed different strategies for survival. Both were lucky to fall under the control of men who, though businessmen through and through, had more than profit in mind. Without a well-managed organisation, nothing else was possible. Both have shown how small professional football clubs can thrive without the single-minded pursuit of quick profits, the one (Crewe) by rearing and passing on young players, the other (Preston) through careful commercial developments in a profitable relationship with the local town. In both cases, the football club has promoted a number of practical community-based schemes. Here and elsewhere, small professional football clubs have thrived where imaginative management and boards have used their position to incorporate their towns. Trusts, partnerships with a local council, jointly owned and jointly used sporting facilities – all this and more have served to integrate a number of clubs more closely with their community. Curiously, it was just such a vision (of a major football club playing a community role, and offering much more to local people than merely one professional game per week) which so excited Matt Busby when he first visited Real Madrid in the mid 1950s.

It is easy to sound romantic about such ideals and schemes, and it is tempting to side with the virtues of football's small-scale civic responsibility against the vices of the elite clubs' vaunting corporate ambitions. Yet it is not solely the editors of fanzines who find such schemes attractive. Support can be found in *all* corners of the footballing world; from grass-root fans, and among people who have spent their lives toiling in the less rewarded and humbler corners of the game. Criticism of the wealthy clubs is universal. It is also worth pointing out that such criticisms mirror almost exactly the growing chorus of discontent about global corporations. At the very time the major English clubs have slipped smoothly into the mode of any other corporate body, global corporations themselves are attracting heavy fire for their rapaciousness and lack of social responsibility. Ironically, the footballing elite have the power – the money, the skills, the personnel (and, above all perhaps, the star names) – both to be good neighbours *and* commercial giants. Yet they have become famous for making money almost to the exclusion of anything else. It is

They have become famous for making money almost to the exclusion of anything else.

true that they often indulge in publicity-conscious gestures, such as dispatching players to children's hospitals. But the photo opportunities afforded by such acts of karaoke conscience should not to be confused with the carefully thought-out (and highly successful) plans devised by smaller clubs in co-operation with their neighbours.

Those people in charge of successful smaller clubs have brought about the reformation of their club's fortunes by much more than mere acumen and imagination. Their work has been characterised above all else by respect for the supporters, a quality which has been consistently scarce in the Premiership. Indeed it has been absent through long stretches of the history of the English game. Major clubs have come to view their fans much as their financial analysts do; as a source of revenue to be tapped by ever more imaginative marketing techniques. When that immediate fan-base is fully exploited, there are the millions of (carefully nurtured) fans on the far side of the globe. Standing in sharp contrast to all this is a vanguard of smaller clubs in the lower leagues who have been forced to live by their wits. That, in its turn, has had the effect of persuading them to return to the very people who spawned the club in the first place; the local community.

> **Major clubs view their fans as a source of revenue to be tapped.**

The initial distress and upheaval in the other leagues caused by the Premiership breakaway has now receded. They manage to get some reasonable income from TV, and the Premiership gives a fraction of its income for the redevelopment of small clubs' grounds and for the promotion of youth schemes. Though some complain when their better players are plucked away by the big clubs, the fees received provide important income. Equally, the smaller clubs also benefit by the flow of players *downwards*. There are gaggles of young players, trained and nurtured by the major clubs, who simply do not make it to the top, and who, having served an important apprenticeship on the edges of the Premiership, find their way to careers with smaller clubs.

Whatever the benefits accruing to the poorer clubs from the Premiership, they have learned to live under the cultural and financial shadow of dominant clubs who, at heart, are not really concerned about their well-being. Clearly, the elite need the smaller clubs, especially as 'feeders' or training farms. But the ideology of the Premiership, conceived in the free market and sustained by the City and investors, has little or no sympathy for clubs that are struggling. In the brutal world of corporate politics, the consequence of financial weakness and bad management is commercial failure. If small clubs go to the wall for whatever reason, so be it. Their assets can generally be put to some other use. Why, so the argument goes, should major clubs bail out the failing clubs, any more than Starbucks should help a faltering local coffee shop?

The ideology of the Premiership has little or no sympathy for clubs that are struggling.

To make matters worse for small clubs, the Premiership has dragged more and more football fans into the gravitational pull of the elite clubs. Football fans have drifted away from local clubs, heading towards the major teams. Large numbers of fans now grow up following teams from the far side of the country, rather than their home-town team. In another illustration of the sway which the Premiership has come to exercise over football, motorways fill with coaches and cars ferrying armies of fans from all corners of the country to watch their favourite Premier team play a 'home' match.

Amateurs

English football is *not* monopolised by the Premiership, even though it casts a shadow across the wider game. There are any number of amateur leagues across the country, some of them boasting teams which are older than many in the premiership clubs. It is here, in often delapidated grounds, that the traditional game continues, much as it always has. Such clubs survive on their wits, on generous backers and whip-rounds, and on a dogged local support. However, given the choice, many fans opt to watch a televised game rather than a local amateur game, and given the frequent and widespread coverage of football on satellite TV, amateur clubs invariably face competition for their spectators.

But it is here, among the amateurs, that we find the real strength of football – alongside its casualties and might-have-beens. Players who dash from their day job to train and play, side-by-side with players whose promising careers never materialised. The lower the league, the more frequent and troublesome the tales of hardship, both for clubs and for the players. Clubs sometimes fold and disappear; more likely, they stumble on, kept together by the gritty loyalty of the people who run the club. Here too voices are raised against the Premiership and its harmful consequences for the rest of the national game. The refrain is universal; a familiar complaint that the money and support which swirls around the Premiership is, in part, diverted from other corners of the game. The exact arithmetic of such claims may be hard to fathom, though few inside the amateur game doubt the end result. 'The bottom line' means very different things at opposite ends of the game. For the top clubs, the bottom line is measured in tens of millions, at the bottom, in petty cash. Amateur officials counting the coins have no doubt that money that once came their way now ends up at Old Trafford or Highbury, at Elland Road or Anfield.

'The bottom line' means very different things at opposite ends of the game.

At the heart of the England's amateur clubs is normally found a determined figure who, with a small band of helpers, manages to keep the team afloat against all odds. Those loyal to amateur football swear by the game's qualities, preferring its honest endeavour and enthusiasm to the lavishly paid skill of the elite teams. At the same time they bemoan the indifference which, they claim, the major clubs display to the game's grass roots. Football seems to be in the hands of people who know the cost of the game, but really do not understand its value.

From its earliest days, modern football was actively promoted as a means of healthy exercise for boys and young men. To a late Victorian society increasingly alarmed about the physical condition of its people, football seemed an ideal antidote to the problems of urban and industrial life. It was easily and cheaply arranged, could be played in the most unlikely of places and offered a means of regular exercise for young men. It also had a host of social qualities. It encouraged boys to play within a team; to channel their energies and skills into a collective endeavour. There were, from the first, some who were better than others. Some who were brilliant. But even they had to be team-players. To be a team-player involved knowing your place, being aware of others, heeding a captain or coach. It is easy to caricature the role of authority and obedience which were fundamental to football and other team games, but such qualities were vital to the enthusiasm which was invested in promoting football. In the late 19th century football seemed to offer Britain a host of social benefits; it brought discipline at the same time as it entertained and encouraged fitness. Millions of boys turned to the game for a very different reason; it was good fun. Eventually football also became a defining experience of childhood and adolescence, part of growing up. True enough there were many who did not like the game, and who never understood its appeal – but there were millions more for whom it was fundamental to their childhood and early adult years.

School sports

The modern codified game of football was quickly grafted onto the new compulsory English school system after 1880. Football quickly took root in the school system and thrived on competitions within and between schools. School football in England (and Scotland) was the nursery for footballing enthusiasms and skills bequeathed from one generation to another for more than a century. At its best, schoolboy football attracted large crowds.

After a century's success in English schools, the story of football began to change in the 1980s. School football and games in general fell victim to the politics of the 1980s. The Thatcherite revolution prompted a fight between an increasingly powerful central government and cash-strapped local (often Labour) authorities. School sports were badly affected. Cutbacks and the selling of assets such as school fields and sports facilities gnawed away at schools' extra-curricula facilities. Between 1987 and 1995, no fewer than 5000 school playing fields were sold off. Of course the worst consequences of this central government-inspired regime of cost-cutting was the decline in the educational fabric itself. Hard-pressed teachers had little time and energy left for the chores of monitoring pupils' games and

> **School football and games in general fell victim to the politics of the 1980s.**

sports. Even when politicians recognised the damage caused, they did little to arrest it. The end result was a dramatic diminution of the nation's sporting stock. It is simply impossible to calculate how many children were denied access to decent sporting and gymnastic training (the value of which no one disputes). School football declined, especially in the major cities. Playing fields were sold, or schools could not afford to ferry children to pitches elsewhere. Organisations to encourage school sports simply collapsed or were undermined by budgetary cuts.

Where schools sports survive (and thrive) they do so because of the enthusiasm and commitment of a small band of teachers and parents. It is however impossible to know how many children are now denied the pleasure of school sports because of the political upheavals of the past generation. Few doubt that the organisations responsible for schoolboy football are thread bare; they survive by shaking their begging bowl left and right. The story is worsened to the point of black comedy by the shadow of football's millionaires. Virtually *nothing* flows back to school football from the millions awash in the Premier League. Even those clubs which benefit directly from local school football – who cherry-pick star footballers – give little or nothing in return. Their indifference adds professional footballing insult to the political injuries inflicted on schoolboy football over a generation.

The problem of school sports is clearly much broader than the story of football. But anyone familiar with the history of football must worry about the decline of schoolboy football. The role of football within the national school system was a peculiarly English arrangement. It was, at one level, a historical accident; a hangover from late Victorian and Edwardian England and its massive social and urban problems. It also served as a means of encouraging a healthy attachment to sport. Having thrived for almost a century, school football (and school sports in general) had effectively fallen apart by the end of the 20th century. In the very years when more and more people in the nation at large were playing sports, there was a catastrophic decline in school sports. As early as 1990, a survey of 1582 schools revealed the sports offered at weekend had declined by 70 per cent, daytime sports by 62 per cent. Sporting skills and enthusiasm which had once been encouraged and taught in schools, were increasingly only to be found in sports clubs. The contrast with the public schools (education's Premier League) could not have been greater, for there the schools' sporting tradition continues to thrive. They have the money, the resolve and the manpower to maintain what they clearly see as a vital aspect of education. The public schools, after all, initiated the whole business and they maintain it to this day. Not surprisingly, ex-public school boys have a prominent place in a range of sports, out of all proportion to their numbers in the population.

> **What has happened in the past twenty years has been the effective strangulation of one of the game's main arteries.**

At the start of the new century, sports in state schools were in a weaker state than at any time since the coming of compulsory education – and that despite a string of government papers and policies designed to reverse the trend. School football had been vital to the broader game itself. Football's grass roots had clearly withered to an alarming degree. The creation of football academies and training schools, sponsored by clubs or by the FA, have scarcely begun to correct the damage. For a start, the establishment of such academies has been designed primarily to spot potential *professional* talent. School football was utterly different, but no less important, for it incorporated millions of boys into the national game throughout their formative years. In fact football became the national game in large measure because of being established as part of the compulsory educational system. There was, of course, more to the popularity of football than the experiences at school, but what has happened in the past twenty years has been the effective strangulation of one of the game's main arteries. Many of cricket's recent problems have clearly been dictated in part by the decline of cricket in English schools, for similar reasons.

Community schemes

The effective bankruptcy of school football (the seed bed of the game) stands in sharp contrast to the opulence of the Premiership. It is a contrast made all the more acute by the refusal of the elite clubs to recognise their debts to schools and the schooling system. They are indebted first for the raw talent for their future professionals, and secondly for the way schools cultivate a national attachment to football. There have been successive schemes for schoolboy football concocted by the FA in cahoots with the Premiership. But they do not inspire confidence. The FA's and Premiership's interest in developing schemes for young boys is to capture players for the professional market, more especially for the top clubs. Such players are always the tiniest of minorities. What about the rest? In all this, the game's hierarchy has lost all trace of football's sustaining links, between the millions who watch and play for fun, and the fortunate few who play for millions.

There are some examples which buck this trend, most notably the 'community schemes' fostered between some of the smaller, less glamorous professional clubs and their local towns. They became a form of 'stake holding' much promoted by Tony Blair's first government. Such schemes have produced some of the most forward-looking and beneficial changes in football for a very long time: campaigns against racism, concern for disabled fans, youth training and, most innovative of all in this masculine game, the encouragement of women's football. These, and summer training courses, have all emerged from a range of partnerships forged between clubs and local authorities. Schemes have been developed to introduce young players – and fans to professional clubs and some are keen to promote the football club's role as a civic as well as a professional body. All this stemmed initially from Lord Taylor's suggestion that the new stadiums should be more than temples for adoring fans, but should, in addition, provide access and opportunities for a wider range of sporting interests in the local community. For their part, local authorities have been keen to improve local recreational facilities without having to invest their own scarce resources. Such partnerships seemed ideal. In truth however they are few and far between, though much trumpeted where successful and undoubtedly important where they flourish. But the simple truth remains, the professional clubs – and especially the elite clubs – have their own single minded footballing agenda.

More interesting to most professional clubs than ties to the community is the potential talent growing up in their own 'catchment' area. Clubs have a proprietorial view towards boys born and raised close by, as if birth and upbringing ought to bring, along with accent and identity, a natural attachment to a local football club. (Critics continue to discuss how

Clubs have a proprietorial view towards boys born and raised close by.

Manchester United 'snatched' David Beckham – Essex born and bred – from his neighbouring London clubs.) Anxious not to miss out on potential talent, especially keen to prevent local boys being snatched from under their very noses by distant clubs, football management use every means available to lure and secure young local talent. If new coaching schemes fail to tempt, there are always football's tried-and-tested inducements to parents. Agents even trawl the schoolboy leagues, looking for young talent, talking to parents, and then parading the boys' qualities to prospective clubs. Low-income parents in particular find it hard to resist the temptations of a new car, or even a substantial lump sum. There is, as we have seen, nothing new in this. Professional clubs have been securing young footballers via offers to their parents since at least the 1950s; today, inevitably, the stakes (and the offers) are higher. More than that, parents realise the value of their boys' abilities, and often come prepared to negotiate the best offer from clubs. Few in the game will talk openly about this. But it is just as hard to find anyone who will deny its existence.

The debate about schoolboy football has been skewed – the whole discussion has concentrated on how best to find and train recruits for the elite clubs. The assumption is that what is good for the Premiership is good for the game as a whole. This is patently and demonstrably untrue. Indeed, as this book has been at pains to point out, what is good for the Premiership has, in many key regards, been bad for the broader game of football. Even more depressing perhaps is that the organisations which had once safeguarded the schoolboy game, notably the FA and its ancillary organisations, have virtually capitulated to their footballing paymasters. That has left the game's local servants, the gaggle of men and women across the country, high and dry; struggling to maintain schoolboy football, ill-rewarded and ill-regarded, and with no one effectively to

> **The organisations which had once safeguarded the schoolboy game have virtually capitulated to their footballing paymasters.**

defend them or speak for them. They look ever more like the remnants of a defeated army, rolled over by the game's big battalions.

Such an image however does them a disservice. Despite their problems, despite their generally hostile reaction to the way the game has shifted over the past decade, the people who run schoolboy and youth teams and leagues know that they do a good, worthwhile job. The pleasure they secure from what seems, to outsiders, unrewarding work is not to be calibrated by the indices which the City has imposed on the professional game; by the state of the shares and the bankability of the clubs. It is two different worlds. The ordinary grass-roots game is played much as it has been for a century and more, rooted in schoolboy life and lovingly guarded and promoted by a relatively small band of selfless adults whose sole interest is a love of the game, and a fierce attachment to the ideals of schoolboy football. These and people like them in other amateur leagues, not the behemoths of the Premiership, are the true guardians of the people's game.

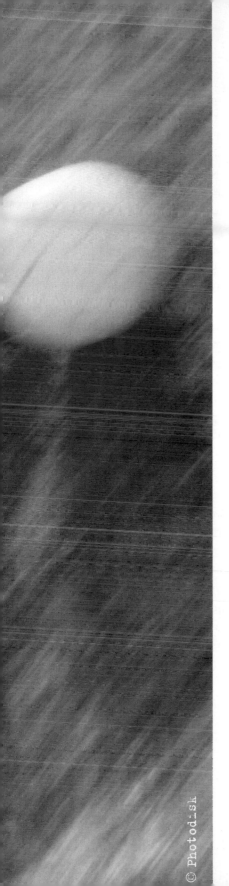

13

Celebrities
in shorts
Football in
the public
eye

Football was more visible, more central to English life in the 1990s than perhaps at any other period in its history. Its major teams and star players were rarely out of the news, though sometimes for all the wrong reasons. The game was a source of massive, expanding, commercial concern – of remarkable public attention. Critics complained that football had become a national religion, played out in the modern secular cathedrals of the new stadiums. At the same time there were residual social problems which refused to leave the game alone, and which inevitably attracted political and public concern. Overt racism, problems of crowd control, fans' misbehaviour, trouble abroad, all continued to attract political intervention and new legislation. The last decade of the century witnessed a political involvement with football, and a consequent police management of the game, to a degree never seen before (apart from the exceptional years of the Second World War). Nor were troubles merely domestic, because English fans continued to inflict their troublesome behaviour on our European neighbours. Fans across Europe displayed local symptoms of 'the English disease', hooliganism. The English tried desperately to keep other footballing nations sweet, and to persuade them that England was, following the post-Taylor revitalisation, a suitable venue for major footballing competitions. The hugely successful 'Euro96' tournament in England proved that English football could manage a major tournament without the troubles of the 1980s. But time and again, despite the efforts of government officials and senior footballing diplomats to show English football and its new stadiums at their persuasive best, small knots of disruptive fans turned up, in England or in Europe, to try to ruin the case. Through all this, football stood out as an object of major public interest. It was no longer merely a game.

The new Premier League dominated the domestic game in the 1990s, a super league for the biggest and richest clubs. It is easy enough to be critical about the Premier League. The vices and failings of the major clubs, especially their avaricious greed and selfishness towards the rest of football, are so obvious, so well-documented, that they scarcely deserve repetition. It is, equally, no great challenge to show how far those clubs have veered from English football's historical spirit, though this is not to romanticise the old, traditional game of football. What is abundantly clear, however, is how fundamental – how revolutionary – were the changes brought about by the Premier League. The elite clubs and the men in charge launched a chain reaction which had fundamental ramifications from schoolboy football to the richest of the major clubs. Yet it would be wrong not to acknowledge the improvements ushered in during the 1990s.

The most visible change was the improvement in the game's physical environment. The unreformed English football grounds were among the ugliest of civic amenities. As a fan said of Port Vale's ground: 'Nowhere have so many different shades of grey been on display at the same time'. The same was true north of the border. Hampden – according to *The Guardian*'s David

Lacey – was, 'The only ground which looks the same in black and white as it does in colour'. They were, with a few exceptions, uninviting, bleak, and in many cases forbidding. And the security systems of the 1970s and 1980s (i.e. fences) made them even more unattractive. The improvements on this front are thanks to Lord Taylor. There are lots of problems associated with many of the new football stadiums – perched at the top of Manchester United's new stand, it is easier to see the Pennines than the players – but these pale into insignificance when set against the squalid discomforts of the crumbling pre-Taylor stadiums. It is difficult, now, to conjure forth that unique experience of trying to watch a football match on a dangerously crowded terrace, packed into a swaying crowd, with no access to the toilets (themselves too disgusting to mention).

> **Perched at the top of Manchester United's new stand, it is easier to see the Pennines than the players.**

New football stadiums came with a highly choreographed marshalling of fans, inside and outside the stadiums, by police and by armies of club stewards. New stewarding proved effective in containing (but clearly not eradicating) many of the social tensions which had rippled through the game in the 1970s and 1980s. Though problems remained and periodically flared, it was obvious enough that football grounds were once again safe places to visit. There is no reason to feel that so dramatic a turnaround would have been effected by the game as it existed pre-Taylor; indeed football had repeatedly shown itself incapable of reform in those areas which mattered most. The remarkable chemistry of the convergence of three factors (the Taylor Report, the Premiership break-away, and satellite TV) served to transform the game as we knew it. The immediate result was that people began to return to football grounds.

Attendances had hit an all-time low of 16,448,557 in the 1985–86 season, but by 1994–95 they had risen to almost 22 million. The Premiership alone (20-team strong after 1995) attracted more than 11 million spectators by 1998. At the end of the 2000–2001 season, Manchester United's greatly increased ground capacity enabled more than two million people to pass through the Old Trafford turnstiles. The cost of redevelopment, passed on to admission prices, was enormous. Football fans everywhere complained about the cost of watching football (and, increasingly, of the cost of pay-per-view TV coverage of the game). On the other hand, the corporate smiles within the elite clubs told their own tale; with the increase of fans, record income flowed into the coffers. More than that, football had gained a new respectability, a social cache, forged in part by a different media treatment and partly by the elevation of major stars to celebrity status. Many of these changes had their origins in the commercial buoyancy of the game. A small band of footballers, certain football teams and, periodically, the national (often faltering) team found themselves caught up in the frenzy of renown. We became accustomed to reading about celebrities in shorts, though often as much for their extra-footballing antics as for their footballing skills.

Marketing and advertising agents created new dimensions and attractions to the game's basic simplicities. So much has come to hinge on personality – on promoting individual stars around whom commercial interests can drape any number of products. Sports equipment, cosmetic produce and clothing, cars and restaurants, even the simple delights of Danish bacon have been promoted by prominent footballers through costly TV marketing. In the process footballers developed a fame far beyond their own sport, their celebrity enhanced still further by invitations to TV shows, showbiz parties, the catwalks of fashion houses and offers to grace the pages of *OK* or *Hello* magazine. Astronomic wages (is this the right word for millionaires?) compounded by dizzying fees

> **Even the simple delights of Danish bacon have been promoted by prominent footballers.**

from sponsorships propelled this relatively small band of young sportsmen into the fluffy world of other superstars, people whose social worlds overlap and rely on each other. There was, too, a natural social drift to the bright lights of London.

The price of fame

Though there had always been a close link between journalism and football, what happened in the 1990s was quite different. In the inter-war years, the press had taken up sport in a major way, the popular Sunday papers sometimes running up to six pages devoted to sport, and even the 'quality' press responding with increased sports coverage. Throughout however the press adhered to certain codes and generally went out of their way to avoid a hint of scandal among sportsmen. Up to the 1950s, newspapers were united in steering clear of stories about the personal shortcomings of sportsmen. There was little hint in the press of sportsmen succumbing to the temptations of drink or sexual entanglements. But all that began to change in the 1960s. Over the next thirty years, the popular press went further and further in seeking and publishing sensational stories about anyone in the public eye. Footballers became fair game, especially when caught with their shorts down. But the tabloid press also changed its approach to the coverage of games themselves. Absurd banner headlines, huge spreads of colour photographs and lurid prose all came to characterise the popular coverage of football and the other major sports. Lauded or denounced for their performances on the field, footballers found their off-pitch activities no less interesting to the men with the telephoto lens and the notebook. Spearheaded by the *Sun*, this new approach was, at once jingoistic (especially about the England team), cruel and utterly ruthless. The press treatment of major footballing figures, who were often not trained to defend themselves against unscrupulous journalism, sometimes drove men from their jobs. This sensationalism also whipped up, among the readers, unreasonable and often hostile expectations (especially against foreign teams), sanctioned discriminatory language (nowhere more frequently and insultingly than against Germans) and, in general, sanctioned a tone of ridicule against failure or shortcomings on and off the field.

Football was slow to learn the obvious lessons of caution, not least because many of the game's more prominent figures also used the press for extra income, or for planting stories. Those at the peak of their careers (managers and players alike – even eventually the tycoons in the boardrooms) found that media celebrity had a price, normally in the form of revelations about personal lives. For the first time, prominent footballers shared the fate of the royals in becoming the means by which newspapers sought to increase their sales and to outflank publishing rivals. Much of this sensationalism had little to do with football itself; it was simply the latest way of selling

For the first time, prominent footballers shared the fate of the royals.

newspapers. Gradually football came to terms with the new press, employ-ing press officers, public relations advisors and, overall, developing a thick protective skin, trying where possible to shield younger, inexperienced players from the risks of too close an exposure to the press.

Despite all this, time and again, football offered itself up to press ridicule. New-found riches easily burned a hole in the pockets of many players, and the celebrity lifestyle to which they naturally gravitated put a coterie of foot-ballers firmly in the public spotlight. Many of them clearly liked it – not least because it was fun and it brought further commercial opportunities; but it brought with it press tales of footballers' drunken excess or sexual misde-meanours.

No English footballer was more celebrated or victimised in this way than Paul Gascoigne, forever in the public eye for his repeated acts of misbehav-iour (drink, vulgarity, domestic violence, lavish spending) or for his talents – and failings – on the pitch. Gazza admittted to being 'daft as a brush', and was renowned for his frenetic activity and for his senseless babble through-out a match, but also for his dazzling skill. In many respects Gascoigne per-sonified football in the 1990s; a wonderfully talented footballer, perhaps the best English player of his generation, drowning in the riches which washed over him, gracing the game with a rare ability but periodically bringing dis-grace and ridicule on himself and his teams. For all that, it was hard not to like him. He was a very ordinary, fallible person, that image established by his tears at the 1990 World Cup. At one point his antics even managed to push the threat of war off the tabloid front page: 'Gazza and fiancé split'. Gascoigne represented many of the new game's failings; undreamed-of riches which many players simply could not manage, personal weaknesses magni-fied and worsened by constant media scrutiny, indiscipline (downing pints and gaining weight) in an athletic world which demanded the tightest of per-sonal fitness regimes. Yet it was a circular problem. The riches, the fame, the public adoration and ridicule, all stemmed from the same forces – from that transformation of a simple footballer into a star of the media circus. Even the wisest of older heads and the most sympathetic of seasoned advisors found it impossible to contain the volatile mix of wealth and public fame which plunged a number of successful footballers into a confusion of celebrity.

Ten years after Gazza, we have David Beckham, soaring to new heights of lavish publicity. There have been better players in the past, yet none –

It helps
- of course -
to have a pop
star wife.

including George Best in his prime – has commanded such public attraction, such ubiquitous fame and publicity. It helps – of course – to have a pop star wife. But even that fails to explain Beckham's status: gay icon, model, face familiar on TV and London underground adverts. He is inescapable. TV stars queue to invite him – and Posh – onto their programme.

The Beckhams have become so accustomed to the mass publicity so vital to their commercial lives, that they tolerate the most intimately intrusive questions into their private lives. Comedians ask them openly about their sex lives – and receive an answer. The Beckhams are media royalty, inhabiting a world of celebrity which seems to have no bounds: no ridicule, no scrutiny, no publicity is too vulgar or brash. It all serves the purpose of promoting their joint fame and fortune. They live in what Leo Braudy has called the 'frenzy of renown'. It seems on one hand as remote from football as could possibly be imagined. Yet Beckham is, today, England's most famous footballer, at home and abroad, and captain of the national team.

Even managers have become celebrities – quite unlike their earlier counterparts. The best of them can command huge salaries (reasonably enough given that their players earn even more). But their tenure remained insecure. Even the most successful could (and did) lose their jobs when Directors grew disenchanted – sometimes despite recent successes. In 1989 the chairman of Newcastle United said, 'Let's kill off the rumours that Ossie Ardilles's job is on the line. If he leaves, it will be of his own volition'. Three days later, Ardilles was dismissed. Even Alex Ferguson is thought to have come close, in his early days at Manchester United (before he showered his club with trophies), to walking the managerial plank. Impossible demands are made of them; success on the field, managing a pool of highly-paid, ambitious and increasingly independent young men (who are more likely to listen to their agent than their manager), trying to plan for the future – and all the while keeping a Board of Directors happy. The glare of publicity compounds the manager's difficulty: press and TV interviews, the requirement to have a word with whomever crosses their path (yet needing always to be guarded), playing host to powerful guests and backers. It is more than most men can take. The best of them make the most difficult job in football look easy. But the tensions and strains often show. Cameras dwell lovingly on the facial contortions of managers during the course of a game – and especially afterwards. Kevin Keegan's inability to contain his temper – live on radio when riled by Alex Ferguson – was a clear sign that he was about to lose the championship clash between his team, Newcastle, and Manchester United. Generally, however, managers prefer to have their temper tantrums behind closed doors.

Generally, managers prefer to have their temper tantrums behind closed doors.

Ferguson's infamous wrath against erring players – never in public – is alleged to 'blister the dressing room paint' (yet another hackneyed phrase from the locker room).

The media cannot afford to allow managers to remain private; they need their words, their cracks and predictions, and sidle up, microphone or camera at the ready. Often the forthcoming pearls of wisdom are memorable and are repeated, time and time again. Some, notably from Shankly, have entered popular vernacular – even when they are patently daft. The greatest managers have rarely been English of course – and Busby, Stein, Shankly, Graham and Ferguson are/were fiercely proud of being Scots.

Shankly began the process, spitting out a string of memorable, home-spun comments which delighted the media with their honest simplicity – and humour. 'We can't play against a defensive team' (when Liverpool lost 5-0). But Shankly operated in a more innocent age, one where the camera (and therefore the football manager) was much less in the public eye. Almost anything a manager says today is recorded in one form or another – hence Ron Atkinson's disclaimer – though odd from a man with an opinion on anything and everything – 'I don't want to say anything – not even "No comment"'.

'I don't want to say anything – not even "No comment"'.

The media presence, and the often faltering or nervous speech of many managers in the glare of press scrutiny, has yielded a veritable lexicon of amusing quotes and malapropisms: 'If we think they will be easy meat we'll end up with egg on our faces', 'He was flapping about like a kipper', 'At half-time I told the lads that the only thing you can't repair in life is death'. Most managers are struggling to find words to explain the inexplicable – to cover or explain their players' shortcomings, 'Their first goal was a foul, the second was off-side and they would never have scored the third if they hadn't got the other two'. Brian Clough again, 'I hope you were as delighted as I was last weekend when Nelson Mandela was freed from a South African jail. But what I hadn't bargained for was the fact that his release was going to cut across the start of our Littlewood's Cup Final'.

Along with the players and managers, football fans were also caught in the unforgiving glare of modern publicity. The habit of chanting in unison is a feature. A simple (often vulgar) refrain chanted by a small group is picked up by others and gathers pace and volume as it ripples round the ground. The same chants are shared between most football grounds: 'The referee's a wanker' being perhaps the most familiar. Sometimes the chant can be funny and self-mocking. Beaten 9–0 by Liverpool, Crystal Palace fans chanted, 'Oh lucky, lucky, lucky, lucky, lucky Liverpool'.

Vera Lynn's wartime favourite was adopted by Sheffield United fans in 1990 to describe their long run without a win: 'We'll win again, don't know where, don't know when'. Even the clubs can sometimes join in. After a 1992 Cup tie at Wrexham versus West Ham, the club tannoy announced: 'Visiting supporters will be kept behind for ten minutes after the final whistle to allow the ground to clear ... the Wrexham fans will be kept in until next Saturday's match with Blackpool.'

Foreign players were usually astonished by the passion and verve they encountered among English fans when they first stepped onto the pitch. It was a passion which often knew no bounds. In 1990, as a key promotion game loomed in Yorkshire, a desperate fan put an ad in a Yorkshire newspaper: 'Man offers marriage proposal to any woman with ticket for Leeds United v. Sheffield game. Must send photograph (of ticket).'

Man offers marriage proposal to any woman with ticket for Leeds United v. Sheffield game. Must send photograph (of ticket).

Fans' fanaticism survived in the most distressing of conditions.

Brian Keenan, enduring inhuman deprivation as a hostage in Beirut, managed to watch the Ireland–England World Cup game in 1990, complaining only that, 'It was a bit hard to jump up and down with the chains on'.

The literature

The 1990s witnessed a new-found interest in the game from more 'serious' literary quarters, though some of Britain's finest sports journalists (Glanville, McIllvenny) had been reporting on football for years. The Italian World Cup of 1990, with England's dramatic exit on penalties (against Germany of course), with its fanfare and finale from operatic tenors, raised the game's cultural stakes. Newspapers dispatched prominent writers to Italy to comment on how this mundane game had been transmuted into global passion. If some of their reports seemed odd (to football fans), they nonetheless told of a widening and more respectable interest in the game. Gascoigne was a special focus of attention, and a host of writers and scholars analysed his each and every on-and-off field foible. The truth remained of course that the *only* notable aspect of his life was his sublime footballing skill; the rest was media-inspired froth.

The Italian World Cup of 1990 raised the game's cultural stakes.

Thus sports journalism went in two different directions – sensational coverage on the one hand, on the other an expansion of coverage in 'quality' papers. On top of this there remained local coverage, that week-in-week-out reporting of humbler, smaller teams whose press coverage was largely restricted to the worthy columns of their local newspaper. Whatever the form, *in toto* it amounted to massive press coverage: acres of print devoted to football, week after week, continuing long after the football season ended, and resuming, only a few weeks later, as a prelude to the new season. It became inescapable for its opponents, unmissable for the fans. Like millions of others, whatever the front page headlines, I turn first to the sports page when my morning newspaper drops through the letter box.

The 1990s saw an unprecedented growth in literature devoted to football, much of it in a familiar format but with some striking new forms of football writing. There had been a long tradition of football fans publishing histories

As much to do with male obsessions as about football, 'Fever Pitch' spawned a host of imitators.

of local clubs, packed with statistics (sometimes of the most arcane kind). Footballing memoirs were another familiar genre. The 1990s however were marked by innovative writing about the game, led by the spectacular success of Nick Hornby's book (and subsequent film), *Fever Pitch.* As much to do with male obsessions as about football, *Fever Pitch* spawned a host of imitators. Certain publishing houses developed attractive specialised lines in football literature. Other publishers, realising the enormous market for all things football, sought to find new angles on a familiar theme. At Christmas, dozens of books about football (mainly ephemeral, about particular teams, or the stars), tumbled into the nation's bookshops (most finding their way to the remainder shops by spring). The clearest indication of the dramatic rise in football and other sports literature was the increased space they now commanded in major bookshops. From what had been a few feet of shelving devoted to sport, by the mid-1990s bookshops had reserved distinct corners for the reading habits of sports fans. There were now specialist bookshops dealing solely with sporting literature.

In the process of this rush into footballing print, the game attracted some compelling contemporary writing and became the occasion for serious social commentary. By the end of the 20th century there were annual awards for the best sports writing and newspapers published regular lists of best-selling sports books. Literature and soccer had come together to create what became known as a new *soccerati*. There was also a staggering academic output on football. Academics who, in the 1970s, had found themselves in a small (and generally ridiculed) minority now found their ranks swollen and their academic interest tolerated. In part this was helped by the changed cultural climate; a feeling both inside and outside academe that football and other sports were a legitimate subjects for serious cultural investigation. In part also it was because football and its attendant social problems were clearly an issue of major social concern. Answers were needed to football's problems, and who better to provide them than a pioneering group of social scientists? Sporting issues also entered the teaching syllabus, with all the associated spread of academic theses, articles and conferences. Not always marked by literary elegance, this recent genre of academic sports writing has nonetheless made a massive contribution towards our understanding of football in all its dimensions. I could not have written this book without it.

Most striking of all was the rise of popular fan-based literature, post-1985. The fanzines, with their contributions from supporters, their challenge to the dominant footballing culture of the 1990s, and their assertive stand against the game's racism and hooliganism created a new critical literature of football. They emerged in the turmoil following the Hillsborough disaster, and the subsequent formation of the Liverpool-based Football Supporters' Association. In essence they are fans' magazines, mainly club-based although others have a national circulation, which from the first sought to break the mould of the club-sponsored match progammes. Such programmes, often described as the 'Pravda school of journalism', had, for decades, trotted out the formal club dogma with never a hint of criticism or even self-awareness. Fanzines also reflected a deep dislike of the way football and its fans were treated in the press. Thanks to new computer technology, a number of cheap critical footballing periodicals found their way into the hands of fans as they headed to the game. Although fanzines are highly individual (some of them foul-mouthed and crude), they *do* speak for sections of football supporters who have traditionally been denied a voice in the game. As the 1990s advanced, football's rampant commercialism (coaxed and massaged by allies in the popular media) threatened to reduce media coverage of football to an uncritical blandness, but fanzines spoke up with a much-needed critical, informed voice, generally to the great discomfort of the rich and powerful within the game.

One fanzine, *Born Kicking*, was devoted to women's football and represented not merely the rise of women's football itself, but the increasingly striking female presence in football journalism, both in print and on TV, itself largely a result of editorial and management decisions to give women a higher profile within the media. Fanzines sprouted to cater for each and every following – women (*Born Kicking*), gay (*The Football Pink*) – but the bulk centred on a particular team. Some, notably among non-league teams, adopted imaginative titles: *Dial M for Merthyr*, *Light at the End of the Tunnel* (Dartford), *The Keeper Looks Like Elvis* (Kidderminster), *The Toothless Tiger* (Worksop Town). The launch of *When Saturday Comes* in 1986 proved important for fanzines, for it provided a noticeboard for them and became a forum for interesting critical essays about football. With sales of 40,000, the success of *When Saturday Comes* persuaded major publishers to launch a string of glossy football magazines; *Four-Two-Four, Total Football, 90 Minutes* and others. Some of the better football writers were snapped up by major newspapers, who themselves tapped into the rising tide of interest in football, for example by launching their own 'Fantasy Football' leagues (initiated by, of all people, the *Daily Telegraph*).

One spin-off of this interest in football was the emergence of a new 'laddish' culture, in print and on TV (*Standing Room Only* and *Fantasy Football*). It was a culture which revelled in what it represented as young men's basic instincts: a leery passion for beer, attractive young women and football – not necessarily in that order. It had enormous commercial potential and was quickly copied in a myriad advertising campaigns. It soon permeated the media, through the proliferation of dedicated radio programmes and sports channels, TV chat shows, quiz shows (*They Think It's All Over* – the title a crib from the BBC TV commentary of England's winning goal in 1966).

When we confront the saturation coverage of football we realise that football's celebrity is both massive and yet utterly transitory. Who would even recognise most of the stars of yesterday; their athletic powers gone, their earnings withered (unless they invested well or developed new skills), their faces no longer of interest to the media or the commercial interests which propelled them, briefly, into the public eye? What survives of football's celebrity, as the show moves on; new clubs, new players, new managers; famous clubs now declined, once-great clubs now on their uppers, yesterday's men now forgotten? Through all these changes, through all the inevitable upheavals and the passage of time, what remains are the fans. For them the game's the thing.

> **Football's celebrity is both massive and yet utterly transitory.**

14

Nationalism and the national game

Jingoism

At the 1998 World Cup in France, English fans taunted their long-suffering French hosts with the chant, 'If it weren't for the English, you'd be Krauts.' It was both crude and historically ignorant. But so too is most popular jingoism; rooted in generally ill-informed views of the past, and shaped by visceral animosity to people who are different. The English (variously represented by Britannia, John Bull, the Union Flag,

'Rule Britannia' and sundry other images snatched from a complicated imperial past) display periodic outbursts of jingoism. Nowhere perhaps is that jingoism more overt, more assertive, than at sporting events. And nowhere has it been more unpleasant than at football matches.

Sport has long been a forum for some very striking outbursts of nationalism. This might seem natural enough when it is specifically organised around competing national teams, say the Olympics or the World Cup. But expressions of nationalism have become so deeply ingrained in sporting contests that sports have too often become the occasion for outbursts of crude jingoism.

Sport was specifically used to further nationalist sentiment throughout the 20th century. European nation-building, and the assertion of national sentiment against outsiders, often turned to sports. Later the habit spread to Latin America. The sense of national identity for the English has been a confusing matter. For a start, as Richard Holt notes, the English often prefer 'to call themselves "British", when they mean "English" and vice versa.' For many years the English dominance within the British Isles helped fudge the issue. It is also true that, notwithstanding the important role of the Scots, many of the sporting and imperial values of the 19th century emerged from *English* public schools. The late Victorian and Edwardian stress on the value of sports, and the drive to evangelise those ideals worldwide (especially within the empire) was distinctively English, even when it was promoted in many areas by Scots. The English at play, especially at cricket, seemed a perfect sporting expression of the virtues of English life. Cricket, W.G. Grace, the village green, with an Anglican church close by; all seemed to blend into an image of idealised English life. By the inter-war years this mythology had found its musical accompaniment in the form of Elgar's music. All this, however, was essentially a southern, very rural, phenomenon. What characterised the north, and northern working-class life, was football (in places rugby league), notwithstanding the northern cricket leagues. If the Anglican church was the Tory Party at prayer, crowded football and rugby stadiums were the Labour Party at rest. Nonetheless until the 1940s it was cricket which seemed best to represent England and Englishness, its major hero, Jack Hobbs, the gentleman batsman, son of a college servant. And it was cricket which took Englishness to the far corners of the globe.

Football was, at first, generally devoid of the more overt forms of patriotism.

From the 1880s, with the development of professionalism and its rapidly spreading popularity in working-class communities, the game was too regional, too class-based, to be an ideal vehicle for national sentiment. Despite its public school roots, football became a regional and urban game of working men. Fans in the north seemed more interested in beating teams from the south than beating a foreign team. This was never true of the Scots however. From the earliest days of the game, they were keen to beat the English, and relished victory whenever they did. They were even delighted when someone *else* beat the English. Before the Second World War, the English were outside FIFA, had never played in the World Cup and had played only 23 international games in Europe. As we have seen, this isolationism ended in the 1950s, with the realisation of just how far the English game had slipped behind the rest of the footballing world. When the English finally began to compete with foreign rivals, they did so to a rising chorus of nationalist fervour, later a shrill jingoism, orchestrated by the media.

They were even delighted when someone *else* beat the English.

English nationalism began to rear its head at football grounds in the 1960s and 1970s despite the fact that English clubs invariably had a scattering of non-English players. Clubs were in fact a mosaic of nationalities and of religions, yet when they played against foreign teams, they were thought to represent *England*. This was also true abroad. The great Real Madrid team of the 1950s and 1960s consisted of players from France, Hungary, Argentina – and Spain, though they have always been remembered as a Spanish team. By the 1990s this issue had become unusually complex, for by then most of Europe's elite teams had become amazingly cosmopolitan: French, Dutch, Germans, Danes, Italians playing alongside British players, with others from South and Central America, the Caribbean, even from Japan. In 2001, Frenchmen managed three of England's Premier clubs, and the English national coach was a Swede. In part this was simply a reflection of football's globalisation, but it also reflected the changing nature of the European economy, and the freer movement of skilled labour within Europe.

To add to the confusion of nationalism in Europe, the concept of *Englishness* was seriously challenged, especially from the 1960s onwards, by the emergence of nationalist movements in Wales and Scotland and, of course, by the

England fans hurl debris from the stand, Ireland v England, 1995
© Shaun Botterill/Allsport

revival of violent nationalism in Northern Ireland. These political movements had ramifications on the way scholars thought and wrote about the history of sport in Britain. A spate of books and articles chose to indicate the local, regional and different histories of sports (including football) in Scotland, Ireland and Wales. The history of football differed greatly within the British Isles.

The explosion of international football over the past thirty years has been extraordinary. Global contests (notably the World Cup), continental championships in Africa and the Americas, and a proliferation of club competitions in Europe (the most lucrative of all being the European Champions League, formerly the European Cup) all provide a rich diet of international football venues. Players have occasionally to be rested by their club side, not because of injury but because of jet lag. A mid-week game in Australia or Central America is clearly not an ideal preparation for a weekend game in England. Even when English clubs began to make their presence felt in European competitions, they were able to do so thanks to key non-English players. From the 1960s to the 1990s the success of English clubs could not have been achieved without the Scots and the Irish in particular. The rise of the super clubs in the 1990s prompted the urge to buy the best players from around the world, but the number of foreign players a team might employ was restricted by both UEFA and by national football authorities. In breach of European labour laws, such restrictions had been set aside by 1991, after prolonged political lobbying, though quotas remained in place for certain competitions from fear of major clubs simply buying success. Once again, the 1990s proved a major turning point. English club football began to fill with foreign players (attracted by the money now on offer). By 2000

Players have occasionally to be rested, not because of injury but because of jet lag.

70 per cent of all foreign players in England came from the European Union, the highest proportion of any country in Europe. Club football in England, and in many other parts of Europe, had effectively become international (though still mainly European).

All this was a world turned upside down. Here were football clubs sporting a specific local or regional name, established over more than a century of intimate association with a specific town or city – or even with a part of the city – now made up of young athletes with no affinity whatsoever to the place itself, nor even to the country they played in. It was if an army of sporting mercenaries had taken over the game. Too often, that was how they behaved. In addition, millions of fans on the far side of the world professed an attachment to a team whose home town they had never even visited. The sense of place, that attachment to locale, the loyalty which had shaped the English game for the best part of a century, had changed. Of course, the core of local support remained just that: local and regional. But it now came wrapped in new layers of support, from across England and from around the world. This account is of course the story of the major clubs, and clearly was *not* true of the smaller clubs which remained recognisably similar to the clubs they had been decades earlier, supported by football fans who did not like the ethos of the Premiership and who preferred their football small scale.

Foreign players

Those elite teams which represented England in major European competitions were remarkably polyglot. In many respects this was consistent with other skilled labour markets in Europe and further afield. Talent followed the opportunities and the money. In the case of football this had the effect of internationalising a game which had traditional local roots. The time had long gone when prominent footballers could live and travel among their local fans; now, their wealth ensured that they were cosseted away, often behind gated communities. Clubs with the

> **Talent followed the opportunities and the money.**

greatest income and resources attract the best players. On the face of it, there is no *obvious* reason for moving from, say, the French Riviera to Newcastle or to Manchester, but wages of £1 million a year prove a powerful incentive. Add to all this the opening of borders in eastern Europe, the flow of players westwards from Russia and the old Communist bloc and more recently from the Balkans, and it becomes clear why western Europe seems awash with exotic footballers. Only a generation ago, black players were an unusual sight in English football. Today, any major team without a black player is unusual. Thus, we have Afro-Caribbean footballers playing alongside Africans, in English teams consisting largely of non-English-speaking Europeans.

Such major immigration of foreign footballers has been criticised notably from the ranks of the players' union; national footballing organisations (in France, Italy and England) have complained that this foreign presence hinders the development of the best local players, with a damaging effect on the national teams. If, say, English players cannot secure places with the best club teams, they will be unable to reach the levels of excellence required to play at the highest international level. Local talent cannot rise and develop if clubs continue to buy mature, quality players from abroad. On the whole however, fans do not object. What they want to see is good, successful football, and if that is produced by foreign players, so be it. In fact the English fans' enthusiasm for the best foreign imports has been staggering. Some – Cantona being perhaps the most obvious – became cult figures. Others have been a merchandising dream. David Ginola's film-star looks and flowing mane of hair have been used to promote a host of items, from shampoo and cars to train journeys.

Despite supporting England at crucial moments, most fans have an attachment to a particular team. People have grown up supporting a specific team, usually because it was their *local* team. Fans who profess to love the game itself, who are happy to watch *any* team and have no firm allegiance are unusual. How else do we explain the noisy crowds, the packed stadiums – and *especially* the sparsely attended games with their huddled knots of spectators? In both extremes the crowds consist of football fans following particular clubs. In the Premier League, teams which had become remarkably cosmopolitan continued to attract local support. In the case of Chelsea, for example, having only one Englishman in the team did not affect their local following.

For all this very local support, football clearly had enormous potential for stoking nationalist fires. It was manipulated by fascist regimes in the 1930s, and in the 1970s by military dictators in South America. On the other hand football could simply involve harmless vocal support for your homeland against an outsider. More often than not, however, it became something altogether more troublesome. For more than a century, the Scots have rarely lost the opportunity to regard football as a means of overcoming

Football clearly had enormous potential for stoking nationalist fires.

'the old enemy' (even the phrase is instructive). There have been regular episodes of footballing nationalism throughout the British Isles, mainly directed against the dominant English, by the Irish, Welsh and Scots, though the story of sporting nationalism *within* the British Isles is a complicated story, not confined to football.

The World Cup

These flashes of nationalist sporting tendencies within the British Isles have been reduced to parish-pump politics by the enormous national clashes which have unfolded in recent years in the struggle to secure football's major international sporting events. FIFA's decision-making process for allocating the greatest of all football's plums – the World Cup – has rivalled the Olympic movement for its levels of back-scratching, skulduggery, lavish entertainment and political arm-twisting. The stakes are almost beyond calculation, and the complexity and nefariousness of the negotiations are appropriately devious. The sums provide a clue. When the Brazilian Joao Havelange became President of FIFA in 1974, he inherited a modest organisation which ran the World Cup, for 16 nations. When he stepped down 24 years later, FIFA itself was worth more than $4 billion, 32 nations competed for the World Cup, and the global game of football had an annual turnover of $250 billion (compared to General Motors' $170 billion). There were, in addition, championships for youth teams, for women, and regional or hemispheric championships – a total of eleven competitions – in all parts of the world. All was made possible by the lavish involvement of the world's leading corporations, whose names and logos appear throughout these various competitions. Havelange had masterminded this extraordinary expansion of the global game with an autocratic style which shocked outsiders. Henry Kissinger, well-versed in the ways of devious diplomacy, said after having negotiated the (unsuccessful) US bid for the 1986 World Cup, that dealing with Havelange 'made me feel nostalgic for the Middle East'. Other politicians too commented on the 'positively Byzantine' world of FIFA politics at the court of Joao Havelange. As he dangled the prospects of awarding the games to this country or that, honours and awards came his way – a Nobel Peace Prize nomination, a *Legion d'honneur*. He circled the globe like a hybrid mix of political sultan and corporate chief, dispensing competitions here and there, claiming to promote peace between warring nations and visceral rivals – and all by the simple prospect of football.

At this level, international football was a world of largesse and favours, of diplomatic and corporate manoeuvring on a mind-bending scale. Since the smallest of nations within FIFA's electoral system (Vanuatu or the Faroe Islands, for example) had the same voting rights as the major footballing nations, the granting of favours to the small and apparently powerless could secure blocks of votes. It was at one level democratic, though few who watched the decision-making unfold doubted that it was a form of democracy lubricated by patronage and favour. The whole process, and the whole history of FIFA under Havelange, came gift-wrapped in self-serving prose, reams of documents praising this decison, that deal – and the President's role in securing the latest (beneficial) advance for football. His career had critics thumbing through their dictionaries to find an alternative to the clearly inadequate concept of *hubris*. It was a shameless and self-regarding epoch in the history of world football. The same process was reflected at every level of the game. Old footballing institutions (clubs and national organisations) were simply bundled into the arms of global corporations. Yet, by its own lights, it worked. Football had never been so popular, had never been watched by

so many people, had never before attracted such vast crowds, throughout the world. And, of course, it had never before, attracted such massive global TV audiences – or sold so huge a range of global commodities. It seemed at times that football was not so much the only game in town, but the only game on earth.

It was a shameless and self-regarding epoch in the history of world football.

Havelange's successor was his nominee, the Swiss Sepp Blatter, whose campaign for the position had been protracted and remorseless (especially among African nations), and highly effective. Blatter came with enormous sporting administrative experience, in the Olympic movement and elsewhere. He had also worked through the ranks of FIFA and had assisted Havelange develop crucial links with the world's major corporations. The voting for Blatter's Presidency was surrounded by controversy, and journalists greeted his victory with a critical chorus. Through all the dubious manoeuvrings of that election, countries were aligning themselves for forthcoming votes on future World Cup locations. Deals, gifts, loans, back scratching, duplicity; it was more like the UN than football. In the event the crucial impending decision (the site for the 2002 World Cup) went to a Japan–Korea axis; the first ever jointly hosted series. Needless to say, Blatter trotted out the threadbare cliches about what football meant. Blatter's litany of moral good (football contributed to education, to good health, and helped to shape a sense of competition), could have been mouthed by the public school men of the 19th century. Indeed the durability of those schools' ideals has been remarkable. Football's core qualities, conceived in small corners of Victorian society, were thought relevant and important in the last years of the 20th century. But Blatter also stressed the game's more visceral appeal

> But, first and foremost, it is an endless source of passion and excitement. It stirs the emotions and can move its enthusiasts to tears of joy or frustration like no other game and it is for everybody.

For the lucky few, football also offered rich pickings. After his election, Blatter promptly suggested his Executive Committee be paid $50,000 a year, on top of their lavish expenses.

Who started the war?

Football was at its most fevered in the World Cup, a competition which, like the Olympics, fostered fierce national rivalries. This was especially striking in England, and particularly in the way the popular media treated the international game. England's international games invariably prompted reminders of past glories, not merely on the football field, but on many another foreign fields. Military and wartime imagery, the vernacular of the 1940s, appeals to a resolute 'bulldog spirit', the evocation of Dunkirk, up and at 'em; these and more rolled off the popular presses in a bewildering and inappropriate stream. Quite what it all meant to the footballers themselves (young men whose grandparents might recall the Second World War) is hard to say. Every conceivable hackneyed idea and phrase (many of them insulting, some of them actionable) was harnessed to the task of puffing up interest in a forthcoming international match. And nowhere was the process more exaggerated – ludicrous even – than for football matches with Germany.

It was the fate of the English national team to be pitched against the Germans in a number of important football matches, never more so of course than the World Cup Final of 1966. The images of that game have all slipped into the popular collective memory (the goal that wasn't, the killer goal in the last moment of the game, the commentator's phrase 'They think it's all over. It is now', the elaborate celebrations on and off the pitch afterwards). It was impossible to forget, not least because the media recycled the whole affair whenever it seemed appropriate – that is, as often as possible. Games against Germany were prefaced by a battery of hostile images. Time and again, the Second World War was conjured forth to remind players and fans alike that this was no normal football match – this was a game against the Germans. The contests were invariably spiced by the simple fact that the German national team was usually better than the English. At major games in Mexico (1970) and Italy (1990), Germany knocked England out of the World Cup. In less exalted venues, the outcome was generally the same, a trend not reversed until a poor England team beat an even worse German team in the European Championship of 2000. It was clear enough that England could not hope to win the World Cup. But for many fans,

> **This was no normal football match – this was a game against the Germans.**

beating the Germans was almost as good. That one single English victory was greeted almost like winning the World Cup itself. Visitors from a non-footballing culture must have scratched their head in bewilderment as they watched the media contort themselves into a communal delight, to the accompaniment of a deep-seated anti-German feeling among the English. What was it all about?

The memories of the Second World War ought to have faded, fifty years on. For all the brutality and unspeakable wickedness of those years, it is hard to see their relevance to a present-day football match. Modern Germany is a thriving industrial giant, a European friend and ally, and a major democratic state at the heart of Europe and the European community. That, of course, may be the core of the problem for many of the English. German's post-war success may explain much of the animus directed towards Germany in sporting events. After the shattering defeat of 1945, ground between the might of Russia and the USA, Germany emerged to become Europe's economic powerhouse and, in alliance with France, the key political player in the transformation of modern Europe. The story of Germany after 1945 is a staggering story of reconstruction and reinvention, of hard work and democratic vision. Of course, Germany in 1945 had nowhere to go but up. We on the other hand, had nowhere to go but down.

1966 World Cup Final, England 4 v West Germany 2 © Popperfoto

Some of the importance which continues to be attached to games between England and Germany was revealed, again, in the autumn of 2001. The 5–1 England win in Munich in a World Cup qualifier was, for any English fan, a delicious sporting moment. For once the Germans were much the worse team, and in Michael Owen, England had a genuine 'Roy of the Rovers' striker. But, once again, the game and the result was greeted by a media blizzard of those hackneyed cliches so frequently used over the previous 40 years.

It is hard not to feel (however difficult to prove) that serious issues of jealousy and resentment lie behind the complex English reactions to Germany. True, English hostility is obviously stimulated by the popular media. But, if so, the media must feel that here is an issue they can use. Yet time and again anti-German sentiment surfaces in English social life. In recent years British television in particular has regaled viewers with an endless parade of programs about the Second World War, and especially about Hitler. In higher education, when students of modern history have a choice, they will opt in large numbers for courses on the Third Reich. It often seems that they would be happy to take a degree in Hitler studies. It is hard to explain why all this should be so. There are clearly overlapping layers of contemporary interest in the recent German past, and deep-seated cultural feelings about Germany which break surface at moments of sporting rivalry.

Offensive epithets ('Kraut' and 'Hun') and hostility are hurled at German teams; preludes to major matches between England and Germany see every hackneyed idea and myth about the two nations paraded in public. Because there has to be a winner and loser, images of warfare easily lend themselves to cheap football coverage. The English are not alone in harnessing nationalist myths and traditions to football, of course. In the case of England versus Germany, however, popular English animosity stands out both as a historical nonsense and as a redundant insult. At a time when the English have been beset by problems of industrial and imperial decline, Germany has transformed itself in one of the world's leading economies and a pillar of European democracy. More than that, Germany has a vision of its future, however troublesome reunification

Images of warfare easily lend themselves to cheap football coverage.

and dealings with the east have been. At a time when some prominent English politicians have discussed involvement with Europe (and Germany in particular) as a betrayal of the English past, Germany has maintained a steadfast commitment to European co-operation.

The contrast is depressing. A buoyant, expansive nation at the heart of a progressive Europe, and a declining offshore island, happy to sing discordant imperial tunes and to congratulate itself on its historical pre-eminence – despite the evidence of material and social decline. The English, then, have many reasons to be jealous of the Germans. And as if to confirm that fact, the German national football team has, for more than three decades, often been better than the England team. A newly united Germany has come to take great pride in its sporting successes. Meanwhile (until 2001), English football has produced a series of inadequate teams, managed by a string of even more limited coaches, perfect fodder for the gross lampooning of the popular press. Nor was it really surprising that Germany, not England, won the FIFA vote to host the 2006 World Cup, thus compounding a deep-seated English animus which accepts no balm save for beating Germany at football.

A national stadium

The English game grew up in the plebeian heartlands of industrial society. Almost without exception, those industries have gone. New stadiums have risen in a unrecognisable post-industrial environment. Others have simply abandoned their former locations completely. The national team has *not* however been able to make the same leap. For more than 70 years the England football team traditionally played at Wembley stadium, a faded and inadequate place by the end of the century. As early as 1925, it was described as, 'A vast white elephant, a rotting sepulchre of hope and the grave of fortunes'. The saga of the abandonment of that stadium and the failure to find a replacement is a perfect morality tale for the story of the national game.

The site itself had bad omens. The Wembley site had previously been occupied by 'Watkin's folly', a tower intended (by its builder Sir Edward Watkin) to rise to 1150 feet. It managed to rise to 200 feet before being abandoned. The Empire Stadium built there, intended for the British Empire Exhibition, was completed in 300 days, and finished only four days before the 1923 Cup Final. Towards the end, Wembley betrayed its age – old, dingy, dirty. A visiting fan described it in 1990 as 'a dried-up old pigsty'. A year later, a journalist remarked, 'If Wembley was a beach, the EC would make it fly a skull and crossbones from the twin towers'. Wembley has now, and not before time,

> **'If Wembley was a beach, the EC would make it fly a skull and crossbones from the twin towers.'**

gone the way of the empire it was designed to celebrate; its twin towers a fond image, but its decayed environment destined for the demolition men. In its place – nothing. More money has been spent on planning a replacement than on the original Wembley construction or on the entire construction of the Millennium Stadium in Cardiff. At the time of writing, the national game has no national home, and is destined, for some time to come, to wander the major stadiums of club sides, rootless and homeless.

Having bought the Wembley site (with a Lottery grant of £150 million), the FA was unable to raise the extra £410 million needed. The government, having already suffered a self-inflicted wound with the Millennium Dome, refused any further help. And there, at the time of writing, the matter hangs. Beholden to the major clubs for a venue, dependent on charitable (Lottery) or government hand-outs, hamstrung by an archaic bureaucracy, and institutionally incapable of effective decision-making, the FA has allowed the debate about a national stadium to make the national game a laughing-stock. That debate was widespread and furious; here once more was another emblem of national failing made all the more painful by successful examples overseas. Looking at the *Stade de France*, for example, or the more recent Stadium Australia in Sydney (even though the latter is effectively bankrupt) provoked a depressing sense of *déjà vu*. Others did these things better than the English. Everyone blamed each other. Many pointed to Blair's government, some to the composition of the planning committee and others to the FA itself.

Through all this the FA was lucky to have a new and young senior executive, Adam Crozier, with experience of business and high finance elsewhere, who bravely brought the tortuous matter of the national stadium to public view. The problem was money. How could a game commanding such vast wealth (admittedly, little of it going to the FA) not be able to afford a new stadium? Yet some of the guiding spirits on the new stadium committee approved of

The national game, more popular than ever, apparently awash with money, unable to afford a national stadium.

plans which allowed the costs to spiral beyond the bounds of reality, alarming the federation of banks planning to loan the money to the point that they backed away. Thus there emerged the bizarre situation of the national game, more popular than ever, apparently awash with money, unable to afford a national stadium.

Few doubt the need for a new stadium. Those who follow international sport closely (especially the fans and the journalists who travel the world) have long realised what is visible to most others only on TV, namely that English facilities woefully lag behind international competitors. This is true for most sports but there is a special poignancy in the case of football. Politicians who had no trouble digging deep into the national purse for the Dome (and perhaps for that reason) refused to look for money for a national stadium. Football itself is unable to raise the necessary cash, yet those clubs whose coffers are bursting are as reluctant as any other plc to share their profits with anyone other than their shareholders. The end result is stalemate. The only game is homeless.

English football in the new century shows all the tell-tale signs of its recent past. The national team is, on the whole, a collection of young talent, its current hopes placed in the hands of a Swede (in the absence of a suitable Englishman). It has no home, nor is it clear even *where* that home should be. Football's former national home, owned by the FA, is derelict. Yet up and down the land, brand-new stadiums are packed, week after week, for games in the Premiership. At the very time the hundred best-paid players in the Premiership earn £100 million a year between them, it is hardly surprising that politicians (and their voters) feel that football should look to itself for money. Nor does it help that the national team continues to attract unruly fans, ugly jingoism and a corrosive racism.

It is obvious enough that the centre of gravity of English football support lies not with the national team but with the clubs. Yet the most prominent of those clubs have been utterly changed in the 1990s, pulled loose from their local roots by the rise of football as a transnational sport. The aim of all major clubs today is to succeed at home, in order to compete in Europe. Clubs whose history has been rooted in particular cities, or parts of a city, for more than a century, now consist of players from around the world, playing for a place in European contests which offer income on an ever-more lavish scale. As a schoolboy I watched in Manchester a team that was predominantly English – with a few Irish or Scottish players. Today that same club is utterly cosmopolitan – British, European and a scattering of West Indian, South American and African players. They strive, year after year, to be champions not just of England, but of Europe. Where I sit at Old Trafford, on the rare occasions I get a ticket, the fans around me are mainly Mancunians, but they bellow their support for an amazingly international team – and even chant the name of a Frenchman long departed. I love being there, love the thrill of the game and the atmosphere. But what does it have to do with Manchester? In the confusing world of local and national identity, it is hard to find anything quite so confusing as modern English football.

15

Politics and false profits

This sporting life

Walking home from work, I cut past the sports centre, invariably filled with sweating young people, and across the playing fields. Sometimes in good weather I have to keep to the path to steer clear of the archery practice. The tennis courts are generally fully booked, and in summer they are flanked by cricket nets. On the other side of the road, the local golf course caters to an older clientele; its crowded car park testimony to the golfers moving around the fairways throughout the daylight hours. But most striking of all are the number of football pitches on either side of the road, including an all-weather flood-lit playing surface. In this part of town, sport is inescapable. Even at work, gaggles of students arrive for classes, sports bags slung over their shoulders, ready for the next game or match. We have never been able to teach on Wednesday afternoon – that is reserved for students' sports.

Wherever you turn, sport dominates the modern landscape. Sportswear has become the dress of choice for millions of people. Shoes have given way to trainers, sports-shirts and tee-shirts have replaced conventional shirts. People dress in any combination of sportswear; variants on track suits, base-ball caps, football shirts – the list is endless. The line between sportswear and everyday clothing has become so blurred that it is often hard to see the difference. In part it is a reflection, part cause, of the greater informality which has crept into all corners of modern life, and partly a change in fashion driven by the massive commercial power of TV and global sports cor-porations whose shops and products dominate the high streets and shopping malls. And throughout modern urban life there lurks the gym, looking to out-siders like modern torture chambers. Their sweaty members spend a fortune as they push, spread, lift, flex and monitor every conceivable body part, on space-age machines designed to improve health, strength – and looks. The evidence of one's own eyes proves what the data confirm – that the nation is keener than ever on sports and physical recreation. At times, there seems no clear dividing line between sport and everyday life. Sports have thoroughly permeated the social fabric of the way we live; the way we look and dress, the conver-sations we hold (even the language we use). In a way, we are all sportsmen now.

There seems no clear dividing line between sport and everyday life.

It was a process which began in earnest after the Second World War. Since 1945 there has been a steady increase in popular partici-pation in most sports. Some sports were effectively reinvented, snooker for example, thanks to television. Rugby clubs increased from 854 in 1939 to 2000 in 1980. In 1989, 6500 cricket clubs belonged to the National Cricket Association. But football dwarfed them all. In the mid-1960s there were about 25,000 football clubs. Twenty years later that had increased to more than 40,000, helped in part by the ending of the ban on Sunday football. Amazingly, Victorian sabbatarianism had effectively thwarted popular pleasures almost to the end of the 20th century. By 1987 an estimated one million adults played in organised English football teams. These are extraordinary figures and they do not even include school football. There had been a huge demand for football pitches for years, but by the 1990s demand was even greater. There were more players and teams in search of a pitch *at the very time* local authorities began to sell off their 'surplus' land. Between 1981 and the mid-1990s an estimated 5000 sports pitches had been sold to developers.

A 1994 census revealed a total of 77,946 playing fields in England. Almost half of them were reserved for football. Not surprisingly demand for pitches was greatest in the major cities, London especially, where land was costly and pitches were especially vulnerable to sale and redevelopment. By the end of the century the story was the same everywhere; too few pitches, and poor facilities with poor maintenance and few (if any) changing rooms. Those involved had no doubt that the state of the nation's football pitches had greatly deteriorated, a process hastened by sub-contracting of maintenance. The story is obvious enough to any casual visitor to a public football pitch on Sunday morning. A line of players' cars and vans serve as changing rooms. As winter advances (which in recent years has meant rain on an almost biblical scale), football pitches are reduced to muddy quagmires. Yet footballers return to play, week after week, often adjourning to a local pub (which serve as footballing headquarters) to relax and plan. The conditions endured by the typical Sunday footballer are proof enough of footballers' passion for the game – often beyond the realms of reason.

Here, again, is another stark contrast characterising the modern game of football. Cities which boast lavish professional facilities find it hard to offer their residents the kind of decent sporting facilities which, only a generation ago, were thought basic to urban life. The decay of the urban infrastructure can be measured not simply in the inadequacy of hospitals, schools and public housing, but in the paucity of civic sporting facilities. There is however little or no political credit to be gained for championing sports fields. Yet this was not always the case. Nor is it true, today, among our European neighbours.

In the post-1945 sporting boom, urban sporting facilities were improved. Even so, they were rarely more than basic, and often became a favourite

Amateur footballers play on Hackney Marshes in October 1962
© Atlantic Syndication Partners

target of vandals. The contrast in post-war Europe could not be greater. Sports facilities, including pitches, were an integral feature of post-war urban renewal. Later, they were enhanced further, thanks to the material improvements brought about by European integration. In the last quarter of the 20th century public sports facilities improved in western Europe at the same time as they declined dramatically in Britain.

There were fewer football pitches – and their condition had deteriorated. Even poor pitches have to be maintained and paid for, and many low-income players could not afford their contributions to their amateur clubs, quite apart from the cost of equipment. Numbers of clubs folded, and even some local amateur football organisations disappeared, though this gloomy evidence has to be set against another, more positive story – there has been a major increase in women's football and a huge growth in clubs for boys under 16. The dedicated servants of the amateur game – the men and women who make it all possible – ruefully shake their heads when discussing their problems and point to the dire influence of the Premier League. Amateur football has been reduced to pauperism in a land of footballing plenty.

Amateur football has been reduced to pauperism in a land of footballing plenty.

In this, football is not unique. We have all become accustomed to tolerating public squalor in the midst of private affluence. In the case of football, this contrast is all the more obvious because it has come about so quickly, so relentlessly, and with little or no regulation. The privatising cult of the 1980s, the transfer of public assets into private hands, was normally accompanied by regulatory agencies, designed to safeguard the interests of the public (though that brought little comfort to, say, the rail traveller). With football, the changes of the 1990s saw a small band of tycoons create their own market, and transform football into a money-making machine of unparalleled success. Little attention was paid to the interests of *other* constituent groups within the game. The end result was that the 1990s saw English football became unbalanced, skewed out of all proportion. Its original shape had both a rationale and an organic purpose. Football had reasonably nourished grass roots which formed a healthy base of a massive footballing pyramid, and which sustained the game, up to its professional tip. In the 1990s this was thoroughly distorted, replaced by a rapacious liaison between television, a small band of rich clubs, and global corporations – a commercial triumvirate which paid no regard to the popular grass-roots game. The contrast is to be seen in any major English city. Millions of amateur players slog their way through games on poor pitches, often only a short distance from the new sporting cathedrals which house the premiership clubs.

Television has enabled elite clubs to thrive, but what would happen to the wealthy if their source of wealth – television – turns its back on football? What would happen if televised football loses its appeal? Or if the TV moguls discover different ways of securing the loyalty of their viewers? For them football is only a means of securing massive audiences. Such worries may seem groundless. Already however, financial critics have begun to warn of football's over-reliance on television for income.

What would happen to the wealthy if their source of wealth – television – turns its back on football?

Let's consider the figures. When the Premiership was launched, Manchester United received £2.42 million from television fees. By 2000–2001, that had risen to £20.4 million. Even Bradford City, relegated from the Premiership, earned £8.42 million from television fees. It is likely that, by the end of the 2001–2002 season, the best-paid team will receive more than £40 million from television. Such increases in income cannot be sustained (it is hard to imagine that television income will increase tenfold again over the next ten years). There are signs that the clubs recognise that they must not become too dependent on their television paymasters. This is compounded by fans' growing concern at the parallel increases in ticket prices. Season tickets which cost, say, £500 a year have had a serious impact on the kind of people who can afford to attend football matches. The game has become too expensive for many of its traditional fans, and a number of clubs have begun to restructure their tickets, offering discounts for the young and the old, for family or low-income groups.

Through all this financial bobbing and weaving, major football clubs have to be alert to the changing markets which have brought them such riches. The temptation is to imagine that television's golden goose will always be available. But what happens, for example, if a club's footballing success begins to slip? The same clubs cannot continue to be successful indefinitely. And if they did, what effect would that have on a game which relies on competition and the unpredictable excitement of sporting twists and turns? (Would the game be quite so exciting if the same band of clubs won the major trophies year after year?) The mighty may stumble, and there are many rivals within the game who would happily help to bring them down. The lower leagues have a number of clubs that could, quite easily, have been in the Premiership had they not slipped at the wrong moment. A bad patch, poor judgement, a profligate manager – all have helped to send clubs tumbling from their once-exalted position. The temptation for the small band of super clubs is to imagine that their current wealth will secure them against the tides of misfortune and failure. Yet football is volatile and unpredictable, which is part of its appeal. Who knows who will be on top, or even viable, a decade hence?

> **Would the game be quite so exciting if the same band of clubs won the major trophies year after year?**

Political involvement

No one seriously doubts that football is the national game, a game described by one critic as having entered the national psyche. For the same reason, football is highly political, subject to the stresses and strains of political involvement. In fact football had long been in the political eye. At critical moments, politicians could not *afford* to stand aloof from the game (quite apart from the fact that many politicians were keen fans). Prime Ministers from Harold Wilson in the 1960s through to Tony Blair today generally had something to say about football. Unfortunately, the most obvious political involvement has been to deal with football's social problems.

The progress of football in the 1990s created political problems of a different kind however. The rise of the super clubs and football's growing commercialism ensured that football would attract growing political attention. As players' wages, transfer fees, merchandising and ticketing spiralled, politicians were inevitably dragged into a public debate about football. As luck would have it, the country had successive Prime Ministers who were sports fans. John Major was a keen cricket fan and supporter of Chelsea, while Tony Blair followed Newcastle United. Both men were alert to the benefits sport could bring both to players and to the country. Major accepted that sports were part of the national heritage, and allocated them to the Department of National Heritage when he became Prime Minister. Politicians could no longer ignore sports, if only because they had become so obviously import ant to so many people. Television enabled millions to enjoy the most dazzling of sporting achievements. The 1990 Italian World Cup and the 1992 Barcelona Olympics, for example, confirmed both the popular appeal and the commercial importance of sport. Politicians also became involved because major sporting events spawned multi-million pound investments. The city of Barcelona had boomed on the back of the Olympics. The old days (notably Montreal in 1976), when the Olympics could bankrupt a city, had clearly gone. As with football, so with the Olympics; new business techniques, the involvement of major corporations, clever TV marketing – all could create a sporting cornucopia. The hope that it might even happen in Britain (and kindled by the success of football's Euro '96) was a tempting political prospect. John Major's government made a massive investment and effort to try to win the Olympic games for Manchester. The bid failed.

Success was not, however, simply a matter of money. Politicians were not about to throw huge sums of public money at unreformed sporting organisations. It was essential that sport reform itself, to widen sporting access, and enable local talent to mature. There was also a parallel demand, accepted by John Major, that school sports should be revived. It was accepted by both sides that school sports had been seriously degraded by Thatcher's political fights of the 1980s between Westminster and local authorities. Those conflicts even affected the quality of school teaching itself. Previously many young people had become teachers because they could both teach *and* enjoy sports. That was no longer the case. School sports posed a political challenge, and it was taken up by Blair's Labour government.

The new Labour government, elected in May 1997, was keen to forge a link with the national game. There followed a variety of initiatives, all designed to enhance British sporting fortunes and to increase sporting access. From the first, however, there was a problem. Anyone drawing up a list of social priorities facing an incoming government would accept that sport ranked well below, say, health or education. In addition it was hard to argue that football in particular needed government assistance when the game was dominated by clubs apparently awash with money, and when star players were millionaires. The government was understandably reluctant to provide public money for football, though it did ensure that some television income was redirected to football's grass roots. Above all, it was reluctant to help a game which had shown few signs of being able to put its own house in order.

By the time the new Labour government took office, it had become clear that football was riddled with problems. At the very time television money was beginning to surge through the game, football was beset by a series of major scandals. Prominent managers were under investigation for accepting bribes in transfer deals. A group of players (in cahoots with foreign gambling syndicates) had been charged with match-fixing. And the infamous incident in January 1995 of Eric Cantona's televised assault on an abusive fan at Crystal Palace helped to confirm the view that the game needed to regulate itself more stringently. Bad behaviour and corruption compounded the feeling that the game was out of control. All of this had taken place in the last years of a

> **Bad behaviour and corruption compounded the feeling that the game was out of control.**

Tory administration which itself displayed similar problems; it lacked firm leadership, it was woefully divided (notably on the issue of Europe) and it was awash with accusations of sleaze. Only the die-hards doubted that it was time for a change – in politics and in football.

By the mid-1990s, football dominated the headlines, it attracted glossy coverage in fashionable magazines, and celebrities of all sorts (including MPs) stumbled over each other to be seen at matches, or to declare themselves a lifelong fan. Basically, football was Labour's natural game; and never had a British political party been so alert to the media and so alive to the need to cultivate its media image. Football, TV and Labour seemed a natural alliance. The Labour Party had published a pre-election policy document, *Charter for Football*, which confronted the game's recent troubles and which sought to tap into the current fashion for football. The Charter had emerged from a series of meetings with all sectors in the game, and it promised a Football Task Force to scrutinise the current game, with subsequent legislation to deal with the game's various problems.

Tony Blair's government roared into office on a landslide victory, positively twinkling with an energetic commitment to reform. Despite all the other problems it faced, the new government could hardly ignore football. It had made a major pre-election promise (though that had rarely proved binding in the past) and football was too high-profile to be marginalised. More important though was the fact that Labour and Labour supporters were football's home constituency. They had a natural social affinity. In addition football might bring the media attention so craved by the men who managed the party. Labour's affair with football would generate publicity at very little cost.

The Task Force consisted of representatives from all sectors of the game, under the surprising chairmanship of David Mellor QC, the former Tory Minister, a well-known football fan and public figure. Given a remit in seven distinct areas, the Task Force was expected to report on each to the Minister of Sport, Tony Banks, himself a surprise choice. They were to report on racism, disabled access, supporter involvement in clubs, ticket prices, merchandising of club brands, players' involvement with communities, and the potential friction between shareholders and fans. It was, in effect, a watering down of pre-election proposals. Each was diluted further in discussion, filtering through a large committee structure, and a protracted debate in London and at various regional visits. Whatever the outcome, the Task Force needed two critical levels of support. First, any proposal required government backing. Second, goodwill and cash were needed from the senior clubs. But both sides, government and elite clubs, had their own agendas to look after.

From the outset, Task Force meetings became a platform for airing grievances (nothing wrong in that of course, but not the best recipe for effective action). There was, too, a jaundiced antipathy towards the Task Force, ranging from outright opposition through to cynical acceptance. Many felt that the confrontational courtroom style of its chairman, David Mellor (already famed as an opinionated radio pundit) would inevitably diminish proceedings. Too big, too all-inclusive for effective action, nursing too dominant a chair, and all under intimate political scrutiny, the Task Force was altogether unwieldy and unmanageable. Even in restructured form, it remained a clumsy beast. Such criticisms ought not to hide the fact that this was an important and imaginative step. No previous government had sought to consider all corners of the game in so comprehensive and open a manner. Previous enquiries into football had been forced on reluctant governments by this or that crisis. This was unique in having so broad a brief, to listen to constituencies within the game previously ignored.

The Task Force submitted a series of reports to the Minister. Most were welcomed, accepted and acted on (on racism, disabled access and links to the community for example). There were the predictable clashes of interest and personalities, with the inevitable public disagreements about proposals. There were too many sectional interests on the Task Force to ensure harmony throughout. In the end, the ultimate divide – the fundamental clash built into the very fabric of the Task Force – was the clash between fans' interests and the clubs. Though it is true that many (generally smaller) clubs had long gone out of their way to consider their supporters' interests, the disregard of the major clubs for anything except their profits created a deep-seated grievance throughout the national game. Fans complained, especially about prices, about merchandising and ownership of shares. More fundamentally perhaps, they complained about being on the outside. The clubs needed their support, but seemed keen only on their money, not their opinions. It was, yet again, a very British phenomenon; of ownership/management on the one side paying no heed to the great body of the rank and file on the other. Elsewhere industrial and commercial practice had changed. Not football.

The ultimate failure of the Task Force was, in many respects, predictable. They found it impossible to reconcile the interests of the fans and the clubs; the gap between the two sides had grown unbridgeable. What exacerbated that divide (widening further as the decade advanced) was the lack of regulation of the clubs. The elite clubs had no interest in regulation, which could only be achieved by government intervention. At heart, the major clubs were unlikely ever to agree to restrictions on their commercial freedom. For their part, fans wanted clubs to show some moderation, some flexibility, towards hard-pressed supporters. The clubs fell back on their well-honed answers; stadiums were full, fans were not obliged to buy their (usuriously priced) merchandise and, on the whole, people could not get enough of their 'product' – on the pitch and on television.

The elite clubs had no interest in regulation.

What sustained the major clubs in their general indifference towards their fans' genuine complaints was the crude free-market ethos which informed their proceedings. They were in effect the last of the robber barons of the 1980s. Worse still, there was no regulatory body to monitor and rein in their activities and excesses. Throughout the economy, supervisory agencies tried to balance the interests of consumers and business; but football clubs could do what they pleased. The ultimate boardroom defence was of course the mealy-mouthed plea of freedom of choice – no-one was obliged to pay for football's pleasures and its (amazingly tacky) products. The boards and shareholders, argued that they, and they alone, needed to be free to decide what was in their own commercial best interests. All this was, at once, true and yet irrelevant. Apart from a dwindling band of zealots (happily now bereft of political or economic power), fewer and fewer British people believed that national well-being was best promoted by the pursuit of untrammelled private gain. The whole political debate about economic policy had moved on, accepting, it is true, the fundamental changes of the Thatcher years, by embracing a broadened base of private ownership, and an end to the massive burdens of nationalised industries. But even Thatcher had accepted the need for *regulation* of her privatised babies. In addition there had been enough recent horror stories from within the City (Maxwell, Lloyds, major insurance and bank scams – and indeed financial scandals within Parliament itself) to remind people of the importance of effective regulation. There was too much money sluicing around, too many sticky fingers, too much temptation, to allow major economic concerns simply to line their pockets at will. Even the USA at its Reaganite apogee accepted the need for regulation. But not the people's game. And there lay football's ultimate – and at the time of writing – major surviving problem.

The Task Force had revealed (through commissioned research) football supporters' widespread dislike of many features of the modern game, notably its rampant commercialism. There was a deep distrust about the way the major clubs run their affairs. As football's finances spiral extravagantly (transfers of £20 million, salaries measured in millions, club profits of tens of millions, TV income measured in hundreds of millions) the fans' unease has come to be shared by more and more people, including many with no special love for the game. At one level it ought *not* to be a concern, for the game is thriving, apart from at the grass roots. Moreover, here is one local product which is avidly sought after by millions round the world; they might no longer want our motor cars or textiles, but they want our football. English football is a massive global success; sold and marketed to, and watched by, untold millions worldwide. There are very few other local products which can make a similar claim. Similarly, Premiership football has become a species of showbiz, and this alone ought to help ease many of the fans' concerns. So what is the problem?

There is an obvious discrepancy between the very nature of football as a working man's game and its multi-million pound business ethos. It is a game played by millionaires, under the control of multi-millionaires, but played out in front of low-income groups. Clearly, the nature of spectatorship has changed enormously over the history of the game. But the changes became more marked in the 1990s as low-income groups often found themselves priced out of their favourite clubs (one of the issues addressed by the Task Force), their places taken by the better paid. All this may seem obvious: the more prosperous taking the place of the less prosperous when prices rise. Complaints do not stop there, however, for television too has been able to raise its asking price, not only to pay for the insatiable financial demands of securing the rights to football, but also, of course, to maintain the profits of News Corporation. Financial matters are uppermost – the need to increase earnings by whatever method seems likely to succeed.

One corollary of all this is that the Premier League and its individual clubs simply refuse to countenance any proposed changes which might eat into their earnings and profits. Task Force proposals (for redistribution of money within the game), suggestions from independent 'think tanks' (such as windfall taxes on clubs' profits), pleas from fans' organisations; all and more have received a generally frosty response from the game's richest organisations. For centuries, it had been one of the traditional obligations of the rich to regard benevolence and care as a duty imposed by their riches – that they should give some of their riches to worthy causes. There is precious little sign of philanthropic virtue within the boardrooms of the Premier League, even though it might ultimately serve their purpose better than the current reign of unbridled profit.

There is precious little sign of philanthropic virtue within the boardrooms of the Premier League.

The end result of all this is a chasm between rich and poor which has grown wider and wider in the course of the 1990s. Worse still, the poor have grown poorer. It is a contrast which worries those with long service in the grass-roots game. Where the Premiership and television have agreed to divert money back into the game, it has constituted a mere dribble, diverted from the major clubs' overflowing coffers. In any case, the major changes agreed by the big clubs have served their own self-interests. What is required through all this is a regulatory body with power to impose controls on such cavalier money-making and to ensure that money is shared more evenly within the game. But football's problem goes deeper even than the financial discrepancies.

Leadership

Today, more so than at any period in the history of the game, there is a striking absence of any clear leadership. The game's natural leaders are the prominent men within the Premiership clubs, the very men whose financial interests create such problems within the game as a whole. This lack of leadership (and the parallel lack of overall vision) is not simply a matter of looking back nostalgically to better times. The structure of the modern game was re-cast, at a stroke, by the inauguration of the Premiership, undermining the traditional structures of the game which had, for good and ill, managed the broader interests of football for more than a century. The FA, and its then chief executive Graham Kelly, were snatched and made captive by the Premier clubs, while the Football League was emasculated by the departure of the bigger clubs. The lower leagues were reduced to the rank of a marginalised and impoverished relative. English football's founding and critical organisations were instantly diminished by a commercial coup managed by a small band of tycoons. In the process the game lost the base from which its natural leaders had traditionally defending football's broader interests.

Since the Second World War two dominant men had spoken up for the game as a whole. Stanley Rous at the FA was a crucial figure in ensuring that football thrived, from top to bottom; that schoolboy and amateur football was nurtured as an integral part of the national game. Rous was also a major figure in the global game, within FIFA (until ousted by Havelange), and he saw to it that English interests were promoted abroad. The Football League, in the person of Alan Hardaker, had a more provincial leader, cautious about Europe, unhappy at the first signs of commercialism but, for all that, a doughty defender of all corners of league football. Hardaker was never beholden to the bigger clubs; indeed, it was the permanent headache of the major clubs, that they were dragged along, year after year by the collective deliberations of small club chairmen, steered by Hardaker. But who, in the 1990s, spoke for the game of football? Which base could anyone use as a platform to address the needs and interests of the national game? Kelly, the man destined by experience in both League and FA, was shackled by the Premiership (and was promptly removed). In any case, who was going to listen to the League anyway? English football was effectively leaderless.

> But who, in the 1990s, spoke for the game of football?

There were and are leaders in abundance within the game. The most powerful are the major managers, although each has his own club to safeguard, and the tycoons and board members within the Premier League. A number of the directors have made considerable fortunes outside the game, and others slip easily between football and other boards in the city and in the media. But all of these men, football's dominant figures, speak not for the game itself; they speak for their own club. When some of them have tried to embark on a more broadly-based venture (for example on the Wembley redevelopment) their inadequacies have quickly been revealed. The game has had a number of iconic figures – most prominently Bobby Charlton – occasionally co-opted for various national duties. But without an institutional base, such spokesmen were merely in transit. The heart of the problem lies in the structure of the English game. For all its millions (of pounds and fans), the Premiership has created a hole at the heart of the game. It has left a trail of debris, of unresolved problems in its wake, problems about the game's financial imbalance and commercialism for example, and yet it is clearly incapable of self-regulation. Why should we expect money-makers to stop making money? The case for outside regulation of football becomes more persuasive by the year. Yet regulation will come only from government decree. And in the hectic welter of government business, what political credit is to be had for curing football of its own vices?

As I finish this book, in September 2001, flush from England's defeat of Germany, with a new TV regime in place for the coverage of English football, the game rolls on. Crowds pack the major stadiums, impending international

games and tournaments are eagerly awaited, and millions round the world tune in every week to watch the English game. Football shows no sign of faltering. But many of the basic problems remain. Even the dominant Premiership is troubled by money worries – especially the gap between the rich and the also-rans. Football continues to attract the headlines – on both front and back pages. But at heart, to most people who watch and who are fanatical about the game, what really matters is the game itself: the anticipation and the post-mortems, the noisy thrills and excitements of winning, the angst of losing, the sheer fun of playing. It remains what it has always been: a simple game, eleven players against eleven opponents. It is the same game my grandfather watched with his cotton-worker mates a century ago. It is the same game I watched my grandson play on a bright Sunday in September 2001 in North Yorkshire: two teams of ten-year-olds, giving their enthusiastic schoolboy-all. It is the same game, then and now; the same game the world over; the only game.

GUIDE TO FURTHER READING

New books and essays on football tumble from the presses with amazing regularity. What follows is not a comprehensive list, but a guide to the literature I have found most useful in writing this book.

John Ballard and Paul Suff, eds, *The Dictionary of Football*, London, 1999.

P.J. Beck, *Scoring for Britain: International Football and International Politics*, London, 1999.

Derek Birley, *Land of Sport and Glory: Sport and British Society, 1887–1910*, Manchester, 1995.

Dennis Brailsford, *Sport, Time and Society: The British at Play*, London, 1991.

J.D. Campbell, 'Sport and the Transformation of the British Army, 1860–1914', *The International Journal of the History of Sports History*, vol. 17, December 2000, No. 4.

D. Canter, M. Comber and D. Uzzoll, eds, *Football in its Place*, London, 1989.

Timothy J.L. Chandler, 'Games at Oxbridge and the Public Schools, 1830–1880,' *The International Journal of the History of Sport*, vol. 8, Sept 1991, No. 2.

David Conn, *The Football Business*, Edinburgh, 1999.

Hunter Davies, *The Glory Game*, London, 1972.

Eric Dunning, Patrick Murphy and John Williams, *The Roots of Football Hooliganism*, London, 1988.

Eric Dunning and Kenneth Sheard, *Barbarians, Gentlemen and Players*, Oxford, 1979.

Eamon Dunphy, *A Strange Kind of Glory: Sir Matt Busby and Manchester United*, London, 1991.

A.H. Fabian and Geoffrey Green, eds, *Association Football*, 2 vols, London, 1960.

Nicholas Fishwick, *English Football and Society, 1910–1950*, Manchester, 1989.

Jon Garland, Dominic Malcolm and Malcolm Row, eds, *The Future of Football*, London, 2000.

Richard Giulianotti, *Football: A Sociology of the Global Game*, Cambridge, 2000.

John Goulstone, 'The Working Class Origins of Modern Football,' *The International Journal of the History of Sport*, vol. 17, March 2000, No. 1.

Sean Hamil, Jonathan Michie and Christine Oughton, eds, *A Game of Two Halves? The Business of Football*, Edinburgh, 1999.

Richard Holt, *Sport and the British*, Oxford, 1989.

Richard Holt and Tony Mason, *Sport in Britain, 1945–2000*, Oxford, 2000.

Nick Hornby, *Fever Pitch*, London, 1992.

Nick Hornby, ed., *My Favourite Year: A Collection of New Football Writing*, London, 1993.

S. Inglis, *The Football Grounds of Britain*, London, 1987.

Stephen F. Kelly, ed., *A Game of Two Halves*, London, 1992.

Charles Korr, *West Ham United*, London, 1986.

Simon Kuper, *Football Against The Enemy*, London, 1994.

Pierre Lanfranchi and Matthew Taylor, *Moving with the Ball: The Migration of Professional Footballers*, Oxford, 2001.

Robert W. Lewis, 'The Genesis of Professional Football', *The International Journal of the History of Sport*, vol. 14, April 1997, No. 1.

Sue Lopez, *Women on the Ball: A Guide to Women's Football*, London, 1997.

Robert W. Malcolmson, *Popular Recreations in English Society, 1700–1850*, Cambridge, 1973.

J.A. Mangan, ed, *Tribal Identities: Nationalism, Europe and Sport*, London, 1995.

Tony Mason, *Association Football and English Society, 1863–1915*, Brighton, 1980.

Tony Mason, ed., *Sport in Britain*, Cambridge, 1989.

Ross McKibbin, *Classes and Cultures: England, 1918–1951*, Oxford, 1998.

Aletha Melling, 'Ray of the Rovers: The Working Class Heroine in Popular Football Fiction, 1915–1925', *The International Journal of the History of Sport*, vol. 15, April 1998, No. 1.

Bill Murray, *The World Game. A History of Football*, Urbana, 1996.

Martin Polley, *Moving the Goalpost: A History of Sport and Society since 1945*, London 1998.

Jeffrey Richards, *Happiest Days: The Public Schools in English Fiction*, Manchester, 1988.

Ian Ridey, *Cantona: The Red and the Black*, London, 1995.

David Russell, *Football and the English*, Preston, 1997.

Phil Scraton, *Hillsborough: The Truth*, London, 1999.

Matthew Taylor, *'Proud Preston': A History of the Football League, 1900–1939*, Ph.D. Thesis, De Montfort University, 1977.

Rogan Taylor, *Football and its Fans*, Leicester, 1992.
Neil Tranter, *Sport, Economy and Society in Britain, 1750–1914*, Cambridge, 1998.
Nick Varley, *Parklife: A Search for the Heart of Football*, London, 1999.
James Walvin, *The People's Game Revisited*, Edinburgh 2000.
Steven Wragg, *The Football World*, Brighton, 1984.

The only game

INDEX